HIGH-VOLTAGE
SPIRITUALITY

Other Books by Bill Tenny-Brittian

Prayer for People Who Can't Sit Still

House Church Manual

Under the Radar: Learning from Risk-Taking Churches
Coauthored with Bill Easum

HIGH-VOLTAGE
SPIRITUALITY

Bill Tenny-Brittian

CHALICE
PRESS

ST. LOUIS, MISSOURI

Cover photo: Digital Stock
Cover and interior design: Elizabeth Wright

Visit Chalice Press on the World Wide Web at
www.chalicepress.com

10 9 8 7 6 5 4 3 2 1   06 07 08 09 10 11

Library of Congress Cataloging–in–Publication Data

Tenny-Brittian, William.
High-voltage spirituality / Bill Tenny-Brittian.
    p. cm.
Includes bibliographical references.
ISBN-13: 978-0-827214-53-8 (pbk.)
ISBN-10: 0-827214-53-7 (pbk.)
1. Spirituality. I. Title.
BV4501.3.T4546 2006
248.4–dc22

2005037542

Printed in the United States of America

Contents

Dedication

I work at the Fairwood Starbucks. No, I'm not one of their employees, but during most weeks you can find me sitting at the end of the bar with my laptop. Many have been the weeks that I worked at my Starbucks more than the full-time baristas. I know every staff member by name, and probably a good percentage of the customers. As I work, I'm frequently interrupted by the busyness of the environment and by the many folks who stop by to share their lives with me. But I enjoy the interruptions because the staff and the customers have come to mean so much to me.

And so, I want to begin by dedicating this book to the staff and customers at the Fairwood Starbucks. Special thanks to Sarah, the manager, who's been there with me through four books now. And to Tyler, Madge, Vee, Robert, Jackie, Jennifer, Jason, J.D., Debbie, Michael, Amy, Anna, Kristy, and Elizabeth—the baristas who remember what I drink and take such good care of me.

But it's not just coffee that keeps me going. My long-suffering, and I mean *long*-suffering, wife, friend, encourager, and completer has stood by me through thick and thin, richer and poorer, for better and for worse. Thanks will never even come close. I love you, Kris.

And to my children, who tippy-toed around those times when Dad actually worked at the dining room table instead of at Starbucks (or who stopped by Starbucks to share a Java Chip Frappuccino or an iced Carmel Macchiato), I love you all: Britt, Shannon, Katrina, Becky, and Toni.

And finally, I've enjoyed the generous support of my House Church Network as I took a month to put this book into its final form. Thank you. May the words of this book make it all worth it.

Introduction

High-Voltage Spirituality. Words like *shocking, electrifying,* and *hair-raising* leap to my mind. It sets an exciting tone for a topic that is traditionally quiet, tranquil, and peaceful. When I think of spirituality, I think Psalm 23 and pastoral scenes of green pastures and gentle waters.

I don't know about you, but I don't live there. My surroundings are anything but pastoral. My calendar reminds me, "Hurry up, you have a deadline plus two appointments this afternoon." My cell phone beeps and says, "You've missed two calls that you need to return." And my to-do list, well, thankfully, it doesn't talk. I actually have to *look* at it to see what I have to do. My life is less about green pastures and gentle waters and more like shooting the Colorado River rapids in a rubber raft with only one paddle and without a guide.

That's why the title of this book is *High-Voltage Spirituality.*

But there's another reason.

Busy people, by definition, are busy. Their lives are filled with responsibilities, appointments, and to-do lists. Their prayer, whether they are persons of faith or not, is for an extra hour in each day, an extra day in each week. Their plates are full and they can't add even one more thing to them, but somehow most of them have difficulty saying, "No." So something else gets the short shrift, such as our family or our faith. So they go through the motions of life without a significant connection into the "Divine Power Grid," the source of our spiritual power.

I was one of those people. I spent many of my years *way* too busy to seriously develop my faith—which was a scary thing, considering I've been in the professional ministry for over fifteen years.

I discovered early on that a life devoted to the work of the church is not the same thing as a life devoted to deep spirituality. Sometimes, being a pastor is like almost any other job. Get up, go to work, be faithful in your responsibilities, go home—typically with some sort of home work or evening meetings—go to bed, repeat. I regularly worked over fifty hours a week, and often over sixty. I was busy. Too busy to spend extended time practicing spiritual habits. Though there's an expectation in the church that pastors and professional ministers are deeply invested in their personal spiritual development, it isn't necessarily so.

Now if ministers have trouble cultivating their spiritual life because they're so busy, it's a cinch that folks who *aren't* in professional ministry may have some difficulty. Indeed, as I preached and taught and extolled the virtues of a deep and satisfying spirituality, I was often disheartened at how few of those in the church "got it."

The problem may have been that I hadn't "got it" either.

I came into the practices of spirituality later rather than sooner. Over the years I had watched my wife, Kris, continuously nurture her spirituality. She'd practiced a number of different habits. She worked with a spiritual director. For a time she was an oblate in a religious order. And she prayed–she prayed *a lot*. I couldn't figure out how she could get all her work done and still have time to practice so many spiritual habits (she is a professional minister as well). But she did.

Now I wouldn't say I was envious of her, but honestly, I did covet her connection with the Divine Power. So I began to look for ways to fit some spiritual habits into my schedule. I had spiritual giants telling me they got up at four a.m. every morning for prayer–I'm a morning person, but I'm not *that* much of a morning person. Others told me about week-long and month-long retreats they went on. I took note of what these sages had to offer and began to incorporate a piece here and a practice there.

My breakthrough came when I learned how to pray. I'm one of those folks who can't sit still, so long meditative practices that require motion-lessness only served to frustrate me. But when I experienced deep, soulful prayer for the first time, my appetite for other spiritual practices was like a black hole that was determined to capture every ray of light it could reach. I found my connection into the Divine Power Grid and my spiritual batteries began to recharge.

What follows is a compendium of spiritual habits adopted and adapted for busy Christians. You'll discover habits you can practice that won't put a ripple in your time. These you practice "as you go." Mostly they just take awareness and a commitment to make them habits to slip into your everyday life. Other habits will take some time, but they can be easily added into your busy schedule because they are particularly suited for multitasking. If you commute to work, if you run errands, or if you're a soccer parent, there are a number of habits you'll love. And then there are spiritual practices that take a significant time commitment. Some you can practice during lunch. Others need to be scheduled. But in my experience, those habits that take extra time are worth the effort–they have the potential to take you deep rapidly.

There's no need to read this book from cover-to-cover like a novel. Each chapter is self-contained, so you can read it in stages. Don't feel compelled to read it straight through, nor to read the chapters in any particular order. In fact, the last chapter of the book breaks down the various habits into a series of tables. For instance, "A.M. Projection" is an early morning practice (for most people), whereas "Imaging the Word" can be practiced almost anytime of the day. Use the tables when you're ready to add a spiritual habit into your life but don't know which one to choose. By deciding whether you want to take on a practice at home or at work, whether you have ten minutes or an afternoon, and so on, you can more easily make an appropriate choice.

You'll also discover that the majority of the spiritual habits are "layer-ins" rather than "set-asides." In other words, you layer them into your daily routines rather than stopping and setting aside a time to practice them. On the other hand, multitasking is *not* a recommended method to engender an effective connection with the Divine, even though some of the spiritual habits in the book can be practiced simultaneously while you are otherwise occupied. Just don't rely solely on multitasking spiritual habits to increase your faith and to put an end to your spiritual power shortage!

Each spiritual habit has been assigned three symbols that tell you how much time the practice takes, whether you need to be in solitude or not, and if the habit is multitask friendly. Below is the key to the symbols.

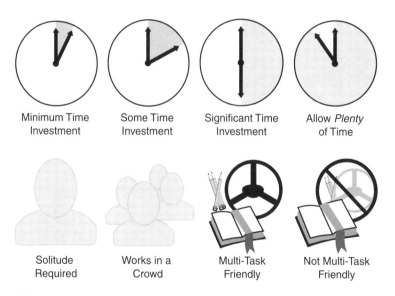

| Minimum Time Investment | Some Time Investment | Significant Time Investment | Allow *Plenty* of Time |

| Solitude Required | Works in a Crowd | Multi-Task Friendly | Not Multi-Task Friendly |

My fondest wish is that these spiritual habits will offer hope that you can have a vibrant connection with the Divine and that your heart, mind, and soul will be empowered.

My benediction for you as you begin this journey is that your desire will outweigh your schedule. May your spiritual batteries capture every amp of God's "yottavolts"[1] so that you experience the promised fullness of life.

1

Power Shortage

There's a power shortage in North America and it has nothing to do with the price of oil or diminishing natural resources. This power shortage isn't darkening the skylines of any metropolitan centers across the continent. No line crews have been dispatched to reattach downed lines, and no engineers have been called to diagnose faulty generators. The lights are still burning brightly in all the suburbs, villages, and hamlets across America. However, this power shortage has darkened the lights of many a church from sea to shining sea, and has even cast dark shadows on the name of Christianity itself.

North America is experiencing a critical spiritual power shortage.

Many people are feeling the pinch of this shortage in their daily lives. In fact, you may be feeling the effects of this power shortage yourself. In the Gospel of John, Jesus tells his disciples that he came so his followers could have an abundant and full life (Jn. 10:10). Yet, for many Christians, that promise seems like empty words–or else a promise meant for someone besides us, the common men and women of the faith. We shrug and wonder where the promised "power from on high" is (Lk. 24:49). Sadly, many of us have been taught that those promises weren't really for *us,* but were only true for those of the early church or for the disciples of the first century. So we've been left with this yearning deep inside, an itch we can't quite reach.

There is a critical spiritual power shortage in North America. But the problem isn't with the Power Supply. God didn't suddenly stop generating the promised spiritual power. And the problem isn't with the delivery system.

The Divine Delivery System has been functioning flawlessly ever since the day of Pentecost.

4

The problem lies with the end user–those who yearn for the power of God but haven't figured out how to plug into the Source.

For a moment, imagine what would happen if we discovered H.G. Wells' time machine and whisked ourselves back in time to the first century Corinthian church. There we pick up the apostle Paul and bring him back with us. Now if you handed him the cord to an electric fan and asked him to "plug it in," he wouldn't have a clue. He'd stare at the plug, the cord, and the fan and probably shake his head with bewilderment. In many ways, the inverse is true as well. When it comes to plugging into God, we appear to be about as baffled as Paul would be with the electric fan. We know how to plug in an electric fan. He knew how to plug into God's power.

Yet that unscratchable itch keeps calling for our attention. We yearn for the touch of the Divine that will enliven our spirit within. We want to connect with the Power Source.

Although most of this book has been written to help you get plugged in, before we proceed, let us consider why it's been so difficult for us to figure it out. Why were the early disciples so "plugged in" and we feel so disconnected?

Because We're Really, Really Busy

I'd like to tell you that I'm a really busy person–and that I'm also really, *really* spiritually mature; that as the CEO of some Fortune 500 company, I fly all over the world wheeling–and–dealing, trading and merging, and yet amid all my responsibilities I manage to balance my work, my family, and my faith; that, to play off of Garrison Keillor, "My wife is strong, I'm good looking, all my children are above average, and I'm plugged into the power source."

But the truth is that I'm probably a lot more like what I envision the average reader of this book is like. I've been in the work force in one way or another for more years than I care to chronicle. From pet store manager to pastor, from Air Force Airman to author, I've pretty much spent my life at work. Most of my life has seemed so busy that making time for anything like a spiritual discipline has been easier said than done. And although I have a great family, far too often I've neglected them for the sake of "the job." I've simply been too busy.

I'd also like to tell you my faith has always been the North Star that I've used to navigate through life. Indeed, if the Gallup Organization had ever polled me with the question, "How important would you say religion is in your own life?" I'd have answered, "Very Important." Never mind that there have been stretches in my life during which I hadn't made it to church, I hadn't spent much time in prayer, and the only reason I could find my Bible was because I'd labeled the box it was packed in.

So I can't tell you that I've always had this unshakeable faith that's never wavered. However, what I *can* tell you is that for several years of my adult working life I've lived more like a "believing Christian" than as a "practicing disciple."

Let me explain. For years I've maintained that there's a difference between a Christian and a disciple, at least in the North American context. According to Gallup, over 80 percent of those in the U.S. claim to be Christian. With all those Christians, you'd expect our world to be a pretty ethical place. However, that same survey also reported that over 75 percent of us think the morality of our nation has been getting progressively worse.[1] There appears to be a disconnect between Christian belief and Christian practice.

Recently, I came across a brief article in *The Christian Century.* It was titled "Christianity Lite":

> Some of the CEOs accused of unethical business practices are also "born-again" Christians: Richard Scrushy of HealthSouth, Ken Lay of Enron and Bernard Ebbers of WorldCom. How did they justify actions that are unethical, if not criminal? Robert S. McElvaine (*Chicago Tribune,* July 17) explains that while Hindus believe in karma—what one does in this life matters for the next life, some Christians believe all you need to do is "accept Jesus and then you can do whatever the hell you want."[2]

Not what you might call a flattering story about the faith. The story begs the question: Why didn't their Christianity guide their decisions? What caused the disconnect between their belief and their behavior? I think there were two key reasons for their lapses.

First, there really *is* a difference between a Christian and a disciple—at least in the North American context. Once upon a time, "accepting Jesus" meant you "invited Jesus" into your life and from that time forth you tried to transform your thinking, your words, and your behaviors to conform with Jesus' life and teachings. However, in our popular culture, accepting Jesus often means little more than assenting to the "fact" that Jesus is the Son of God, which, unfortunately, for many is sort of like believing that Abraham Lincoln was the sixteenth president of the United States. Though it may make for interesting conversation (or not), "believing in" Abraham Lincoln doesn't really affect our day-to-day life. In North America, the words *accept, believe,* and *assent* have become synonymous with acknowledgment rather than with practice.

This troubling development is why I make a distinction between a Christian and a disciple. I define a Christian as someone who "believes" Jesus is the Son of God. A disciple is someone who "believes" Jesus is the Son of God *and* demonstrates that belief by his or her behavior. In other words, disciples are *Practicing* Christians; they practice what Jesus preached.

This doesn't happen overnight, because the key part of "Practicing Christian" is *practice* (which, not coincidently, is what this book is about!). So the first reason I believe these CEOs failed, and why many other "Christian" leaders have failed, is because they were *believing* Christians rather than *Practicing* Christians.

Being a Practicing Christian is difficult even during the best of times. However, when Christians—leaders or not—get too busy to *practice* their faith, moral and ethical lapses are simply the natural consequences of that busyness. The busy factor distracts us, steals away our time, and gets in the way of our relationships.

The Art of Distraction

I'm not a magician, but in a "past life" I was involved in clown ministry in Atlanta. I could twist balloons into poodles and parrots. I was a master at pratfalls. But I was never really good at doing magic tricks. You see, I could never master the art of distraction—of getting people to look the other way while I worked my "magic."

On the other hand, great magicians are *masters* of distraction. Your eyes follow the tightly closed hand you *thought* the handkerchief was in—while the magician's other hand surreptitiously tucks it safely under your hat. On the stage of life, the most talented magicians aren't named the Incredible Kazaam or the Amazing Houdini. They're called *responsibilities, tasks, chores,* and *jobs.* They are "master distracters" that keep us so occupied that we lose sight of what's really going on. And when we do, the really important stuff slips out of sight, out of mind.

Distractions lead us to live on autopilot, facing decisions and making choices without taking adequate time to consider faith-filled ethics and morality. Just like watching the magician, we're so busy with the distractions that we miss opportunities for practicing truth.

Grand Theft Burglary

The second reason busyness hampers our faith is because it's a cunning thief. In the world of thievery, the most admired are the art thieves (at least in the movies!). The "best" art thieves don't just snatch and dash. Instead, they discretely replace the priceless masterpiece with a fake so no one notices the switch until it's too late and the thief gets away safely.

Original Renoirs, Monets, or Picassos are masterpieces said to be "without price." It's funny that Sotheby's and Christie's auction houses regularly auction off these "priceless" paintings for very large sums of money. Pricey? Yes. Priceless? Apparently not. In fact, Lloyd's of London somehow manages to insure these "priceless" art pieces, again for rather large sums of money. But "priceless"? Hardly.

However, each of us is creating a unique piece of art that, although still a work in progress, really *is* priceless. Time is the canvas we paint on, and life is the paint. But "Busyness" is the most cunning of all the world's thieves. The canvas of time is so valuable that Sotheby's can't auction it and Lloyd's can't insure it, but Busyness can steal it. And Busyness is so good at it, we don't even notice the theft until it's too late.

Busyness robs us of time, and not just extraneous time that might otherwise be wasted. Busyness robs us of the time we desperately need to practice our faith. Busyness pressures us into thoughtless, knee-jerk reactions. And Busyness keeps us from pausing long enough to seek wise counsel. Without adequate time to reflect on the decisions before us, the canvas of our life becomes but a distortion of the masterpiece we could be creating.

Busyness Gets in the Way of Relationships

The third way Busyness hinders the practice of our faith is that it gets in the way of relationships. If we hope to move further along the road–to move from a believing Christian to become a more effective, Practicing Christian–we must let nothing get between God and us. However, in a recent article for the *Regent Business Review,* Christian leaders were asked about the correlation between the busyness of their lives and their relationship with God. Their responses are revealing:

> To the statement "The busyness of my life gets in the way of developing my relationship with God," three out of four Christian leaders indicated that this is "often" or "almost always" true of them. Looking more closely at the data, I also found that female leaders report even more of a challenge in this area than do their male counterparts.[3]

Three out of four leaders are so busy that their relationship with God suffers. I suspect virtually all of the "Christian" leaders who suffer moral and ethical lapses would confess they let their busyness get in the way of their relationship with the Divine.

Busyness is not a friend to relationships. It is one of the underlying grounds for the break-up of many marriages. Good, healthy relationships take time, and not just any old time, but time *together.* Good, healthy relationships take significant, intentional time together...alone. When two people spend time together alone, they grow together. Now that doesn't necessarily mean that they grow *closer* to each other, but they both grow alongside each other. Conversely, when two people in a "relationship" *stop* spending time together, absence doesn't make the heart grow fonder; in time it makes the heart wander. Relationships that aren't nurtured with time together drift apart.

The same is absolutely true with our relationship with God. If we don't spend significant, intentional alone time with God, our relationship will wane. The busyness of life will come between us; it will seduce us, and in short order we'll discover we're creeping along a slippery slope instead of traveling on the straight and narrow.

All this is to say that if we aren't experiencing the promised power from on high, if we are scratching our heads wondering where the full, abundant life is, then perhaps we might want to take an inventory of our life. Possibly, we've let busyness distract us and get in the way of our relationship with God.

Because We've Mishandled Our Priorities

Sometimes I think the apostles had it made. After all, they were Jewish men who didn't have the burden of scientific knowledge. They didn't know Earth was round. They simply had no concept of outer space—they believed the stars were angels perched up on the cosmic dome looking down on them. The apostles thought storms and droughts, floods and famine were God's way of punishing people—they had no concept of low-pressure zones, El Niño or La Niña, or global climate changes. In short, the apostles lived convinced that everything they saw in creation, every natural event or wonder they experienced, and every blessing they received came directly from the hand of God. In other words, for the apostles there was no dichotomy between the sacred and the secular.

If you and I didn't know about Earth's rotation and were convinced that the sun only came up because of God's good graces, we *might* not take all our blessings so much for granted. When we pray over our meals, we might be a little more deliberate and sincere in offering our gratitude to the Lord if we believed the food came literally from God's hands. And if we didn't know about germs, and if we thought disease was generally a curse sent by God on the unrepentant, we just might make God more of a priority in our lives.

But we all know Earth is round; the sun rises because Earth is rotating; the stars are infernos of pressurized gases; weather patterns are relatively consistent and largely predictable; good hygiene takes care of most germs; and food comes from the supermarket. Because science has explained almost everything, we no longer see God behind every tree, in every storm, or even very present in our lives. So God gets Sunday morning from ten-thirty to noon—and not a moment longer, thank you very much.

The worldview that every natural phenomenon is a divine supernatural event has passed. In that old view, the Israelites and the early Christians saw God, literally, in every aspect of their lives. God got credit for the blessings, and God regularly got the blame for the hardships. And since they recognized the hand of God in everything, the hand of God was never far from their minds. God was a priority by default.

Today, even for most Christians, God is more like an afterthought than a priority. It *isn't* natural for us to recognize the working of God in everything we see and experience, even if, on some level, we know it to be true. If we're brutally honest with ourselves, we'll acknowledge that although God may be *one* of our priorities in our lives, our relationship with God isn't often number one.

The Eroding Divine Priority

The slipping Divine priority isn't just the result of a changing worldview. The modern church has had its fingerprints all over it as well. Although God is supposed to be our first priority, a different "truth" has permeated our church culture and has been taught from our pulpits, from our curriculums, and from well-meaning peers. As heretical as it may seem, the notion that God is the priority in our lives has been seriously undermined. Although the erosion has been communicated in a variety of ways, the teaching has been particularly pernicious in two areas.

① The Priority of Church

First, the rise of the church as an institution has had a part in subordinating God. Although everybody "knows" that the church is people, not buildings and institutions, our practice and language belie what we proclaim. As a people, we still talk about "going to church" as if church is a destination. Additionally, over time, theologians and church leaders have come to understand and teach a difference between sacred space (church buildings) and secular space (essentially any place that *isn't* a church building). This unfortunate dichotomy has confined God to the church and weakened the conviction that God can be found anywhere and everywhere—even though we all "know" better.

The understanding that God can only be found in the church (i.e., in a church building) has led to the blurring of the lines between God and church. A commitment to God has come to mean a commitment to the church. In fact, in most North American churches, when someone "of age" gets baptized (not an infant or a young child) they are not only making a commitment to the Kingdom of God, they are also "joining the church." This is most clearly seen in the many churches that give their newly baptized "members" both a baptism certificate *and* a box of branded church offering envelopes.

There are many good reasons why a newly baptized person should be a member of a congregation, but there's another point to be made here. When our commitment to God and our commitment to the church is fuzzy, we internalize the notion that the needs and work of the church are synonymous with the needs and work of the Lord. In other words, to make God a priority in our lives means to make the church a priority in our lives.

On the surface, the understanding that a commitment to the church is the same as making a commitment to God seems legitimate. After all, Paul wrote that the church is the body of Christ (1 Cor. 12:27). The commitment lineage looks like this: God=Jesus=body of Christ=church. The logic seems inescapable. But for the first couple of centuries, membership in the church meant something entirely different than it does now.

The early church understood itself as a people who were committed to Jesus Christ and to doing what he commanded, especially in fulfilling the Great Commission. When you made a commitment to Jesus, it meant you were willing to lay your life on the line for the sake of sharing the gospel. When you made a commitment to the church it meant you dedicated yourself to practicing the "one anothers" with your fellow Christian sisters and brothers—people for whom you would gladly sell your house to help out financially if it was needed; people for whom you would literally jeopardize your own life in order to protect and serve. This commitment took *very* seriously Jesus' instruction, "A new commandment I give you: Love one another. As I have loved you, so you must love one another. All...will know that you are my disciples if you love one another" (Jn. 13:34–35).

However, as the church transitioned from a movement of people committed to each other and became an institution, the meaning of church commitment changed. Today when you "join the church," it means you've made a commitment to show up at Sunday worship and weekly Sunday school. It means you'll bring a bucket or lawnmower to the all-church work day to maintain the church building. It also means you'll pledge a fixed sum of money for the church's ministry and that you'll give extra time to attend committee meetings...board meetings...teacher's meetings... building-and-grounds meetings...planning meetings...and, well, you get the idea. The church needs all this because the work of the church is headquartered in the church building. The church has made itself responsible for the education and spiritual maturity of its members, as well as becoming the ministry clearinghouse on their behalf. The institution has subsumed personal responsibility for ministry.

In North America it's been difficult to make God a top priority because a commitment to God means a commitment to church. Ultimately, that means putting church meetings and church tasks over and above our families, our careers, and even over our own spiritual development. Many of us just aren't that committed to the church. We aren't finding a spiritual connection in committee meetings, so the church, and thus God, gets relegated on our priority list.

The Priority of Me

As I pointed out before, today's worldview is significantly different from that of the first-century Christians. In the minds of the early believers, God was in, and a part of, everything. Not only did they have a very different understanding of creation and the cosmos, they had a different under-standing of the scriptures. As they heard the stories of the faith, they took seriously making God the priority above all else. The scriptures taught it, they believed it, and they experienced it as a fact of life. The early Christians universally understood this, even when it wasn't universally practiced.

However, as the years passed and the empirical sciences and the social sciences gained prominence, the church's teaching of scripture slowly began to accommodate the findings of the scientific communities. In some cases, these concessions came with serious conflict, such as discovering that Earth was *not* the center of the universe. In a few cases, however, accommodations were made almost without notice. One of these was the accommodation of social priorities.

I'm a "card carrying" member of the *Me Generation*. My generation was raised with the conviction that self-actualization is the ultimate goal of life. This conviction was my generation's societal norm. Self-actualization, as defined by society, meant at least the following:

- My needs are more important than your needs.
- I should get–I *deserve*–whatever my heart desires; therefore, my desires are more important than your desires (and thus more important than your needs).
- Society as a whole is responsible for helping me to become self-actualized by keeping me informed of what I need and desire through advertising, peer pressure, and creating social norms.

Ouch! I suspect you'll agree that *none* of those reflect Christian values, but if we honestly take a look around the church, we can put names and faces on each bullet point. And if humility is a part of our genetic or spiritual makeup, we might see our own face there. These beliefs play themselves out in a variety of ways in the church, but the most pervasive is in the area of priorities. Self-actualization *always* puts me at the top of the priority list. If I have to endure church music I don't like, I couldn't possibly become the person God's ultimately created me to be. That music makes me cranky and I can't worship to it; if I can't worship then my walk with God suffers; if my walk with God suffers, then I can't be the person God created me to be. Therefore, the church *must* accommodate my musical preferences…or else. My priority is to meet *my* needs and to get *my* personal desires met rather than to put God's priorities–or anybody else's–above mine, even for the sake of the gospel.

Although church leadership decries self-centeredness, this mind-set is so ingrained for most of us that it seems foreign and even unhealthy to think otherwise. Those willing to make do with less in order to meet the needs of others are labeled codependent. The thought of making a real sacrifice for the sake of the church is considered aberrant and draws criticism at best and a mental health assessment or even institutionalization at worst.

Recently at a church gathering we were discussing Acts 4:34–35:

There were no needy persons among them. For from time to time those who owned lands or houses sold them, brought the money from the sales and put it at the apostles' feet, and it was distributed to anyone as he had need.

As we discussed it, I made the comment that if one of our fellow church members had a legitimate financial need that was so great we couldn't meet it, that I expected members of the church to sell their cars (virtually all of the members had multiple vehicles) in order to meet that need. Another pastor I know later asked me if I meant what I said. I did and I still do—it's a matter of having a different priority.

In Jeremiah we read that we'll find God only when we seek with our whole heart (29:13), when the quest to experience God becomes our uppermost priority. Experiencing the power of God and the promised abundant life isn't going to be a reality in our lives until we make God *the* priority in our lives.

 Because We Don't Know How to Connect

Few observers of the North American church are unaware of its spiritual power shortage. On the other hand, in almost every congregation there are at least one or two people who are clearly "plugged in" with the Divine Power Source. These people are *Practicing Christians.* Whether they're the quiet type or the high-energy type, they live their faith. Many of them are no less busy than you and I. Oh sure, they still make mistakes; they still fall short of the glory of God; but when they do, they admit it and do what they can to make it right. These folks are Christians all day long and they're both the proof and the hope that we too can make a connection with God that will make a difference in our lives. But the question is…how?

This brings us to the third reason there's a power shortage: we don't know *how* to connect with God.

I had the opportunity to offer a workshop on alternative prayer practices based on my book *Prayer for People Who Can't Sit Still.* I asked the organizers how many people I should expect and they replied their experience suggested I could count on twenty-five participants, thirty at the most. So I printed thirty-five handouts, just in case. On the day of the workshop, I set up tables and chairs for thirty people and had ten chairs in reserve. I knew it would be tight if forty people actually showed up, but I knew it was doable. Besides, how much interest could there be about prayer?

The hour came, and the first participants made their way into the room. I casually chatted with a couple here and there as I watched the chairs begin to fill. I was feeling pretty good about the prospects when I noticed someone had to reach for one of the extra chairs. *Good thing I printed thirty-five handouts,* I thought. But people kept coming in the door. We ran out of chairs, we were running out of space, and then the organizer stepped into the room and told me we needed to change rooms. I really didn't see the need for that, but they insisted and I grabbed my notes and followed them into the hall where I was confronted by a line of people trying to get into my workshop. One hundred and sixty-eight people later I was able to begin to a standing-room-only workshop on prayer.

Why the heightened interest? Where did all those people come from? The reality is there's a renewed hunger to learn effective spiritual practices. Jesus' disciples asked him to teach them *to* pray (Lk. 11:1). Their request indicated that they already knew *how* to pray—what they needed was to get a handle on their busyness and to straighten out their priorities. Remember, they were raised in a culture in which God was thought to be a part of everything, so they already knew how to pray.

On the other hand, as I pen these words, I am very aware that we live in a time that's at least two generations from the church. The first mass exodus from the North American church was in the 1960s. Although those born before 1942 generally stayed with the church, many of their children drifted away. These children, commonly called the "Baby Boomers" (my generation), didn't generally return to the church to stay. Though the majority of us have a "church memory," we didn't spend much time practicing anything that looked like spiritual disciplines. And so *our* children were generally raised outside of the church and have no church memory to call upon. With the exception of the occasional funeral, wedding, or a visit to their grandparents' church, they haven't seen anyone really pray, or practice any other Christian spiritual practice. Today, this generation is birthing children who will, by and large, have even less of a clue about Christian spiritual disciplines.

Why was there such an interest in the workshop on prayer? I suspect it's because many of us don't really know *how* to engage in prayer. And if we don't know how to pray, it's a cinch that we don't know how to practice other spiritual disciplines either.

And that brings us to the hope of this book—to introduce you to some spiritual habits that will facilitate a connection to the Divine, no matter *how* busy you are. There's a long and dignified history of spiritual disciplines that have been practiced by the church for nearly two thousand years. From monastic living to contemplative prayer practices, there are many spiritual disciplines that can help transform our lives in spite of your busyness.

SPARKS AND RESISTANCE ⸺⸺⸺⸺⸺⸺⸺⸺⸺

Questions for Discussion and Reflection

1. What are some of the clues in your church that there's a spiritual power shortage? What about in your life?
2. How would you characterize the spiritual power levels in your life? (1) The lights are burning brightly at my house; (2) I'm in the midst of a

"brown out"; (3) The lights are flickering–sometimes they're on, sometimes they're off; (4) I'm in a spiritual blackout.

3. What do you think is the main reason for the spiritual power shortage in North America?

4. Consider for a moment the statement that the church has had a hand in promoting society's value of "self-actualization." Where have you seen signs of this in the church? in your life? What would you offer as evidence to refute this suggestion?

5. It has been said that everyone gets a suitcase with twenty-four hours in it; however, some people seem to know how to pack theirs better than others. How well do you pack your "daily" suitcase? What have you packed into your day that you could live without? What do you wish you could add (besides an extra hour)?

2

The Spiritual Habit of Projection and Reflection

On August 14, 2003, the East Coast experienced the largest blackout in North American history. Beginning at about two o'clock in the afternoon, a power surge shut down a power plant in Ohio. The effect of that single outage snowballed as transmission lines failed, breakers tripped, and generating plants shut down until just after four o'clock, when the dominoes finally quit falling. The blackout left forty million people in the U.S., and ten million in Canada without electricity. The effect of the blackout was so pronounced that it could be seen from space. And, although power crews from across both Canada and the U.S. responded rapidly, full power throughout the region wasn't completely restored for five days.[1]

The Canadian Prime Minister blamed a lightning strike in northern New York. New York responded by saying the outage didn't originate in the U.S. A former head of the U.S. Department of Energy complained that the U.S. was a superpower with a third-world electricity grid. Political pundits blamed the deregulation of the energy market. Fingers pointed at everybody. And nobody took responsibility.

So what happened? Aren't the electric companies supposed to be projecting power needs and making sure they provide enough for the demand? In Washington, my home state, we are host to ten aluminum plants that make incredible demands on the power grid. But Bonneville Power keeps in constant contact with the aluminum companies in order to project their power needs. Did the Eastern Seaboard power companies fail to project their customers' needs? Granted, the power needs of the Northeast are greater and far more complex than those of the state of Washington, but could projections have been better? In the end, the U.S.–Canada Power System Outage Task Force was created to reflect on the incident, review the facts, and make recommendations.

Projection and reflection: These are the twin tools that ensure you and I can turn on the lights in the middle of a dark and stormy night. They're also important tools you and I can use to prevent a power failure in our spiritual lives.

The Power of Reflection

Socrates told his disciples, "The unexamined life is not worth living." And though absolutes never prove true, if we don't take an opportunity for reflection, we're doomed to repeat our mistakes. Whether it's a life lesson, or ensuring there's adequate electricity for tomorrow's power needs, there are several reasons why reflection is a power-*full* tool.

Spare Yourself from Déjà Vu

Déjà vu is that funny feeling you get when you're sure you've been there, done that. It's the feeling I get when I make the same dumb mistake I've been making for as long as I can remember. Reflection can relieve the causes and symptoms of recurring *déjà vu*.

A good friend of mine has a theory about the trials of life. She believes we have the capacity to only learn one significant life lesson at a time. So when hardships beset us, she advises discovering what lesson we're supposed to be learning, since we won't move on to the next lesson until we master the first. If we don't learn it the first time the lesson comes around, we'll only have to repeat it. The same problems will come back to bite us again and again, until finally we *do* learn.

In our world of busyness, however, few people take the time to reflect on much of anything. A careless word here, a thoughtless act there, a promise left unfulfilled, a task left undone all go unnoticed by the cad–but at what cost? What havoc do they wreak? Behind them they leave a trail of hurt feelings, mistrust, and chaos. The problem is, this cad is you and me whenever we don't "notice" what we've said, done, or left undone. And when we *do* finally discover what we've done, it's often too late to do anything about it. There's nothing left but regrets. William O'Rourke wrote, "Regret is an odd emotion because it comes only upon reflection. Regret lacks immediacy, and so its power seldom influences events when it could do some good."[2] By taking the time for timely reflection, we have an opportunity to put things right before thoughtlessness turns to regret. Plus, we have an opportunity to learn a life lesson, giving us an advantage over many people–most folks don't know life's trying to teach them anything.

Taking time to reflect over our day, and especially over the mistakes we've made, lets us study the circumstances surrounding our behaviors. As we do, we can often discern what it was that "set us off," or the events that precipitated our goof.

Wise Decisions Are Better than Knee–jerk Decisions

I'm one of those people who work well under pressure. Somehow I manage to muster motivation best when I taste an upcoming deadline. For instance, as I write these words I'm very aware that my editor is sweating. He's concerned that I may not be able to complete this project by the deadline. And though there is lots of work to do, I'm not sweating it. I relish the pressure.

But there's a difference between working well under pressure and making decisions under pressure. The only decisions I have to make while writing this book are word choices. And as important as the "right" words may be, no one (except maybe my editor) will be concerned if an adjective here or there isn't the exact, precise one "I" was looking for. Besides, that's the beauty of synonyms. On the other hand, many of my business friends have to make critical decisions that affect dozens, and sometimes hundreds, of employees, and cost many thousands of dollars. *They're* under pressure. But those who are successful in business have learned by experience how to make these decisions with aplomb born of reflection. These men and women make good decisions under pressure for one of two reasons: Either they've reflected *before* making their decision, or else they've spent significant time reflecting and learning while making the same kind of decisions in the past. In either case, reflection has been a part of the decision-making process. Those in business who constantly make shoot-from-the-hip decisions either don't stay in business very long, or else they're very, very lucky (and luck only carries you so far in business).

The fact is, life is decisions. We make decisions at home, at work, at school, and at play. Although not every decision is critical, each one represents a different path that we'll be taking. By taking the time to reflect on them, your chances of avoiding a significant power shortage is lessened.

Make Today Your Best Day

When we think of reflecting, we naturally think about looking back. I mean, after all, isn't that what a "reflection" is? Something looking back at you in the mirror? But if you'll forgive my liberties, I want to talk about a different *kind* of reflection: reflecting on those things that are *going* to happen.

Each day presents us with an incredible opportunity to practice our faith. We have decisions to make: how we'll spend our time, how we'll spend our treasure, and how we'll invest our talents. We're going to meet people: some we know well; others we're meeting for the very first time. To paraphrase Robert Frost, everyday we have promises to keep and miles to go before we sleep.[3] How we respond to our responsibilities, how we interact with those around us, and how we get God into our day are important opportunities–too important to leave to chance.

My wife has used an e-mail signature for years that reads, "There is no such thing as coincidence." She recognizes each day is filled with Divine appointments. Every day we have the opportunity to make a meaningful difference in our world, which is why reflecting on your day *before* it happens is important.

When the U.S.–Canada Power System Outage Task Force offered its initial findings in November 2003, they blamed the East Coast power outage on overgrown trees. Apparently, a utility company failed to keep the branches trimmed over some high-voltage lines in part of its Ohio service area. The Task Force concluded that when high electrical demand strained this set of high-voltage lines, they came into contact with untrimmed trees. The transmission lines shorted out, causing a nearby generating plant in Cleveland to shut down and go off-line. These events created a cascading failure that shut down much of the power grid across the Northeast.[4]

Although I'm certain utility company officials learned much from the "reflections" of the Task Force, imagine how much better off the whole Eastern Seaboard would have been if someone had had the foresight to do some reflecting in advance. Perhaps *someone* would have taken tree trimming a bit more seriously.

Projection and reflection are the twin tools for maintaining your spiritual power grid. When you take the time to reflect on your life and on the potential for each day, you reduce the risk of a cascading failure: spiritually, morally, and ethically.

Reflecting the Future: Projection

There's a popular quote that goes, "If you say you can, you can. If you say you can't, you're right!" Most of us have experienced the effects of self-fulfilling prophecies in our lives, both for the good and for the not-so-good. Whether we're speaking into existence something already brewing deep down inside, or hearing the still, small voice of God, self-fulfilling prophecies can be powerful realities in our lives.

To the oblivious, a self-fulfilling prophesy is an act of serendipity. But coaches, psychologists, and motivational speakers know better. Thoughts that bubble up from our unconsciousness, drift into our awareness, and become words we speak aloud have the capacity and the potential to change, not just our lives, but the world around us. This is why projection is such an important spiritual habit to develop.

The Spiritual Habit of A.M. Projection: Starting the Day Off Right

 When we look at the spiritual habits Jesus practiced, one of them was taking time to reflect on the day before him and the decisions he needed to make. One of the best scriptural examples is when Jesus had to choose who would become his apostles from the crowds that tagged along with him nearly everywhere he went:

One of those days Jesus went out into the hills to pray, and spent the night praying to God. When morning came, he called his disciples to him and chose twelve of them, whom he also designated apostles." (Lk. 6:12–13)

If Jesus needed to spend time reflecting on the day to come, it's probably a good idea for us to take a closer look. After all, there's never been a more connected, spiritually aware person!

When we wake up in the morning, we normally have a good idea how we're going to spend the day. If it's a work day, without much thinking we know we're going to crawl out of bed, brush our teeth, get dressed, find our way to work, face the day, have lunch, deal with the rest of the day, come home, have dinner, spend our evening doing whatever we do, go to bed, start over tomorrow. There's not much projection in that. However, if you think about your upcoming day a little more specifically, you'll realize you actually have a much better idea what's coming. For instance, if you're married, you should know who you'll wake up next to. If you have a job you go to, you probably know who you'll be working with, who you're going to see, what appointments you have, and maybe even the important decisions you're facing. If you have a family at home, you know you're likely to spend some time with them after work. Without much effort, you can project most of the day before you, whether you're going to work or spending the day at home. It's the ability to project what the day holds that makes "A.M. Projection" such a powerful spiritual habit.

Practicing A.M. Projection

In 1967, Dionne Warwick sang about saying a prayer "the moment I wake up, before I put on my makeup."[5]

In a nutshell, these are the instructions for practicing the two keys to A.M. Projection: first-things-first and prayer. I'm one of the blessed (or cursed!) ones who doesn't need an alarm clock to wake up in the morning. Most of the time, regardless of what time I go to bed, I wake between 5:30 and 6:00 in the morning. But I'm like most folks I know–just because I wake up doesn't meant I automatically jump out of bed. It takes me a couple of minutes to get my mind moving and to stretch a bit to get my ol' body moving. It was during one those first moments of the day that I learned about A.M. Projection.

Whether or not you need an alarm clock, begin the practice of projection by stretching both your body and your mind. Remember, though, the goal is to spend a few moments in planning prayer, not to snooze and catch an extra ten. I have a personal theory that one of the reasons we have a hard time getting out of bed is because we haven't unfurled our muscles. So take a lesson from the birds. When they first wake, they stretch their wings as far as they will go before they take to the skies. As you wake to the new day, stretch out your legs, your arms, and finally your neck. When you do, your body is more likely to cooperate when you pray.

Once you've stretched and your body is ready, get your heart, mind, and spirit centered through a few moments of centering prayer. (For a full introduction to centering prayer, see chapter 3.) Centering prayer is less a spoken prayer, and more an exercise that takes you into an attitude of prayer and receptivity. It's almost like a guided meditation, except you are your own guide. To practice centering prayer time, get yourself comfortable. (Since you're still in bed, hopefully you're already pretty comfortable). Take a few slow, deep breaths. Focus on your breathing, listening to the sound of your breaths, feeling the rush of air through your nose and throat, and feeling your chest rise and fall. As you do, concentrate your thoughts on your senses and listen intently—some people learn to hear their own heartbeat with practice. When you are fully aware of your breathing, begin to shift the focus of your mind to the Divine Presence in and around you. As you make the mental shift, allow your thoughts to image God's presence. Some imagine a deep and dark cosmos with a distant point of light rushing toward them like a long-lost loving parent with wide open arms. Others like to image a warm light that engulfs and enfolds them. Still others see Jesus standing at the foot of their beds. Whatever it is that helps you sense God's holiness and presence is an appropriate image. When you feel you're in the presence of the Spirit of God, you're ready to practice A.M. Projection.

From this centered place, offer the next few minutes to God as a gift. Start with a brief prayer that lets God know you're ready for some Divine input. You might pray something like:

> Good Morning, Lord. For the next few minutes I'm going to look forward to my day with you. As I do, remind me of the appointments I have, the people I'll meet, and things I need to do. Help prepare my heart, mind, and spirit so that I can be a faithful witness in everything I do.

While you're in this place of prayer, begin to preview your upcoming day and commit yourself to being Christlike in every action and interaction. Ask the Spirit to remind you of each appointment, of the people you'll encounter, the decisions you'll be making, and the tasks you will be accomplishing. As each one crosses your mind, take a moment to envision how you would like each interaction to go. Project yourself into the situation and visualize the preferred results.

For instance, if you know you have a meeting with a client, project yourself into the appointment—let it play out in your mind's eye. What will you say? How will they respond? How will you present yourself as an empathetic listener? If there is a particularly "sticky" issue to be addressed, how will you present it? How will you resolve the appointment? What will be the results? Visualize exactly how you'd like the appointment to flow. Most importantly, as a Practicing Christian, project how you will exhibit faithful ethics, morals, and values. Finally, take a moment to commit your words, actions, behaviors, and attitudes to the Lord.

Repeat this exercise for each of your appointments–including the informal appointments you have, such as riding with your car pool, picking up a latté from your corner coffee shop, or picking up the dry cleaning. In your mind's eye, see yourself at each one and commit your words and actions to God.

This is especially important on those mornings when you wake up and realize there are strained relationships that need mending (whether with family, a coworker, friend, etc.). How will you be a healing presence rather than a source of contention? Project how *you* will be a blessing and how you can bring peace and serenity to the relationship.

As you project your day, don't forget the time you will spend with family. We have a tendency in our society to sacrifice our families on the altar of our careers. When we do, our families suffers from neglect. It's also far too easy to bring our pent-up anxieties and frustrations home and vent them in the "safety" of family. Whatever you do, resist this temptation– learn to leave work at work so you can be fully present with your loved ones. So as you project your day, include your family.

At the other end of the familiarity continuum are the opportunities we have for building new relationships. There are people you interact with on a daily basis whom you don't know well, or at all. Take a few moments to project your interactions with these people as you review the day ahead of you. Paul reminded the Colossians to "Be wise in the way you act toward outsiders; make the most of every opportunity" (Col. 4:5). As a Christian, your faith is on display for better or for worse. The truth is, Christianity in North America generally has a sullied reputation; however, today you may have the opportunity to change someone's mind. That's why it is so important to project yourself into what you might consider insignificant interactions–they may not be as insignificant you think.

Now you may be concerned you'll be spending an extra forty-five minutes each morning in bed. However, I find it typically takes no longer than five minutes to run through my whole day. The mind plays each scene in an amazingly short period of time. Certainly, I occasionally obsess on an important appointment I'm facing, but since I'm in a prayerful place, I can count on the Spirit to quickly point out how to approach the interaction. Then I visualize the appointment with the preferred outcome and commit my words and behaviors to the Lord.

As you finish the spiritual habit of A.M. Projection, close your prayer time with a word of thanks for the opportunities you have this day. Then, take another chance to stretch, and slide out of bed to face your day.

Learning from History: Reflection

I suspect that the person who adapted George Santayana's quote and said, "Those who don't study history are bound to repeat the past," was probably a history professor trying to convince a freshman class there really *is* value in studying the rise and fall of the Carolingian Empire. As important as the ancient past is, it's what you did today that is going to most impact your tomorrow. At the end of the day, taking ten minutes to reflect on how you spent your time, what you accomplished, and who you touched will influence your tomorrow more than a Ph.D. in history. Perhaps the saying should be, "Those who don't study their todays are bound to be stuck in their yesterdays." The mistakes we made, the bad habits we practiced, and the interactions we mishandled today will resurface tomorrow if we don't learn to do things differently.

The Spiritual Habit of P.M. Reflection: A New Beginning's End

The hit single *Closing Time* by Semisonic has a cryptic line that has always intrigued me: "Every new beginning comes from some other beginning's end."[6] When we take time to practice the spiritual habit of P.M. Reflection, we bring a fitting end to our day. We're also preparing our heart and mind for a new and fresh beginning on the morrow. That's a lot of return on, but a little investment in, reflective prayer.

Every year, U.S. consumers spend over $2.1 billion on prescription sleep aids.[7] Although many consumers suffer from insomnia caused by physiological causes, many others–perhaps most of us–can't sleep because of the stress and anxieties we bring to bed with us. And though it won't help you sleep when you suffer from a sugar high or too many cups of coffee, with regular practice P.M. Reflection *can* be a non–narcotic sleep aid.

Beyond the benefits of getting a good night's sleep, P.M. Reflection offers a much richer reward: the opportunity to learn and grow as a Practicing Christian–and remember, it's the Practicing Christian who experiences a steady flow of spiritual energy from the Divine Power Grid.

Practicing P.M. Reflection

Whereas A.M. Projection gets you ready for the day, P.M. Reflection helps you learn from what you've already experienced. This is where we take seriously Socrates' observation that an unexamined life isn't worth living. By taking a look at our behaviors and interactions we ensure we're not heading for a cascading failure in our spiritual life.

In my opinion, the best time to put P.M. Reflection into practice is during the last few minutes of wakefulness. At that moment, you've pretty much had all the interactions you're going to have for the day, with the exception of this last one with God. This, of course, makes it possible to reflect on literally *every* interaction during your day.

However, for some people, as the blankets come up, the eyes close, and the mind switches off. My wife is one of these people, so she practices P.M. Reflection earlier in the evening, when she's less likely to fall asleep. I know of others who reflect on their day during a nightly soak in their hot tub or in a warm bath. These lucky souls not only let go of their day through their reflections, they get to experience physical relaxation as well. I *highly* recommend the practice.

However, there is another reason why you may want to wait until the last possible moment of your day to practice your P.M. Reflections. Research has shown that whatever you put into your mind just before you go to sleep will stay with you through the sleep cycle and into the morning.[8] Not only will it help internalize any decisions you make, you will be well prepared in the morning to practice A.M. Projection. Remember, every new beginning is another beginning's end. That's never more true than when you spend the last few minutes of your day in prayerful reflection.

Whenever you put P.M. Reflection into practice, start by getting comfortable and taking a few minutes in centering prayer. Once you've found your center and connected with the Divine, say a prayer as you begin your reflection time. Your prayer might sound something like this:

> Lord, as I wind up my day, I offer you the next few minutes. Help me recall the words I've said, the things I've done, the people I've helped, and the people I've hurt. Remind me how I brought you honor and how I brought dishonor. You've seen my day; you've never left my side. Teach me how to be a better follower in this time of reflection.

From this place of prayer, begin to reflect on your day. Start by recalling your morning's projections and compare each one to the reality of your experience. It is generally best to review your day chronologically so you don't miss a decision or interaction that may have had a significance you missed at the time. "Relive" each event in your mind's eye. Watch the scene as it happened and ask yourself these questions:

Did the outcome match my morning projections?
  • If so, what did I do right that I want to remember so I can repeat it?
  • If not, what happened? Did I get sidetracked? Was I reactive when I should have been reflective? Did I allow my "buttons" to be pushed and responded in less than helpful ways? Or did I simply misread the whole scenario this morning so I was unprepared?

What can I learn from this interaction?
  • This could be something you learn about yourself, or it might be an insight that you glean about the other person. For instance, besides

learning what you did right or what you could do better next time, you may discover you get defensive when someone is critical of the way you organize your desk. Or perhaps you will learn that when you listen more than you speak, you get better results. Keep your heart and spirit open and listen for the whisperings of God as you reflect—you never know what may be revealed!

Is there something I need to do to follow-up on this interaction?
- Did I make a promise or agree to do something? If so, make a commitment to follow through.
- Do I need to ask forgiveness, make amends, or build a bridge to mend a relationship? If so, commit not only to make it right, but decide *when* you're going to make it right.
- Do I need to touch base to offer words of support, encouragement, or comfort? If so, make a commitment to do so.

Were my words and actions consistent with my faith?
- Was I ethical?
- Was I moral?
- Was I loving and kind?
- Could others see Jesus in my words and actions?

Though this may seem like a lot of questions, and that you may be at this all night long, the reality is that as you practice P.M. Reflection you'll discover you move through the events of your day fairly rapidly. At times you will agonize over a decision you made or an interaction you took part in, but in these cases you will have experienced an important life lesson and will want to take enough reflection time to understand and internalize what the Spirit is trying to teach you.

As you bring your reflection time to a close, take a few moments to confess where your words, deeds, and attitudes were less than faithful and seek Divine forgiveness. Remember, however, that confession isn't the same as repentance. It's fine to say you're sorry. It's another thing to take the next step to make it right. So in your last few breaths before sleep, review the commitments you've made and offer them to the Lord.

When you take the time to practice the spiritual habits of A.M. Projection and P.M. Reflection, you're opening yourself up to one of the most effective tools for growing as a Practicing Christian. Not only will you be enabling self-fulfilling prophesies that reflect the character of Christ, but over time you'll find your decisions and interactions bubbling up from a Christlike spiritual center. When you get plugged into that center, you'll discover an effective connection to the Divine Power Source.

SPARKS AND RESISTANCE ————————————————

Questions for Discussion and Reflection

1. Do you think Socrates was serious when he said the unexamined life isn't worth living? Do you agree with him? Why or why not?
2. What are some of the shoot-from-the-hip decisions you've made in the past? What did you learn from the results?
3. What life lessons have you had to repeat over and over again? What hardships did you have to endure? What changes did you have to make in your life to move on? What changes do you need to make now?
4. What self-fulfilling prophesies have you seen in your church? in your life?
5. Take a moment to reflect on tomorrow. What do you hope to accomplish? Now answer the question, "If you were to look back one hundred years from now, what is it you would wish you had done with the day?"[9] What will you do about that?
6. How would the spiritual habits of A.M. Projection and P.M. Reflection be helpful in your life? How will you incorporate these into your daily practice tomorrow?

3

The Spiritual Habit of Prayer

The North American power grid is a pretty amazing thing. There are over 10,000 power plants that generate the electricity flowing through 157,000 miles of high voltage lines.[1] Those lines carry between 400,000 and 765,000 volts from sea to shining sea, or at least to the local substation where the voltage is stepped down to reasonable 7,200 volts. Seventy-two hundred volts: That is how much power crackles along the typical wooden power pole that stands outside your house. All that electricity flows into the gray cylinder that hangs atop the power pole (or else into that green, metal box near the curb) and gets stepped down to the modest 240 volts that flow into your fuse or breaker box.

The Divine Power Grid is no less impressive. God generates an incredible quantity of spiritual energy in the person of the Holy Spirit. Just for the sake of illustration, we'll say the Divine produces seven billion spiritual yottavolts[2], which is about one yottavolt for each person on the planet. That, of course would be way too much spiritual energy for us to survive if we accidentally made a direct connection (perhaps that's why Exodus 33:20 warns that no one can see God and live). To keep us from a spiritual meltdown, Jesus became the Divine power transformer, taking all those yottavolts and stepping them down to a manageable level so we can actually connect with the power of God and survive. When we *do* connect, our spiritual batteries are charged, the light goes on within us, and we reflect the glory of God (2 Cor. 3:18).

So if God is the spiritual power generator, the Holy Spirit is the power released from God, and Jesus is the transformer that makes it all accessible, then prayer is the transmission wire that carries the alternating current back and forth between us and the Divine. Indeed, prayer is the *only* connection we've been given for reaching beyond our physical existence and into the spiritual realm.

It's generally assumed that Christians know how to pray. I suppose on some levels that's true. As children many of us were taught the standard table grace:

God is great
God is good
Let us thank him for our food. Amen.

Then, if we were raised in the church, we learned the Lord's Prayer. And though we may have heard other prayers here and there, the weekly "pastoral" prayer probably made a huge impression on us. You know, the prayer the minister offered that sounded so *very* holy. In fact, it may have sounded *so* holy it intimidated us and we vowed never to pray out loud in front of anybody. We may even wonder if God bothers to listen to *our* paltry, simple prayers at all.

Yes, we learned *how* to pray…sort of. But what about the kind of prayer that incites the power of God and changes lives? Most of us are clueless. No one taught us *that* kind of praying. And so we listen in awe when someone shares that God spoke to him or her. If by chance they confide that God has a "word" for us, we don't know how to respond. Shock? Consternation? Admiration? Fear? We may wonder *how* they're hearing God. Does the Divine "speak" aloud to them? Do they close their eyes, open their Bible, and point at a random verse, assuming God is directing their index finger? We wonder how *they* got a hotline and all we get, or so it seems, is a busy signal.

The Importance of Praying

In the first chapter, I mentioned an experience I had while leading a workshop based on my book *Prayer for People Who Can't Sit Still.* I was told to expect thirty participants, but ended up with one hundred and sixty-eight folks, many willing to stand against the walls for an hour-and-a-half so they could learn to pray in different ways. There's a serious desire for a touch from God: our spiritual batteries are running low and we're scrambling for a viable connection to the Divine Power Grid.

Take even a cursory glance through the New Testament and you can hardly fail to notice the emphasis on prayer. Jesus modeled it; the disciples wanted it; and Paul told his readers to never stop doing it. Even those raised outside the church know how important it is. In a national survey, the Barna Research Group reported that 82 percent of Americans claim they pray to God.[3] We *know* how important prayer is, we just need some help "running the wire."

It's been widely reported that Martin Luther said, "I have so much to do today that I shall spend the first three hours in prayer." Those who live busy lives (and maybe even those of us who don't!) shake our heads in either disbelief or resignation at his words. If we take a moment to think about what time we'd have to get out of bed for a three-hour prayer session, our head-shaking would turn from bemusement to determination: no way!

Paul told his readers to pray without ceasing (1 Thess. 5:17). His words typically evoke one of two responses. Either we feel frustration over how we'd fit faithful prayer times into our day, or we live with a complacent belief that our whole life is prayer. And though "whole-life-prayer" is a nice sentiment, mostly it's a rationalization for ignoring God most of the day.

We need both. We need intentional times of faithful prayer *and* we need whole-life-prayer. But we're faced with two problems. First, most of us live in a time crunch. When people get busy, their spiritual practices are often the first things that get dropped. We worship less, read the Bible less, and worst of all, we pray less. When we pray less, our spiritual battery meter slips from the green, to the yellow, and finally to the red.

The second problem is the how. Though we may know the Lord's Prayer, and even how to ask God for something or other, most of us don't have many prayer tools on our tool belts, let alone enough to even bother with a toolbox. And, frankly, we don't really understand that whole "pray without ceasing" thing.

Since this whole book is about fitting spiritual habits into the reality of our time crunch, let's tackle the second problem. When you learn some "how-to prays," you'll see how to fit them into your schedule.

To begin with, there's a difference between "prayers" and "prayer." Prayers are those things we *say* to God. Prayer, on the other hand, is a state of being.

Prayer

What's the best way to define a state of being? Philosophers have been giving it a shot since before Socrates. But I'm not much of a philosopher, so you'll have to put up with pictures. The best metaphor I could muster is that prayer as a state of being is like a couple who's been married for a long, long time and decided to take a drive across the interminable plains of the Midwest. Once the conversation ends, after they've passed through Wichita and the scenery is nothing but endless prairie; after hours of driving alone together, they needn't speak a word. There's a silent understanding between them, a palpable presence they both feel, but seldom enters their minds. Yet, there's an eternal assurance that hovers faithfully just within the periphery of their spirits, an awareness of their togetherness, their oneness, and their love.

"Prayer" isn't about the spoken, but the unspoken—there's an awareness that you're in the Presence of God. Brother Lawrence of the Resurrection, a seventeenth-century monk, penned a series of letters and opened his thoughts to his abbot (the overseer of the monastery) about this very thing. Those who knew this unassuming monk recognized a deep spirituality that accompanied his daily tasks. He spent virtually every waking moment aware that he was in the Divine Presence. People came from far and wide to seek his guidance, as if he possessed some secret wisdom that God had entrusted only to him. But nothing could be further from the truth. There was no gnosis, no hidden rituals or rites. The truth was neither shrouded in mystery nor reserved for the sacred mystics. Brother Lawrence simply did what the rest would not:

> We establish ourselves in a sense of God's Presence by continually carrying on a conversation with Him…In order to form a habit of continual conversation with God and referring all we do to Him, we must first intentionally pray and seek His Presence with some diligence; but that after a little practice we'll discover that His love beckons us into His Presence without difficulty.[4]

It was his continuing conversation with God that made the greatest difference in Brother Lawrence's life. Instead of praying first thing in the morning and last thing at night, he would pray "as if" God was with him while he worked.

Whenever he started a task, he would pray, "O my God, since you are with me, and I have to turn my thoughts to these outward things, grant me the grace to continue in your Presence. As I work, bless me with your assistance, watch carefully over what I do, and guide my attitude."[5] Then, as he began his work, he maintained an ongoing conversation with his Maker, imploring God's grace, and offering everything he did to God.

When he finished, he examined how he had discharged his duty. If he felt he'd been faithful and had done well, he gave thanks to God. On the other hand, if he felt he'd done otherwise, he prayed for forgiveness and then without being the least bit discouraged, he set his mind right again and continued his practice of being in the Presence of God, as if he had never stopped. "Thus," he said, "by getting up after I fall, and by regularly offering acts of faith and love, I've arrived at a place where it would be as difficult for me to *not* think of God, as it was difficult for me to *think* of God when I first started the practice.[6]

The fact is, I can't add much more to what Brother Lawrence said. Being in the continual Presence of God, that is, existing in a state of prayer, takes practice. If you want to run a marathon, you don't begin training the week before and, then, on the day of the race expect to get much farther than the registration table.

A marathon is a leisurely stroll if you compare it to your spiritual journey. *That* race takes a lifetime to finish, but, with consistent practice, you can expect to get your spiritual batteries fully charged so you can keep on going, and going, and going...Like the longtime married couple in the metaphor, it takes lots of time to nurture and experience the ever-present Presence. It means making a heroic effort to be in conversation, that is, in saying prayer*s* (talking with God) until it becomes so natural that it becomes difficult *not* to recognize you're in the Presence of God. It is then that words transcend the core of the relationship. The *unspoken* becomes the comfortable silence that you share as you cross the interminable plains of life with the Divine.

Prayers

If "prayer" is the comfortable silence you learn to share with God, "prayers" are the dance of intimacy that gets you there. Our couple traveling across the Midwestern plains experienced each other's "presence" because they were confident in each other's love, they trusted each other, and, indeed, they knew what the other was thinking without uttering a word. But that silent understanding took years of gentle, and sometimes not-so-gentle, conversations. They knew more about each other than their own parents ever dreamed of knowing. They'd shared their hopes and dreams. Together, they'd laughed in the joyful and held each other weeping through the tragedies. From idle chitchat to deep discussions, they spent years speaking from the heart.

That's what "prayers" are. The Psalms are full of them. In that one prayer book, virtually every human emotional outburst is expressed in words we can read, recite, and pray. From being giddy with happiness (Ps. 149:2–5); to the heartbreak of betrayal (Ps. 55:12–14); from suffering (Ps. 88:1–5); to your fiercest anger (Ps. 109:4–12).

No matter what the human condition, Psalms pretty much covers it. Some dare to speak the unspeakable–you'll not hear Psalm 109 read from the pulpit very often. But what a powerful prayer it can be when you've been betrayed, oppressed, or abused! The good news is that when you've read those sentiments prayerfully, even in your anger–even though you may have meant every one of those words–ultimately, you've left it in God's hands. Your prayers, even your angry ones, don't require God to act. Besides, do you really think God doesn't already know how angry you are? (Or how hurt, disappointed, sad, frustrated, or depressed?) Honesty in your prayers is a *good* thing; anything else is *dishonesty.*

"Prayers" are words, whether they be words of anguish or joy, blessing or curse, need or desire. Prayerfully reading a psalm when the needed words escape you can be both powerful and comforting.[7] But there are many ways to "say your prayers," and we'll explore several chosen to fit into the lives of those who are very, very busy.

The point is, it will take more than a misguided theory that everything you do is prayer to make a solid connection into the Divine Power Grid.

Like Brother Lawrence, you'll need to begin with "prayers," and then practice, practice, practice. Only when you do will you discover the power of "prayer."

The Spiritual Habit of Prayer

When I was a child, my mom or dad would come to my bedside every night to hear my prayers. Those were important moments in my life and I can still remember word-for-word what I used to pray:

> Dear God,
> Thank you for today; thank you for tonight.
> Help me to be good; forgive me when I do wrong.
> God bless Mommy and Daddy, David and Kathy, Grandma and
>   Granddad.
> In Jesus' name, Amen.

Today, my prayers are a bit more sophisticated, but probably no more faith-filled. But if that bedtime prayer was the one I still depended on today, I would be a poor, poor man. In the words of Paul, "When I was a child, I talked like a child, I thought like a child, I reasoned like a child. When I became a man, I put childish ways behind me" (1 Cor. 13:11). I have no doubt whatsoever that God heard and cherished my boyhood prayers. But a vital connection with the Divine takes more than a daily fifteen-second monologue, even when it's offered with childlike faith.

When it comes to making a solid connection into the Divine Power Grid, one of the most important things prayer accomplishes is reducing our resistance. In a regular power grid, the amount of resistance multiplied by the amperes equals the available voltage. This law is analogous to what happens with the Divine Power Grid.

The flow of electricity is like the flow of water through a pipe. In this illustration, if you apply pressure to the plunger, water flows through the pipe. Now it flows along pretty well until it meets resistance, such as a clog. When that happens, the amount of water getting through is reduced. But think about it—what happens if you put your thumb over the end of a hose while washing your car? The flow changes from a bucket-filling stream into a pressure spray that you can use to hose the soap off—or drench your car-washing partner. Although there is less water flowing through the hose, the water pressure overall hasn't changed. The same pressure from the faucet is pushing water through a smaller opening, so it makes a water-jet instead.

I= Amperes (Pressure/Power)

V=Voltage

R=Resistance

The same thing happens with electricity. A generator, like a plunger, pushes electricity through the wires (the "pipe" used for electricity). The measure of that pressure is called an *ampere,* or an *amp,* and it's what we normally call "power." However, when the flow meets resistance, less electricity gets through–just as in a pipe with a clog. We call the amount of electricity getting through a *volt.* Just like the water, the resistance doesn't change the pressure (amps), but it *does* change the amount getting through: More resistance, less volts.[8]

As I said earlier, this law is analogous to what happens with the Divine Power Grid. We're told we have the same "power" Jesus had–that the faithful followers of Jesus will do what he did (Jn. 14:11–12). But when that power meets resistance, fewer Divine volts get through. For some, they're getting less than a trickle, not even enough to get the lights on. For others, the light may be on, but there's not enough to charge their spiritual batteries for when the storms of life roll in. However, for a few, the Divine voltage so emanates through them that they glow spiritually. Their spirituality is evident for all to see.

Most of the resistors that reduce God's power are found within us. Sin, guilt, shame, baggage, addictions, poor self-image, and the wounds from our past block the Divine yottavolts. The only effective way to reduce resistance is to engage in prayer. As you do, you'll find some resistors are easily removed; others may take considerable effort on your part. The good news is that if you practice, as Brother Lawrence advised, you may be assured that the Divine Power Grid will never fail to light up your life.

Centering Prayer

 Virtually every spiritual habit begins with centering prayer. When you find yourself in your center and then surrender it to the Divine, your prayer time is more productive.

Although you can practice centering prayer in a noisy, crowded environment, it's easier to learn how to find your center in a quiet place with few distractions until you get used to it. Once you've experienced centering prayer a few times, you'll probably be able to experience it no matter what's going on around you.

The same is true for multitasking. Once you've practiced centering prayer a couple of times, you will probably be able to find your center even while driving in rush hour traffic; however, in the beginning, start by giving the prayer your full attention.

Especially when you first learn centering prayer, you will want to eliminate as many distractions as possible, and that includes leg cramps or backaches. So begin your centering time by getting comfortable. If you're sitting, put both feet on the floor and sit up straight. Rest your arms comfortably and close your eyes. Do a quick inventory of your comfort and shift your position if you need to make any adjustments. While your eyes are still closed, take a deep breath, pause, and exhale slowly. As you do, listen to the sounds of your breath. Continue to take deep breaths and focus all your thoughts on your breathing. Concentrate on these sounds and listen carefully.

As you breathe, release all your thoughts and "visualize" only the dark stillness. Don't force a lot of energy on chasing thoughts from your mind. Instead, when a wayward thought floats into consciousness, rather than diverting attention to give chase, simply let it pass unobtrusively as you refocus on the quiet darkness. When your mind is clear, your body relaxed, and you're fully present to yourself, begin to shift your focus from you as the center of the universe to the Divine.

In this step you're doing nothing less than surrendering your selfness, your "centricity," to the Spirit of God. Begin by visualizing the Divine Presence as a single point of light in the darkness, like a distant twinkling star. Focus on the Divine Light and open yourself to the Holy, inviting it to draw near. As it comes closer, feel the warmth and allow God's immeasurable peace to fill your heart and mind. Visualize and allow your spirit to be enveloped by the light, the calm, and the Presence of God. Take a few moments to simply bask in that place, enjoying unspoken prayer with the Divine.

When you have arrived at this place and you feel the Presence of God within your spirit, you've reached the center and, most importantly, you've surrendered your self-centered place to God. It will be from this place, with the Divine firmly established within your heart and mind, that you can move into the practice of any of the other spiritual habits.

Listening Prayer

It's been said that prayer is a dialogue, but most of the time you'd never know it. Our prayers tend to be a monologue—it's all about *us.* Oh sure, we give God some outs like, "Lord, if it's your will," as if God was going to do something outside of the Divine will anyway, but generally, most prayers seem to be shopping lists of what we want God to do for us. Let's face it, even confession and repentance are asking God to forgive us, that is, to *do* something for us. Even when we ask for God's guidance to make good and faithful decisions, we still tend to end the prayers with a perfunctory "Amen" and then go about our business. It's as if we hope God will give us some sort of a sign so we know what we're supposed to do. Wouldn't it be nice if God spoke clearly so we could listen?

Surprise! That's exactly what the Divine wants. God has been desperately trying to talk to you. The problem is, most of us missed the class on how to tune in God amid all the static of our own thoughts. There's all that thinking, all that noise in our heads that confuses us. Which of those voices is God's voice and which is my id, ego, and superego? Sorting through the voices in our minds is the purpose of listening prayer. However, like centering prayer, listening isn't a prayer that tends to stand alone. Finding the still, small voice of God amidst the chatter is a key practice to many, if not most, of the spiritual habits.

If listening prayer feels like a foreign concept, don't be too alarmed. It's not one of those subjects North American Christians tend to get much training in. Listening to God isn't the same as listening to a friend chatting with you. For one, it's typically not an aural process. Only a very few people, even if you count all the folks in the Bible, get to *hear* the voice of God physiologically. And even those who *have* "heard" the voice of God don't hear it very often; indeed, seldom more than once in a lifetime.

So how can the rest of us *know* when we hear the voice of God inside our heads? It's not as difficult as it might seem—though again, it takes practice. First, you should be aware that there are only three "voices" going on in your head. You only have to discern between the voice of God, the voice of evil or darkness (Satan, the devil, however you identify the dark side), and your own voice. Normally it's pretty easy to figure out the dark voice in your head: that's the voice of self-depreciation, doubt, fears, and all things unloving. That leaves only two voices—yours and God's. Sometimes knowing the difference between those two can be easily discerned—the Divine voice may be loud and clear. But especially when listening is a new practice, it may be difficult to be sure of the difference between your thoughts and God's word for your life. Until you get some clarity, here are some "test" questions to help you tell the difference.

1. Is this thought calling me to my very best? As fallible people, we most often settle for good, even though God calls us to our best.
2. Does this thought call me to repent and/or to make amends for something I've said or done? Admitting we're wrong and/or taking responsibility for mistakes, failure, or sin seldom comes from our own sense of well-being. We'd much rather rationalize it away.
3. Does this thought call me to stop doing something I already know deep inside is wrong? God doesn't wink at sin. God doesn't give us permission to work on one sin at a time. God *does* regularly tell us to *Stop*. Now.
4. If the thought requires me to do something, will it bring honor to God and be considered a loving deed, not only to those who might see, but to those who experience the deed? God's words are nearly always for us to clean up our act or to do some great deed.
5. Does this thought require more of me than I can possibly accomplish on my own? God's vision is bigger than we can imagine on our own.
6. Does this thought reflect something Jesus would say or do? If so, listen carefully.

As the voice of God speaks, you will find yourself compelled to take some action, to adopt some new attitude, or to make a new commitment. Rarely is God interested in leaving us with "gee whiz" knowledge. When God speaks, you'll receive more than an interesting tidbit that makes no practical difference in the fabric of life. God speaks with purpose and conviction. Take the time to listen intently for what God has for you.

Conversational Prayer—Talking with God

Most of us learned how to pray by listening to other people pray aloud. If you were raised in the church, you heard the pastor pray, you probably heard other church leaders and teachers pray, and you may have prayed together as a congregation—such as reciting the Lord's Prayer. Whether you were raised in the church or not, you've probably heard prayers at mealtimes, bedtimes, and even occasionally on a television show. We learn to pray by what we hear, so when it comes time to pray one-on-one with God, some sound like a page ripped from the *King James Version* of the Bible. But nobody talks like that anymore, and you certainly don't have to pray that way.

Brother Lawrence's invitation to practice the ongoing Presence of God is an invitation to the spiritual practice of conversational prayer. Imagine for a moment being "shadowed" at work by a close friend who was interested in getting to know you and your career path better. As you spent the day together, the two of you would have a variety of conversations, not the least would be an introduction to what you were doing or what you were going to do. That visualization pretty well sums up conversational prayer, except that the Divine Presence walks with you 24/7 and bids for your attention. As you will see from the upcoming hints, this method is simple, easy, and extremely effective.

Hint 1: When to Pray

When is an effective time to practice conversational prayer? Whenever you choose to realize you're in the Presence of God. The key to being in the Presence of God is recognizing you're already there. Becoming mindful of that Presence is a matter of consistently jogging your memory, taking a moment to recenter yourself, and bringing the Divine Presence into your awareness.

Over the years, I've been introduced to a number of ways to remind myself to practice the Presence. For instance, office supply stores sell packages of file dots—colored quarter-inch sticky-backed circles used for marking file folders; my wife bought a package of green dots and has stuck them in unobtrusive places around the house, in the car, and in her office. Every time she sees one of those dots, it reminds her to continue her conversation with God. Take a look around our house and you'll find these dots in the corner of our bathroom mirror, on her computer monitor, and in the lower righthand corner of her car's rearview mirror. I learned about another kind of reminder from a doctor. She told me that whenever she hears a siren, she takes a moment to recenter and pray, always remembering to lift up the emergency workers as well as those needing assistance. A Buddhist acquaintance shared that every time he sees a red light it reminds him to pray. You might be surprised how many red lights you'll come across in any given day–stop lights, brake lights, warning lights, digital clock LEDs, and so on. Other possibilities include reminding yourself to practice the Presence every time you hear your digital watch or PDA beep on the hour (when you've developed the habit of praying every time you hear the beep, increase the frequency of the beeping by setting your device to go off every half- or quarter-hour). Practice whenever you hear a car horn, ringing bell, or any sound you will hear regularly. The opportunities to practice the Presence are actually endless.

Hint 2: What to Say

In the North American church culture, there's been a lot of confusion about what we should or should not pray about. Back in 2000, Bruce Wilkinson released his book *The Prayer of Jabez: Breaking Through to the Blessed Life,* and created quite a stir.[9] He suggested that we pray the Jabez Prayer every day: "Oh that you would bless me and enlarge my territory! Let your hand be with me, and keep me from harm so that I will be free from pain" (1 Chr. 4:10). When we do, God will bless that prayer with opportunities. Wilkinson was careful to say this wasn't a get-rich scheme, nor did it manipulate God so we could get whatever we wanted. Nonetheless, many critics lambasted both him and his book as advocating materialism and relegating God to a vending machine, Santa Claus, or the Tooth Fairy.

Although the prayer may be formulistic and presents the potential for being misappropriated (as if God is somehow obligated to grant us anything and everything we ask), underlying the backlash was the notion that it's not okay to pray for prosperity–that somehow God disapproves of our prayers unless we're praying for world peace.

Hogwash.

Remember Psalm 109? (If not, go take a look at it.) That's hardly a call for a peaceful solution to anything. And though I'm sure praying for world peace pleases the Ever-Present Divine, I'm equally sure that bringing about world peace is more our responsibility than God's. Besides, the scriptures are filled with admonitions to pray for everything from forgiveness to the desires of our hearts and virtually all points in between.

So the topic choice is wide open when it comes to conversing with God. However, in the midst of our day-to-day activities, our conversations are more genuine and effective when we pray about whatever task is at hand. Brother Lawrence's prayer is a great example. As he was about to step into a new task he (1) explained what he was going to be doing, (2) asked God to help him continue his awareness of the Divine Presence, (3) asked for assistance in the task, and (4) asked God to guide his thoughts and attitudes.

A more up-to-date example comes from Steve Necessary, vice president of video production of Cox Communications. Steve is a Practicing Christian who takes his faith seriously and engages in several spiritual habits. In a recent conversation, he spoke of conversational prayer:

> I've been inspired by Cecil Day, the founder of Days Inn. I heard of his faith back in college and was struck and remember to this day that it was reported that he would pray before going into a business meeting. I remember thinking at the time, "Boy, that's an odd thing to do." I couldn't imagine doing that. But it placed a seed in my mind that God has nurtured. So today, many times during business situations, during the course of the day, I'll pray. And I *will* pray right before I go into a meeting; I won't pretend to say that I always do, even though it's always a good idea, but many, many times I do.[10]

As you see, seventeenth-century monks aren't the only ones connecting with God while they work. If you learn to continue the conversation each time you start a new task or go into a meeting, you are well on your way in your practice.

Finally, I have a suggestion about *how* to say it. Although we are not, and never will be, peers with the Divine, we've been invited to approach God as we would approach our daddy (Gal. 4:6) or a friend (Jn. 15:14). There are times you may choose to approach the Divine more formally, but if you're going to be spending all your waking hours chatting with God as you go, don't let yourself get hung up on the "hows" of addressing the Lord. Just talk.

Hint 3: Add a Conversation Companion

Although adding a conversation companion to your prayer time is one of the hints for conversational prayer, it nearly qualifies as a different kind of prayer altogether.

Most of the time when we hear someone pray, she or he is praying on behalf of a group. For instance, in our family we pray at every meal, but only one person voices the prayer aloud. The same goes for the pastoral prayer in church and so on.

But that's not the only way to pray. One example would be during a small group prayer meeting. In most prayer meetings, the participants take turns praying. Sometimes the order of praying is random, while at other times the order moves intentionally in a circle of seated participants. Occasionally, but not often, the prayers become spontaneous, prayers build on each other, and it almost sounds like a conversation. In my opinion, this conversational prayer is one of the most enjoyable group prayer practices.

Most of what I know about conversational prayer with a companion I learned from Rosalind Rinker in her book *Prayer: Conversing with God.*[11] Think about it—what does an animated conversation between three people sound like? Do you dutifully take turns speaking? Does the conversation shift topic with each new speaker? Of course not. In a real conversation, each person builds or adds to what the previous person said. There are interruptions, exclamations, interpolations, and so on. Topics change, essentially, by group consensus, but without discussion—no one asks, "Have we completed that topic? Are we ready to move on?" Instead, someone tangents the conversation and away you go, only to be brought back if someone returns to the previous topic later.

Adding a prayer conversation companion is not only enjoyable, it's an especially effective way to pray. There is an extra spark of power in prayer when two or three are gathered for prayer (Mt. 18:20). Further, having a prayer companion holds you accountable to prayer. It's sort of like exercise. If you leave it to me on my own to follow an exercise regimen, I'll get up on the first and maybe even the second morning to work out. But by the end of the week, I'll be lying in bed *thinking* about working out rather than doing it. However, if I have a workout partner who agrees to meet me at the gym three mornings a week, I'm obligated to get up. The same goes for praying. If I have a prayer partner I've committed to meeting on Wednesdays for lunch and prayer, I'll show up for my prayer time—the other person is counting on me.

For us busy folks, adding a half-hour weekly prayer conversation may seem extraneous, but if you'll try it four weeks, I'm confident you won't quit. It will become an important and powerful time between you, your companion, and God.

Getting started is as easy as finding a conversation companion, which is easier than you might think. There are actually a lot of us who would be excited to add this practice to our lives if we only had a willing companion. We just don't know who to ask and, frankly, we're a little intimidated about asking—people might think we're fruitcakes. However, you see, the problem with *not* asking is that there really are a bunch of people out there who would love to have someone to pray with (or who would teach us to pray).

The problem is, no one's asking. You'll just have to be the bold one. A nonthreatening way to gauge somebody's interest would be to bring up this book. "I was reading about conversational prayer, and the book suggested finding a conversation companion. Have you ever heard of such a thing?" If the person's eyes light up and the conversation goes well, suggest a trial run. If they look at you as if you're a fruitcake, go ahead and chat with someone else about it.

You don't *have* to limit the number of conversation companions to just two or three, though the number should be limited. Although a dozen people in a room may carry on a discussion of sorts, intimate and animated conversations are carried on between two to four people. Start with just one or two conversation companions to see how it goes. You can always invite others later if you'd like.

Once you've got a companion or two and you're ready to start, use the following guidelines:

1. If you're on a schedule, set a timer. Time often flies during conversational prayer.
2. Begin by centering.
3. It may help to visualize Jesus sitting in and listening to the conversation.
4. If there's a particular issue you and your companions are aware of, start there.
5. Treat the prayer time as a conversation. Build on the thoughts of each other.
6. Don't be so formal that the group gets caught praying one at a time, politely listening to the others and waiting for an appropriate amount of silence before jumping in. Just jump in. (On the other hand, don't be rude either—treat the conversation as a conversation).
7. Move from topic to topic as the Spirit leads. If you have something to add to a previous comment, don't hesitate. You would if it was in a regular conversation!
8. Remember that the conversation is with the Divine. Don't let your thoughts neglect the image of Jesus sitting there and listening in.
9. Bring the conversation to a close when you've run out of things to say or when the timer goes off. You can always pick up where you left off, either in your personal conversations with God, or later with your companion(s).

I've often scheduled time with a conversation companion during lunch. And, though many business folk like to keep their lunchtimes open for "networking," I've discovered that the most powerful network is the one I nurture with God. Expanding that network by inviting a conversation companion or two has always brought great rewards in terms of connecting with the Divine.

Praying the Lord's Prayer

Probably the best-known prayer in the world is the Lord's Prayer.

> Our Father which art in heaven, Hallowed be thy name.
> Thy kingdom come, Thy will be done in earth, as it is in heaven.
> Give us this day our daily bread;
> And forgive us our debts as we forgive our debtors.
> And lead us not into temptation, but deliver us from evil.
> For thine is the kingdom, and the power, and the glory forever.
> Amen. (Mt. 6:9–13, KJV)

Yes, it's in old English but frankly, that's pretty much how most of the English-speaking world recites it, with a few changes. The Roman Catholics stop at "deliver us from evil." Several denominations say "trespasses" instead of "debts," but my church always said "debts."

When the disciples asked Jesus about prayer, they were looking for a way to pray. "Lord, teach us to pray" (Lk. 11:1). But for all the world, it looks as if Jesus gave them a prayer to recite. Did he expect the disciples to pray those words whenever they prayed? I don't think so. In fact, Jesus had some harsh words to say about those who spent their time praying the same phrases and words over and over and over again: "When you are praying, do not heap up empty phrases as the Gentiles do; for they think that they will be heard because of their many words" (Mt. 6:7, NRSV). If you've prayed the Lord's Prayer every week in church since you were seven years old, you might be able to relate to the words *empty phrases*. Whenever our prayers become rote and we pray them without carefully considering what we're saying, we are in danger of heaping up empty phrases.

So what did Jesus mean when he presented them with the Lord's Prayer? I believe he gave them a model to use that would keep their prayers fresh, meaningful, and would even whet their appetite for more.

"Huh? How do you get that from the Lord's Prayer?" you may ask.

My answer is twofold. The first has to do with structure. I've come to see the Lord's Prayer as a topical outline on which to hang my prayers. It looks like this:

I. Adoration: *Our Father which art in heaven, Hallowed be thy name.*
II. Commitment: *Thy kingdom come, Thy will be done in earth, as it is in heaven.*
III. Petition: *Give us this day our daily bread.*
IV. Reconciliation: *And forgive us our debts as we forgive our debtors.*
V. Protection: *And lead us not into temptation, but deliver us from evil.*
VI. Surrender: *For thine is the kingdom, and the power, and the glory forever. Amen.*

The second part of my answer stems from a question Jesus asked Peter:

"Simon," he said to Peter, "are you asleep? Could you not keep watch for one hour? Watch and pray so that you will not fall into temptation. The spirit is willing, but the body is weak." (Mk. 14:37–38)

Jesus had asked his disciples to keep watch, that is, to stand guard while he prayed on the night of his arrest. Clearly he expected them to be able spend the time both watching *and* praying, so he was disappointed when they couldn't even pray for an hour.

One hour of praying seems like a very, very long time in our culture. The first time I heard someone tell me they regularly prayed for an hour a day, I silently wondered what they could *possibly* be praying for that took them an hour to get it across to God? I felt pretty good that I could communicate pretty much everything I wanted to pray about in ten minutes.

But it was that last thought that arrested, charged, and convicted me. I was praying about everything *I* wanted to pray about. When I began to pray the Lord's Prayer, I discovered that *God* had more for me to pray about than I could have imagined on my own.

The first few times you practice praying the Lord's Prayer, set aside about a half-hour. But as you add to your prayer list, you'll discover you need to add more time. I recommend adding additional time until you are praying an hour or so each time you practice this habit. By personal experience, and from the experience of those who regularly pray over an hour, there is something special about spending that amount of time in devoted prayer to God.

Before you begin practicing this prayer, invest in some sort of prayer journal. Whether you use a journal specially made for keeping track of your prayers, or just use a spiral-bound notebook, listing the people, situations, and decisions you are praying for will help you keep track of who and what you're praying for.

Prepare yourself for praying the Lord's Prayer by finding a comfortable place where you won't be disturbed for at least an hour (or a half-hour for the first couple of times). Spend a few minutes in centering prayer and then begin to pray using the words of the Lord's Prayer as your outline.

I. ADORATION: *Our Father which art in heaven, Hallowed be thy name.*

The Lord's Prayer begins with worship and adoration. In short, this means offering prayers of praise, thanksgiving, and acknowledging the attributes of God. During this time I often start by recalling some of the names of God in the Bible and reviewing how I've seen the Divine Presence work in those ways. For instance, when I think of God as the "Rock of Our Salvation" (Ps. 95:1), I offer words of thanks not only for my "eternal salvation," but for the ways I've experienced God's deliverance through difficult times. While you're praying in adoration, take some time to literally count your blessings and to present words of gratitude for each. Use your journal as you pray to jot down some of the things you're especially grateful for on this day.

II. COMMITMENT: *Thy kingdom come, Thy will be done in earth, as it is in heaven.*

This section of the prayer closely follows adoration because it is the "so what" part of the prayer. Spend this time committing yourself to the Divine's plan for your life. Take a few moments to recognize that God not only wants what is best for you, but for the whole world. Pray for God's will to be accomplished both in your life and throughout the world. Commit yourself to achieving God's will in your life. Think about the decisions you're facing and ask the Lord to show you the "right" decisions (and spend some time listening). Ask the Spirit to reveal where your life is out of line and listen for a response (I almost guarantee you'll hear an answer to this one), then make a commitment that honors the Divine. As a reminder, note in your journal what you have committed to do—and don't forget to go back to your journal to see if you're being faithful to the promises you've make.

During this time of prayer, you will also want to pray for leaders who are making decisions. Pray that God will direct their hearts and minds, and pray especially for those who are not or may not be Practicing Christians. Ask for God's blessing and guidance for your church leaders and denominational leaders. Pray for your supervisor, your employer, and your company. Offer prayers for your civic leaders: city and county council members, the mayor, and the chiefs of public services such as police, sheriff, and fire; your state representatives and senators, and/or your provincial ministers; your governor; your federal representatives, senators, and/or ministers; and your President/Prime Minister. Pray also for other world leaders, including both religious and governmental. If you don't know the names of some of these leaders, find out who they are and pray for them by name. Write their names in your journal so you can remember to pray for them.

III. PETITION: *Give us this day our daily bread.*

Only after adoration and commitment is it appropriate to begin asking God for favors. Asking for our "daily bread" means to seek Divine provision. However, the scriptures invite us to take both our needs and our desires to the Lord in prayer. James, the brother of Jesus, reminded his readers that they often didn't get what the wanted because they weren't bothering to ask for it, or when they did ask, they were asking for desires clearly outside the will of God (Jas. 4:1–3). Perhaps this is why Jesus taught us to pray that God's will be done *before* making our desires known. On the other hand, don't be afraid to ask God for what may even seem self-centered. On two occasions I've known business people who were hesitant to ask God for more customers. However, I assured them that it was okay to ask. (It's always all right to ask for God's blessings on our ventures, so long as they are legal, moral, and ethical). They discovered God apparently *wanted* them to succeed and in both cases their businesses improved. Remember, God already knows what you want anyway, so you might as well go ahead and ask.

This is also the time to make all those "And God bless _____" requests, as well as praying for those who you've committed to pray for (you know, those people who told you their troubles and you said you'd pray about them). Again, use your prayer journal to jot down these prayer petitions. First, it will remind you to pray again for those in need of prayer, and second, it gives you a record of the requests you've made. As you see the results of your prayers come to fruition, make a note by each. These make great opportunities for offering prayers of thanksgiving and adoration.

IV. Reconciliation: *And forgive us our debts as we forgive our debtors.*

There are two parts to this section of prayer: a request for God to forgive us, and a call for us to reconcile with those whom we need to forgive. I'm afraid we often don't take these words seriously enough. Jesus was adamant that we're not *getting* forgiveness unless we're willing to *give* it to others (Mt. 6:14–15). Period.

Begin the first portion by praying for your own forgiveness. Take some time to make a personal inventory of your shortcomings and times when you've stepped out of God's will. Ask the Spirit to remind you of your sin—and once again spend some time listening. As each transgression comes to mind, jot it down in your journal and note who you need to make amends with, and think about what it will take to put things right. Making amends is often the part of reconciliation that gets left out. It's pretty easy to confess our sins to the Lord; we figure God already knows anyway. On the other hand, the consequences of our sin may be considerable when we take the next step. What will it take to make things right with our spouse, a coworker, the boss, or a large constituency of our clients that we wronged when we allowed greed or selfishness to guide our decisions instead of letting God's will be done? Doing right is seldom an easy thing, which is why this is such an important time in your prayer. Don't be afraid to take your concerns and fears and share them honestly with God. Nonetheless, take this time to note your sins, to confess them, and make a commitment to put things right.

There's a second inventory that's necessary during this time—who are you angry with? And who are you harboring ill will toward? In other words, whom do *you* need to forgive? Again, ask the Spirit to bring these folks to your mind, and, as you're reminded, write down the names. In some cases, forgiveness can be pretty easy to give; however, you may have someone or even a couple of someones whom you've been unable to forgive. An abusive relative or spouse, someone who betrayed you, or the perpetrator of some crime against you or against someone you love. These can be difficult folks to forgive, but forgiveness must be forthcoming. If you're having trouble with it, you may benefit from speaking with your pastor, a counselor, or a therapist. You might not be able to make the leap to forgiveness right away, but if you can't, you might as well tell God about it–God already knows anyway.

Ultimately, the point of all this confession and forgiveness is reconciliation–making things right between you and God, which starts with making things right between you and the rest of the world.

V. PROTECTION: *And lead us not into temptation, but deliver us from evil.*

Unless you're a teenager, you're not invincible–and they only *think* they are. This part of the prayer is your opportunity to recognize your vulnerability and to seek Divine protection. Temptation comes in all kinds of flavors, virtually all of them tasty, tantalizing, promising, and seductive. The *real* problem with temptations is that they're so darned tempting! In fact, they can be so tempting that they're difficult to resist, which is the point of this part of the prayer. Notice the subtlety in this phrase. You're not praying for God to step in and deliver you when you discover you're in the midst of a temptation; you're praying for Divine intervention to keep you out of the situation altogether. If you're never in a compromising situation, you'll never compromise your values.

So begin this section by getting honest about your temptations. Remember that God already knows what they are, so go ahead and shoot from the heart. Are you addicted to something? (And here's a hint: If you live in North America, you probably are.) Drugs, alcohol, and tobacco are the "big three" addictions that receive a lot of press, but there are many, many others. Addiction to food or to particular foods is one of the most pervasive enslavements in North America. Bad relationships are another. How many people do you know who keep marrying the same "person"–except with a different body–over and over again? Codependency. Gambling. Sex. Pornography. Video games. Greed. Television. The list goes on and on. Whatever it is that keeps tempting you, spend some time in prayer about it. Ask the Spirit to show you how to avoid your temptations–and listen carefully. Record your temptations, specifically and generally, and what you hear the Lord whispering about how to avoid them. Then make a commitment to steer clear.

However, temptations can't hold a candle to evil. Temptations can trip us up, but evil can swallow us whole. Like temptation, evil comes in a variety of packaging. Circumstances and situations can harbor evil. Evil can sink its tentacles into systemic organizations and processes. And it can come prepackaged in people. We can be minding our own business and evil may just show up uninvited in the form of antagonistic people, unfortunate circumstances, illness, disease, and disaster. In North America, we tend to take evil too lightly. But consider this portion of *St. Patrick's Breast-Plate* prayer:

I bind to myself today
God's Power to guide me,
God's Might to uphold me,
God's Wisdom to teach me,
God's Eye to watch over me,
God's Ear to hear me,
God's Word to give me speech,
God's Hand to guide me,
God's Way to lie before me,
God's Shield to shelter me,
God's Host to secure me,
Against the snares of demons,
Against the seductions of vices,
Against the lusts of nature,
Against everyone who meditates injury to me,
Whether far or near,
Whether few or with many.
I invoke today all these virtues
Against every hostile merciless power
Which may assail my body and my soul,
Against the incantations of false prophets,
Against the black laws of heathenism,
Against the false laws of heresy,
Against the deceits of idolatry,
Against the spells of women, and smiths, and druids,
Against every knowledge that binds the soul of man.
Christ, protect me today
Against every poison, against burning,
Against drowning, against death-wound,
That I may receive abundant reward.[12]

As you can see, Patrick did *not* take evil lightly. Allow yourself time to pray for protection for yourself, for your loved ones, and for your church. Pray for those who are ill and for those who are suffering. If you aren't aware of anybody in particular who's in need of a protective prayer, open a newspaper and pray for those facing difficulties. And don't neglect praying protection for those who protect you: the military, police officers, fire professionals, medical personnel, and others.

VI. SURRENDER: *For thine is the kingdom, and the power, and the glory forever.*

End your prayer as you began—acknowledging the Divine. In the end, everything we see and everything we are belongs to the Lord. Take this time to surrender yourself to that inevitability. This isn't necessarily an easy part of the prayer, since surrender isn't one of the words we embrace in our culture of self-reliance and independence.

Begin with a litany of the things you hold near and dear: your family, your health, your job, your home, and those possessions you particularly treasure. One by one, write them in your journal and give them into the care of God. Pause as you surrender each one to listen for the Spirit's insight.

- Some of the things you hold dear, God gave you to care for. Care for them well.
- Some of the things you hold dear are baggage and chains. Divest yourself of them thoroughly.
- Some of what you hold dear God gave you, but is expecting you to use them differently. Do the right thing.

As you listen, put into ink what the Spirit is saying so you don't forget.

Close your prayer by taking a few moments simply to acknowledge that God is God and you are not. The Lord has a corner on it all: the Kingdom, the power, and the glory. Affirm this truth deep within you as you say your "Amen." Then as you return to the rest of your life, remember that it's not about you—God has it all under control.

Using the Lord's Prayer as a model rather than an incantation is one of the most powerful prayer habits you can develop. For me, the most helpful thing about it is I've already got the prayer memorized, so the outline is always there for me. Once you've read the instructions above, you'll probably be able to pray the outline without needing to refer back to the book. However, reread the section now and again to remind you of some of the nuances.

I've listed the prayer as a solo prayer; it can be even more effective with a conversation companion. Simply use the prayer as the outline and enjoy a conversational prayer on each topic. But be cognizant of the time. A couple of times I've missed appointments because I was so engrossed in the conversational prayer that I lost track of time. Set a timer if you have to get on with life after you pray!

These are just a small selection of the available tools for your prayer tool belt. No matter how busy you may be, you can find a prayer practice that fits into your schedule. If you'd like to explore more prayer practices, I'll be bold enough to point you to my book *Prayer for People Who Can't Sit Still* (St. Louis: Chalice Press, 2005). The book covers ten different prayer methods that can enrich anybody's prayer life, even if you're someone who *can* sit still!

SPARKS AND RESISTANCE

Questions for Discussion and Reflection

1. Do you think prayer is the *most* important spiritual habit? Why or why not?
2. How often and how much do you pray? How does this support or refute question #1?

3. How did you learn to pray and what were you taught? Did this chapter offer any surprise lessons?

4. Do you agree that there's a difference between "prayers" and "prayer"? Why or why not?

5. Discuss Brother Lawrence's process for moving from prayers to Presence. What habits do you need to develop to achieve that kind of connection? Which will you add first?

6. Are you willing to pray aloud in the presence of other Practicing Christians? Why or why not? What would it take for you to be comfortable enough to prayer aloud with them?

7. What prayer style was the most inviting to you? the least inviting? Why?

4

The Spiritual Habit of Study

My dad is a retired senior research scientist. I'm not sure exactly *what* he did—he told us it was spectral analysis, which means he analyzed chemical compositions through absorbed or emitted spectra. Yeah, whatever. But I do remember he had a computer back in the 1960s. His computer took up a whole room at his laboratory and it "read" punch cards, thousands of them. Every so often he had "homework" and he'd bring home a couple of boxes of these cards. I was too young to know exactly what he did with those cards, but I do remember he was *very* concerned that my brother, sister, or I might knock them off the table and jumble them up. It looked complicated, but he told us that computers were amazing pieces of equipment.

Then, in the very early 1970s, Dad came home with a scientific calculator. After dinner he set it in the middle of the table and we got a look at it. We weren't terribly impressed until he clued us in: this calculator not only replaced his lab-sized computer, but it could do the calculations instantly—something his full-size computer couldn't do.

In the early days, Dad could explain to us how a computer worked. We didn't understand him, but he could explain it. Today, pretty much only highly trained engineers understand what goes on inside a computer. Sure, we know it's all ones and zeros counted by chips and processors, but for many of us, even that much makes our heads hurt. We don't care how it works, we just want to be able to plug it in, turn it on, and make it work—and if our PC doesn't give us any blue-screen, fatal-error messages, we'll be happy.

But how do you make a computer work? Hopefully, you read the manual and do what it says. (Okay, most of us guys don't read the manual until we have to.) But in North America, when it comes to our faith, even guys get hung up in the manual. It's as if we bought a new car and fell in love…with the owner's manual. We pour over the manual with a critical eye, soaking in its every nuance. It's as if we have some insatiable passion to understand even how the most insignificant options work before we'll put the key in the ignition. That's how we treat our faith. We're more interested in studying the manual than in doing what it says.

It all starts when we're children in Sunday school. We hear the stories of the Bible–God creating the heavens and the earth; Noah and the ark; David and Goliath. In worship we hear sermons that teach us the finer points about God, complete with Hebrew and Greek language aids. By the time we're adults in the church, we know a lot *about* God. We know more than we put into practice. Christianity in North America suffers from a dilemma: We have way too much information at our disposal, and way too little commitment to practicing what we've learned. We're educated beyond our obedience.

This brings us to the issue at hand: the spiritual habit of study. With what you've just read about education over obedience, you may have concluded that I think "study" is overrated. But that's not the case. We *need* biblical scholars and historians. It's important for those called to teach and preach to be more than just casually conversant in the Bible. However, when it comes to making a connection with God, it's not mining for information that plugs us into the Divine Power Grid–it's "living" with the scriptures and allowing them to rouse our spirit within.

Traditionally, the spiritual discipline of study has been taught as a time-consuming practice. Most sources suggest setting aside a half-hour or more a day for this discipline. And though spending a half-hour or longer in a daily devotional Bible study may be ideal, many of us can't untangle ourselves to take on another thing. But let me introduce you to some habits you can begin today no matter how busy you are (and if you can make some time, I've included some other options as well). But first, let's look at the power we can get from studying the Bible.

The Power in Study

Let the word of Christ dwell in you richly as you teach and admonish one another with all wisdom…(Col. 3:16)

God speaks to us in a number of ways, but one of the most common is through the reading and the study of the scriptures. However, many American Christians don't put much emphasis on reading and studying the scriptures on our own. We've come to depend on the professional clergy and Sunday school curriculums to tell us what the Bible says, rather than reading it for ourselves. We complain it's too convoluted. We're afraid we'll misinterpret it. And besides, who really understands Elizabethan English with all those "thees," "thous," and "the-others"?

For many, the Bible seems to be an intimidating book, to be sure. It seems intimidating because we've bought into the notion that the scriptures are so "holy" that they must be handled with care. I can remember as a young child hearing my grandmother casually mention during a Sunday school class that nothing should be above the Bible. For years I kept my Bible on my bedside table and would nearly panic when another book or magazine was set on top of it.

A second reason we may find the Bible intimidating is because of how it's taught in church. Many times I've heard sermons from well–meaning pastors who expound on the root meaning of a Greek or Hebrew word. Though this is helpful information on any number of levels, whenever I hear it I'm aware that the congregation has just been assured that *they* don't have the background to read and understand the Bible for themselves. The unspoken message is that if you don't know Koine Greek or Masoretic Hebrew, you don't know enough to *properly* study the scriptures.

Finally, the Bible is intimidating because when we've tried to read it we may have been plagued with difficulties. We encounter words we don't understand and would never use in a conversation, sentence structures that are nearly incomprehensible, and far too often we started reading as if the Bible was any other book: We began at the beginning and tried to read to the end. But about the time we reached the genealogies we were ready to surrender. We didn't understand why they're there, we really didn't care, and besides, how in the world do you pronounce *Naphtuhim* and *Sabtechah?*

Let me assure you, however, that reading, studying, and musing on the scriptures can be a joy-filled experience. Neither God, nor those who penned the Bible, intended to confound us. What good is a message if nobody understands it? Remember, God has been trying to connect with us since the garden of Eden. Befuddlement isn't the point.

The Spiritual Habit of Study

Besides the intimidation of Bible reading, there are plenty of excuses why we don't "do" devotions. For one, the only devotional practice some of us have heard about is the sunrise "quiet time." We've been taught that *proper* devotionals include using a Bible reading program, a lengthy period of silent prayer, and perhaps some time for journaling. And, of course, to be *proper* devotionals, you have to practice *every* day without fail.

Let me assure you, those are all myths. In truth, there are as many different ways to practice devotions as there are imaginations. And I've done the research: There's not a single commandment in the Bible that says, "Thou shalt keep a traditional devotional life every day under penalty of hellfire." So feel free to pick and choose your practices—with so many different spiritual habits to choose from in this book, there's no need to feel guilty if you don't practice any particular one every single day of your life. Go ahead. Let yourself off the hook!

Audible Devotions

According to the U.S. Census Bureau, Americans commute an average of about twenty-four minutes to work.[1] For those who live and work in urban areas, that number jumps appreciably. Here in Seattle, the "official" commute time is 23.8 minutes,[2] but most commuters I know will tell you their rush hour commute is between thirty to forty-five minutes, unless of course there's a fender-bender (and there always seems to be). Then all bets are off.

Regardless of your personal commute time, or lack thereof, North Americans seem to be in love with their cars, so we spend significant time in them. Once upon a time, we either listened to the radio or we were lost in thought as we drove. Today, though, many take work with them to do in the car. Cell phones and PDAs have staked a claim on our drive time. Nonetheless, the commute offers an unparalleled opportunity to spend time developing the spiritual habit of study.

With the advent of the Bible on tape, CD, and MP3, you can listen to the Bible as you drive, ride the bus, or vacuum the bedrooms. For those who haven't managed to fit a dedicated "quiet time" into their lives, or for those who want to spend additional time in the Bible, this can be an ideal way to develop the practice.

However, those I've spoken to about audio Bible reading have admitted that, though they listen to the Bible faithfully while they drive, it hasn't helped them make a power-filled connection with God. Something seems to be lacking. Part of the problem is when we multitask and listen to the Bible while doing something else we tend to simply let the spoken words wash over us in an unending stream. We "hear" the words, but we aren't always *listening* to them. So passage after passage and thought after thought dance through our minds, but none has an opportunity to stick. If we don't take time to pause and muse on a particular thought, we only hear the "big picture." Though that's not such a bad thing, it tends to short-circuit the Spirit's "still, small voice" that whispers the secrets of life into your soul.

The obvious "fix" is to listen to smaller portions of scripture. For instance, an appropriate serving could be a single story, such as the parable of the good Samaritan, the battle between David and Goliath, or the feeding of the five thousand. Another suitable excerpt would be one of the Psalms or perhaps a paragraph or two from the letters, such as James' exhortation about faith without works or Paul's instructions about communion. Even a passage as short as a single verse from the book of Proverbs may be suitable. Whatever the length, the point is to allow your mind to wrap itself around a single theme, topic, or thought so the Spirit can have its way with you.

You can practice audio reading in almost any setting. Of course, it's especially suitable while in your car, particularly if you're alone or in the presence of others who would like to develop the habit along with you. However, you can easily practice it on the bus, in your office between appointments, on a treadmill at the health club, or while doing housework. In other words, you can practice audio Bible reading almost anywhere and anytime you're able to multitask.

Let's turn to some study habits you can practice.

Lexio Divina

 *Lexio Divina* (pronounced LECK–tee–oh dah–VEE–nah) is one of the oldest scripture reading practices known to the church, dating back to the desert *abbas* and *ammas* (fathers and mothers) of the fourth century. Although some speculate that the practice was once widespread, until recently the *Lexio* was generally reserved for monastics. However, the rising interest in North America of all things spiritual has coaxed the *Lexio Divina* from behind the closed doors of the cloister and into the public domain.

Historically, there are four elements of the *Lexio Divina: lectio, meditatio, oratio,* and *contemplatio,* roughly translated from the Latin as reading, meditation, prayer, and contemplation. We'll use this same four-step monastic process, but adapt it for our fast-paced culture.

Begin the practice of *Lexio Divina* by choosing a passage. If you have a copy of the Bible in front of you, this is a fairly easy decision to make. You can either open up the Bible randomly and choose a "complete" passage (story, paragraph, or thought), decide to begin in a specific book and read through it passage by passage, or use another Bible reading plan that suggests a *single* story, passage, or thought. However, when you're going to *listen* to the Bible, it can be difficult to be spontaneous. The various audio formats tend to dictate you choose a particular book or section of the Bible in advance. Most CDs and MP3s are formatted so you can make a selection by chapters, but the only convenient way to use a cassette is to listen from the beginning of the tape. It can become rather difficult to get more specific than that. However, don't let that deter you. If you have the ability to choose book and chapter, feel free to do so. If not, just go with the flow. It's amazing how the Divine can intervene no matter what technological shortcomings there may be.

A note about safety here. If you're going to multitask and practice *Lexio Divina* while driving, choose your selection *before* you leave the driveway. Trying to find the CD with Psalm 121 on it, get it out of the case, into the player, and then find the right track as you're navigating the neighborhood or weaving through traffic is a hazardous practice. Get your player loaded up and ready to go *before* you turn the key.

1. CENTERING. Okay, you've made a selection, it's in the player, and you're ready to go. The first thing to do is to get your heart, mind, and soul centered. This time, however, closing your eyes won't work (on the other hand, if you're on a treadmill, go ahead and close them). Take a few deep breaths and relax. Listen to your breathing and center your thoughts on the Divine Presence. It may help to picture Jesus sitting with you in the car (on the bus, in the living room). When you feel the Spirit's Presence, offer a brief prayer asking God to speak to you through the scriptures. You might pray something like this:

> Divine Lord, for the next few minutes I'm going to spend some time in your Word. As I do, open my mind so I can listen and learn whatever truths you want to speak. Help me to listen well so I can connect with you and hear what you want for me and from me today.

2. READING *(LECTIO)*. Remember that the point of this practice is to capture a single passage or thought. In the traditional practice of *Lexio Divina,* you would read a passage from the Bible, close your eyes, and roll the words around in your mind. To practice with audio, listen to the passage and then press the pause button on the player. Now take a few moments to think about what you just heard. Think about the passage as a whole and ponder what you think the main point of the passage is. If any particular thought, phrase, or word sticks in your mind, let that thought hang there for a time. Don't dwell too much on it just yet. Again, in the traditional practice, you would read the passage over a couple more times. With audio, this is relatively easy to do if the passage happens to be at the beginning of a track—simply press the previous track button on the player and it will restart the passage. However, if the passage is midway through a track, or if you're using a cassette, repeating a passage is an inexact science at best. Don't get too wrapped up trying to get it exactly right—obviously it's more important to keep your eyes on the road. As you listen to the passage a second or third time, listen specifically for a thought, phrase, or word that captures your attention. When one has, you're ready to move to the next step.

3. MEDITATE *(MEDITATIO)* The word *meditate* may conjure up images of lotus positions and someone chanting "Ohhhhmmmmm." Of course, this is far from what the word means, but a lot of baggage is attached to it. *Meditate* simply means to calmly reflect on something, and that's what is called for here. Once a thought, phrase, or word from the passage has your attention, take a few moments to meditate on that thought. Ask yourself why this particular thought has claimed your consciousness. Is it addressing some issue you've recently been dealing with? Is there something rooted in your past you've been reminded of? Has some fear, anxiety, concern, joy, or relief been addressed? Pay attention not only to your thoughts, but to what you're feeling. Your emotional feelings may be revealing. Continue to meditate on the passage until you feel compelled to move on.

4. PRAY *(ORATIO)*. Although praying is often defined as a conversation with the Divine, most of us practice it as a monologue. We talk, God listens. But that's hardly the biblical example and practice. When Jesus went up the mountain to pray, he went looking for guidance and answers–which he got (Lk. 6:12–13). Today, listening in prayer seems almost like a long-lost practice. However, it's an integral part of the *Lexio Divina*. Once you've spent time in meditation and feel ready to continue, take some time to seek direction from the Spirit. Ask for insight into the passage. Ask what the Lord is revealing to you here. And then simply "listen." (For more on how to listen, see chapter 3.)

5. CONTEMPLATION *(CONTEMPLATIO).* The last step comes only after you've taken the time to prayerfully listen to the Divine. In the traditional practice of *Lexio Divina,* contemplation means to move from meditation to the next level of presence with the Divine:

> Sometimes, by the infused grace of God, one is raised above meditation to a state of seeing or experiencing the text as mystery and reality; one comes into experiential contact with the One behind and beyond the text. It is an exposure to the divine presence, to God's truth and benevolence.[3]

The key word there is *sometimes*. I *do* know people who reach that particular level on a consistent basis, but they don't do it while driving their car or doing the dishes. The contemplative practice that takes the few into an encounter with the Divine demands the ability to give your whole heart, mind, soul, and body to the experience. If you are practicing the *Lexio Divina* in solitude and have the time to devote to it, there is nothing better than to go there. However, when you're multitasking (or if you're like me and don't have the disposition for contemplative prayer), then practice this fourth step differently.

After spending time prayerfully listening and discovering what God has to say to you, use this last step as your response. Far too often, God speaks and we want to look the other way. At first we may make a valiant attempt to ignore what we're hearing, but if we practice tuning God out, we eventually get good at it. This is why we may find it difficult to hear God when we try to reengage. So when you hear the voice of God *this* time, ensure you take this last step: Contemplate how you're going to put what you've heard into practice. This step is more than just offering a short prayer that says, "Okay, God, I hear you. I'll take care of it." Take the time to contemplate *how* you're going to implement God's leading. If you need to repair a relationship, how will you do that? Will you make an appointment? Write a letter? Pick up the phone? And if so, when? If you have a habit or an addiction to let go of, when will stop? Are you able to do it on your own? If not, who can you call on to help?

As you contemplate, examine the plans you make to ensure they honor what God's said to you. Remember, it's our nature to rationalize away, to distort, or to water down what the Lord says. If you'll honestly listen and heed the Spirit's nudges as you plan, you can be confident that the Divine will empower what lies before you. As the ancient proverb says: "Commit to the LORD whatever you do, / and your plans will succeed" (Prov. 16:3).

The practice of *Lexio Divina* may seem time-consuming and the instructions overwhelming. However, if you drive the average commute time in the U.S., you will probably discover there's enough time for all the steps, especially if you began your trip with your scripture selection ready to go. Occasionally you may find yourself so caught up in one step or another that you aren't able to finish by the time you arrive at your destination, or by the time you finish on the treadmill. Stay with the prayer time if you have the extra few minutes. If your schedule won't allow, don't get uptight or feel guilty. God understands. Simply make a commitment to take up where you left off later on, perhaps on your way home. And though you may have to get on with your day, remember, you're not leaving the Presence of God. You couldn't do that even if you wanted to.

Imaging the Word

 Do you have a longer commute or a bit more time on your hands? Feeling a bit adventurous? What would happen if you stirred prayer and television together? How about mixing daydreaming and devotions? Intrigued? Then, in the words of Monty Python's Flying Circus, "Now for something completely different."

Imaging the Word is a scripture study practice that dates back nearly five hundred years, but was probably practiced long before. The first instructions we have to this practice are found in the *Spiritual Exercises* of Ignatius of Loyola. This particular study habit is radically different because it uses a function of the brain traditionally regarded by the church as taboo—the imagination.

Imaging the Word is a unique spiritual practice because it isn't word-focused; instead, it depends on images—or, more precisely, imaging. Those practicing Imaging the Word sometimes say it's like watching TV inside their heads or daydreaming through the scriptures. But your in-the-mind TV surpasses even a fifty-five inch flat screen high definition plasma on-the-wall television with a twelve hundred watt super-bass Dolby® surround sound, as contemporary as all that may be. Imaging the Word is limited only by your imagination. Vivid colors, multisensory experiences, surround sound, infinite portability, and besides all that it's interactive.

A quick word for those seeing red flags and signal flairs going off when you hear the word *imagination*. I remember my grandmother warning me about the spiritual consequences of idle minds, daydreaming, and the imagination. She may even have suggested that the imagination is off limits to Practicing Christians because of Ezekiel's words:

> Say to those who prophesy out of their own imagination: "Hear the word of the LORD! This is what the Sovereign LORD says: Woe to the foolish prophets who follow their own spirit and have seen nothing!" (Ezek. 13:2–3)

And though I agree that the mind can imagine all sorts of evil–and it regularly does–it also imagines all sorts of incredible good.

The fact is, your imagination is a gift of God that you can use for better or not. It's like any other God-given gift, from grapes to gab. You can make wine from grapes and drink until you can hardly stand, or you can have a nice chardonnay with dinner. Your words can bless or they can curse; bring comfort and hope or destroy a reputation. According to the psalmist, *everything* in the world is a creation of God (Ps. 89:11). On the other hand, according to John, *everything* in the world is under the control of the evil one (1 Jn. 5:19). The point is, we were given the responsibility as stewards of the earth to care for the resources on this planet, and we can use them for good, or we can use them for bad. The choice of how to use the resources God entrusted you with, including the imagination, is yours. As Paul instructed the Corinthians, "Whatever you do, do it all for the glory of God" (1 Cor. 10:31). The point of Imaging the Word is to do just that: to make a connection with the Divine in order become more Christlike.

To practice Imaging the Word takes a bit more time than the average commute. Plan on spending at least thirty minutes, though as you get familiar with the practice you may want to plan on even longer. I tend to practice for forty-five minutes to over an hour.

Although *The Spiritual Exercises* use virtually any scripture passage for the practice, I recommend beginning with narrative passages, that is, stories rather than instructions, lists, and so on. It may take more imagination than we can muster to create an interactive image of the purity laws in Leviticus, so choose a passage that has characters, whether they're people, angels, animals, or God. The popular stories such as Noah and the ark, the birth of Jesus, or the prodigal son are great. Don't neglect the lesser-known stories such as Balaam's conversation with his donkey, or Joseph's conversation with the baker and the cupbearer. There are literally thousands of Bible stories you can turn to. If you're not familiar with the wealth of stories in the Bible, consider picking up one of the children's Bible storybooks. These generally include stories written in short vignettes, and some contain literally hundreds of stories, so you'll not run out anytime soon.

I again recommend choosing the scripture passage and getting it cued up before you hit the highway for the sake of safety. Once you've made your selection and have it cued up, you're ready to go.

1. CENTERING. Whether you're going to read the scriptures at the kitchen table or listen to them while fighting traffic to the mall, begin by taking some time to get centered. (See step one of the *Lexio Divina* for instructions if you need to be reminded how to find a centered place on the go.) Once you find a centered place, you will want to offer a prayer something like this:

> God, for the next few minutes I'm going to be spending some time in your Word. As I do, guide my imagination and my thoughts so that all I experience honors you and helps me become even more faithful to you. Let my thoughts be your thoughts, and only your thoughts. Show me your truths and how to walk in your way.

Once you've committed your mind to the Divine, you're ready to enter the scriptures.

2. READING (OR LISTENING). When you read the Bible for the *Lexio Divina*, you focus on listening for a thought, phrase, or word that makes a claim on your attention. However, for the practice of Imaging the Word, you need to hear the passage as a whole. Press play and listen to the big picture, follow the plot, and let the storyline carry you along. When you get to the end of the story, press pause and review the story in your mind. Live with it for a few moments, musing over what you've heard and taking stock of your feelings. After a few moments, rewind the passage and listen again. This time listen for details. How many characters are there and who are they? Are there onlookers nearby? What's the setting? A marketplace? A city? The temple? A village? A pastoral field? Is it daytime or night? What's the weather like? Of course the words you hear might not supply all the answers; you will have to let your imagination supply them. Listen to the story at least three times so that you're comfortable enough with the chronology of the events and details that you could faithfully tell the story to a four-year-old who knew the story so well they'd correct you if you left out something important. Note that I said *faithfully* tell the story—that doesn't mean verbatim or word-for-word. Faithful retelling means getting the plot and storyline right. It *doesn't* mean getting every detail correct, so relax. When you're comfortable enough with the story that you can replay it in your mind without relistening to it, you're ready to move to the next step.

3. IMAGING. Here's where your imagination *really* kicks in and the fascination begins. You've heard the story at this point at *least* three times and you're confident enough you could retell it to a four-year-old. Now begin picturing the story in your mind (as if you were daydreaming). Start with the setting (day or night, hot or cool, city street or rural pasture). Then add the characters of the story, but with one difference: Put *yourself* in the scene. Remember, your *imagination* is coordinated with and protected by the Spirit (you gave God permission, remember?), so let yourself go.

As you image, you can choose to be anyone in the scene you're comfortable with being. For instance, in the story of Noah and the ark you could be Noah, his wife, one of his children, or a bystander in the crowd who drowns when the rains come. Regardless of who you choose to be, in the words of every great drama coach, "Stay in character." If you're Noah, be Noah. If you're you in the crowd, be you. However, staying in character doesn't mean you can't ad-lib. Regardless of who you choose to be in the story, you get to interact. You can ask questions and listen to the answers. You can take a stroll and see what there is to see. And you can examine your emotions, that is, the feelings of your character, as you experience the story unfolding. Remember, stick with a faithful rendering of the story, but allow yourself room to ad-lib. The goal of this exercise is to allow God to reveal and/or to share with you insights that are pertinent to your life in the here and now.

Let me share an example from my own experience. The very first time I tried this spiritual habit, I was at a junction in my life when I was trying to figure out my future. I had been pestering God to show me what was next in my life, ostensibly so I could make appropriate decisions and draw up some detailed strategic plans. On a lazy summer afternoon after work, I walked out into a wooded area of the neighborhood, sat down, and opened my Bible. I randomly turned to the Gospel of Luke and began reading the account of the angel Gabriel's announcement to Mary. When I put myself into the scene, I decided to be a bystander. I was in the room where Mary, a young teenage girl, was sleeping on a pallet on the floor. There was a single opening in one of the stone walls and moonlight spilled into the room. Suddenly Gabriel appeared. He didn't have wings or a halo, but he was dressed in white. He began his spiel, "Hail favored one–the Lord is with you." Mary woke with a shake and was clearly startled by this presence in her room. (Would you blame her?) I listened to their conversation and Mary was obviously filled with joy and excitement knowing her son was going to be King over Israel. It was also clear to me she didn't have a clue about "the rest of the story." I knew the end of the story. I assumed Gabriel knew it too. So when he finished, but before he departed, I asked, "Why don't you tell her? Why don't you tell her the truth, that her son is going to die a tragic death and she's going to live to see it?"

Gabriel glared at me. You may not have ever been glared at by an angel, let alone an angel who actually stands in the presence of God, but let me assure you that it isn't terribly pleasant. I shrank back a bit, and then he spoke. "Let her be. She knows what she needs to know for now. Why trouble her with the future? Leave her with her joy today." And the scene ended.

As you relive *your* story, it's important that you're more than just an omnipresence watching from afar. Put yourself into the scene, even if you're an extra bystander rather than a character in the story. The experience of being a part of these Bible stories is unmatched. It's vital that you interact, that you ask questions, and that you pay close attention to what you're feeling and to what you're experiencing. It's this experience–what you see, hear, and feel–that the Spirit will use to teach and to guide you.

The actual practice of Imaging the Word typically takes the longest time. In the past I've spent nearly an hour just living in the story, watching it unfold, interacting with those I meet, and so on. It can be quite invigorating and I often didn't want to it to end. But there will come a time in your imaging when it is clearly over. It could be an abrupt ending to the story like I experienced with Gabriel. It could be that the crowd just wanders away. Sometimes an image seems to either freeze or a part of the scene skips like a record and plays over and over. However you experience it, when you know the story is finished, it's time to move to the next step.

4. MEDITATE. When you've finished the story, it's time to return cognitively to the Divine Presence to consider what God may be telling you. Begin by meditating on what you experienced. What did you feel as the story unfolded around you? What surprised you? Were there any "aha!" moments or new insights you came away with? As you ponder these questions, listen closely to the Spirit's whisper. What is it God may be trying to say?

I've discovered that typically when I come away from imaging, I have a pretty good idea what God is trying to get across to me. Most of the time it's rather obvious. In the story of Gabriel's conversation, God was saying: "The future in mine, not yours. Live in your today and leave tomorrow to me." It was a hard lesson to hear, and to be honest, it's a lesson I'm trying to apply still today. But the fact is, when I finished my reading, meditation, and contemplation time, I felt a release from drawing up a strategic plan on a future I couldn't know.

As you listen, expand your meditation time from understanding to obedience. What is it you're being called to *do* about what you've experienced? Is there a misdeed to confess, repent of, and make amends for? An addiction you need to release? An attitude you need to adjust? God rarely speaks to us for the sake of building up a file of interesting information. When the Lord speaks it's nearly always to call us into action or to make some change. Apparently none of us are so mature, complete, sinless, and finished that God has nothing better to do than offer idle chat. If you're not feeling compelled in some way, stay in a quiet listening mode until the Spirit speaks.

5. CONTEMPLATION. This last step is identical to the one outlined in the *Lexio Divina*. This is the time to contemplate what God has said and to make a commitment to put those words into practice. Whether it's about letting go of the future, how to handle that annoying neighbor, making amends to the barista you blasted when she got your latté wrong, or standing up against an unethical corporate decision, take a few final minutes to make a commitment in prayer. Then make sure you accomplish whatever it is you've said you're going to do. As Jesus said, "Simply let your 'Yes' be 'Yes,' and your 'No,' 'No'" (Mt. 5:37).

My wife and I have been leading small groups in the practice of Imaging the Word for nearly fifteen years. Occasionally someone will tell us they simply don't have the imagination for it, but by far the most common response is something like, "Wow! Wait 'til I tell you what I saw."

The practices of *Lexio Divina* and Imaging the Word are both suitable to practice in a crowd (assuming you can tune a crowd out). By using an audio Bible, both practices are usable during a commute or while doing other tasks that can spare divided attention. Of course, both work even better if you can give them your *undivided* attention–but don't wait for those times. Start your practice today (or on tomorrow's commute).

Desktop Devotionals

Before Augustine was a saint, he was pretty much like the rest of us. His life was filled with the everyday and, though he had plenty of potential, he wasn't living up to it. On one of his more angst-filled days, he sat on the back patio trying to figure life out. The afternoon breeze carried the sounds of the neighborhood, lightened by the joy of children playing in the street. But Augustine paid no attention to their childish games or their giggle-voices; a heavy, swirling fog enshrouded his thoughts, occupied his heart, and beset his mind. But in spite of himself, his deepest spirit heard their playful chants: "Take up and read, take up and read." The mist parted just long enough for Augustine to hear the Divine's invitation. He picked up his mother's Bible and began to read. His life was forever changed that very day.

Reading the Bible can be a life-changing event. But for many in the North American culture it feels like a chore, not a catalyst. It may feel that way because of how we were taught to read the Bible. For one, from the first grade, we were taught the best way to read a book was to start at the beginning and read straight through–not a good way to read the Bible. To get past that hurdle we may decide to use a Bible reading program such as *Through the Bible in a Year*. Though it may be good to read the Bible at breakneck speeds, the purpose of the spiritual habit of study is to open the door to the Divine Presence. This is best accomplished by living with and in the Word–not by speed-reading. There is a third reason Bible reading may feel like a chore and not a catalyst, especially for those who have visited a college class or two. Rightfully so, our educational system teaches us to read critically for information, but that's not an appropriate way to approach the spiritual habit of study. The Word is not a textbook, and we're not facing midterm exams (though there *will* be a final–not on what we know, but on what we've practiced). The Bible is a *living* book, the Spirit speaks to us differently each time we "take up and read."

Reading from beginning to end, speed-reading through the scriptures, and studying with a critical eye to accumulate knowledge are not healthy practices in the spiritual disciplines. Couple these with laboring through a four-hundred-year-old translation and you have a recipe for stale flatbread rather than the bread of life.

One last thing before you open the Bible: learn the rules for reading the Bible. Rule #1: There is only one rule, and that is, "A single Bible verse or thought does not a theology make." In other words, it's not appropriate to take a verse or thought out of context to try to make it stand alone as "a truth." That's exactly how many cults and sects have started–someone took one verse out of the Bible and convinced themselves and others that it was the chief rule for life or the truth on which the Bible depends. The goal of the spiritual habit of study isn't to start a new religion, so when you read, don't make a verse into more than it is.

Although there's really only one *rule* for reading the Bible, some helps will make your time more fruitful. First, choose a translation of the Bible that's written in a version of English you understand. Although the *King James Version* is one of the most beautifully written works of prose in the English language, it was the "Good News for Modern Man" back in 1611. It was written in the poetic language of the day (think Shakespeare) that beautifully reflected the spoken language, so when people read it or heard it read, they understood every word. But language is ever evolving, and the vernacular of 1611 isn't just uncommon today, it's barely understandable.

A number of great translations have been released over the past few decades that are very readable, as well as several paraphrases. *The Good News,* recently better known as *Today's English Version,* was one of the first easy reading versions in North America; however, translated in the 1960s, even it is somewhat dated today (though still a very easy-to-read version). Other contemporary versions that use today's language include:

1. *The Contemporary English Version*
2. *The New International Reader's Version*
3. *The New Living Translation*
4. *The Message*

Other versions are being worked on even now, so before you make a choice you will want to make a personal comparison to see which one you best resonate with. Choose one that is pleasant both to the eye and to the ear and you'll discover your time in the Bible becomes more and more fruitful.

A brief note for those of you who, like me, may be so familiar with the Bible that reading it can occasionally seem dry. Recently I discovered that reading one of the more contemporary versions significantly widened my horizons. I had the fortune to pick up a copy of *The Message* and read one of those seemingly all-too-familiar passages. *The Message* not only updates the language, it uses current idioms that introduce a freshness and spontaneity of thought I hadn't experienced since I was a teenager. So if you've been using the NIV, NRSV, or one of the other more "technical" versions and you'd like to add a new dimension to your spiritual practices, consider changing versions–at least for the devotional times in your busy life.

When it comes to "helps" in your Bible reading time, one of the most common may not really be much of a help at all. There are many different Bible reading programs available that have been designed to help readers systematically read their way through the scriptures. One of the most commonly known, *Through the Bible in a Year,* emphasizes reading a good bit of scripture every day. There is nothing wrong–and lots that is right– about reading copious quantities of the Bible in a designated period of time. As Paul reminded Timothy, "All scripture is inspired by God and useful for teaching, for reproof, for correction, and for training in righteousness" (2 Tim. 3:16, NRSV). I suspect he meant *all* scripture, and thus there's plenty to recommend getting familiar with the whole Bible. However, it's not the amount of scripture you get through, but the amount of scripture that gets through to you. Although a couple of spiritual habits in this chapter require reading considerable portions of the Bible, until you have prioritized your schedule to include significant time devoted to reading and study, I'd suggest avoiding most of the Bible reading programs.

On the other hand, devotional books tend to use short passages of scripture and couple them with a devotional thought of the day. These *can* be helpful for some of the spiritual habits introduced here. However, even these can get in the way of making a connection with God, since they tend to steer the reader's thoughts to a particular conclusion...It could be that the Spirit has a very *different* conclusion to offer you. So don't be too hasty to add these into your reading time, but also don't rule them out either. (How's that for paradoxical thinking?)

How much time can you carve out of your schedule for a quiet time with God? Now I know this could be a guilt-inducing question, but the only person you have to be honest with here is yourself. You may be at a place where you feel like you can't add one more thing, even if it doesn't take up *any* of your time, let alone a few minutes. In that case, give yourself a break and move on to another chapter. No guilt, you can always come back when you get a break. But if you can set aside as few as ten minutes a day for a one-on-one devotional appointment with God, then read on.

Okay, if you're still reading, either you can set aside an extra ten minutes, or you're a dedicated sequential reader and the thought of skipping a chapter seems sacrilegious. But since you're here, let me share a couple of "desktop devotionals" that have the potential for connecting you with the Divine high-voltage lines.

Don't let the term "desktop devotionals" mislead you. You can practice these spiritual habits anywhere you can park yourself for a few minutes. That may be at your desk at home or work, or it could be on the bus or sitting at your local coffee shop. If you're the kind of person who can't focus through the noise and potential interruptions around you, you'll want to find a quiet place, or at least close your office door. However, I almost always practice desktop devotionals at my local Starbucks. Sure, it's noisy and I'm there so often that all the staff and many of the customers know me and have no concerns about stopping to chat, but the time I spend in study and prayer there has always been fruitful. It all depends on your personal sense of space.

The following desktop devotions were chosen based on two criteria. First, they needed to have enough potential to generate a real connection to the Divine Power Grid. Second, they needed to be time sensitive in order to fit into a busy schedule. Though I'm sure there are others out there that meet both criteria, I've had experience and success with both of these.

R^3 Desktop Devotions

In *Prayer for People Who Can't Sit Still*, I introduced the R^3 (R–cubed) Journaling Exercise as a kinesthetic prayer practice. This desktop spiritual habit is especially effective for those who want a particularly powerful experience and have limited time to invest. However, the practice will demand ten minutes or more of your undivided attention. Most people fit it into their morning rituals, but many of the rather busy folks I know practice it during lunch or on another break. Whatever time you choose, the key to its effectiveness is your ability to be attentive for the allotted time. When you have limited time, interruptions not only break your chain of thought, they steal your time. So close your office door, put the kids down for a nap, or look *really* preoccupied at the coffee shop and take out your Bible. You'll also need a pen/pencil and either a journal or some other paper to write on. (See apppendix B for a reproducible journal page created for the R^3 experience.)

1. Centering. As usual, the first thing to do as you get ready for any time with God is to find your center. This time, since you're not driving or otherwise occupied, you can fully devote your mind to the task. When you're drawn into the Presence of God, spend a few moments there and offer a prayer asking the Lord for guidance and insight as you turn to the scriptures.

2. Reading. Once you've centered and called for Divine guidance, open the scriptures to whatever passage you've chosen. I generally don't recommend randomly opening the Bible, though I suppose almost all of us have done this at sometime in our lives in the hopes that God will speak just the right words we need to hear. However, the Spirit has the ability to guide us to the passage we need even if we're using a regimented reading program. Personally, I like choosing a book in the Bible and reading one chapter or a section at a time until I've read the book through. I tend to read a New Testament book followed by an Old Testament book, and then back to the New Testament. Since the Old Testament has thirty-nine books and the New Testament twenty-seven, that means I begin repeating New Testament books before I finish all the Old. But since I don't feel compelled to read the books of the Bible in any particular order, or even to read the Bible all the way through by some timetable, I just listen to what the Spirit whispers and choose whatever book I feel led to. In any event, the length of the passage you choose to read should be proportional to the amount of time you have to give.

As you read the passage, "listen" for verses, phrases, or words that leap from the pages and demand your attention. Underline or highlight these so you can readily find them later. When you finish reading, allow your mind to quietly rest for a few moments. Let your eyes wander back over what you've just read and pay attention to where they're drawn. More often than not, a single phrase that you've underlined will monopolize your gaze and thoughts. But don't be afraid to embrace a couple of phrases if you're drawn to more than just one. You just never know what God has in mind.

3. R³—RECALL. Although the R³ process can be practiced solely as a thoughtful exercise, the process of putting pen to paper is cathartic and stimulates the senses in ways that can expand your initial thoughts. Once you've "chosen" the phrase, or more accurately, once the phrase has chosen you, take pen in hand and jot it down in your R³ Journal—don't forget to record the reference so you can find the passage in context later.

4. R³—REFLECT. Begin this next step by reflecting on the phrase that captured your attention. Let your words flow across the page as you ponder why this passage claimed you. Remember, this isn't an academic exercise, but a spiritual one. God is less interested in how much you know and infinitely more interested in growing you as an effective Practicing Christian, so let your reflections move from the head to the heart. Ask yourself what the Spirit is whispering to you through the passage. Were the words disturbing? confusing? Did they evoke an emotional response? Is there something going on in your life that the passage may relate to? As you reflect, allow some time to consider the Divine perspective. What is it God may be trying to say to you? How do the words apply to your life? What are you feeling called to do? Is there something you need to confess, to repent of, or to make amends for? Is there a relational bridge you need to build with someone? Finish your reflection with whatever insights you've gained.

5. R³—Respond. The last section of the journal is your opportunity to make the leap from insight to conversation, and into action. This is an opportunity to be brutally honest with God about whatever insights you may have gained. (It's okay, God can take it.) Whether your reflections hit a raw nerve or heal a wound, let your writing mirror your heart. I've discovered that the more honest I am with God in this prayer, the more I gain. The Divine knows what I'm feeling and thinking anyway, so being honest is a relief—and, in my experience, God honors honesty. Wind up your desktop devotional time by reserving the last line or two of your journal for offering a commitment to action. Whatever it is the Spirit whispered, write out what you intend to do in response.

Finally, close your time with just a few final moments to sit in the presence of God. Close your journal, close your eyes, and just breathe. Then with a quiet "Amen," turn your attention back to your busy life. As you do, allow yourself to bask in the confidence that though you leave your devotional time, you're not leaving the presence of God.

It probably takes more time to read the instructions for the R³ Desktop Devotions than it takes to practice it. Although I have leisurely spent an hour or more at a time reading, reflecting, and responding, the fact is, I often spend as little as ten-to-twelve minutes from centering to amen. I intentionally designed the R³ Journaling page with only a few lines per section in order to limit the writing space, which limits the time it takes. If you need to write more, but time is limited, you can always continue writing later.

If you've never seriously engaged in a Bible study devotional time, I can't recommend this particular practice highly enough. It only takes a few minutes, but it has the potential to make a life-changing difference in your connection with God.

Discovery Desktop Devotions

If you have just a bit more time for the spiritual habit of study and you'd like to more fully explore the scriptures, Discovery Desktop Devotions may be the answer. This practice uses an adaptation of discovery questions[4] that have been used for starting and leading small group studies around the world. And though they are quite effective in small groups, they are equally valuable when used for personal study.

The basic practice is nearly identical to the R³ Devotions, except the six Discovery Questions expand the reflection step. Once again, you can choose to simply think through the questions, but your study and prayer time will be significantly enriched with the addition of journaling.

The following instructions are less detailed, since most of the information has been covered previously in the chapter.

1. **CHOOSE A SCRIPTURE PASSAGE.** Again, use whatever method you're comfortable with to decide what to read in your study time.
2. **CENTERING.** Find your center, move into awareness of the Spirit's Presence, and commit your time to God.
3. **READ.** Underline or highlight passages that demand your attention.
4. **RECALL AND REFLECT.** This is the step that's significantly different from the R³ devotions. For your study time to be most effective you will want to have pen and paper or a journal in hand. (See appendix C for reproducible Discovery Devotions Journal pages.) Begin this step by recording the passage reference and copying whatever verse, phrase, or word that commands your attention. This will help when you read over the journal entry in the future. For the rest of your reflection time, ponder each of the Discovery Questions and record your answers. Note that each discovery question includes a number of sub-questions to stir your musing.

   1. What did you like about what you read?
      What was the best part of the reading? Did you discover a new insight? Was something particularly helpful?
   2. What did you *not* like about what you read?
      What was the most disturbing part of the reading? Did something bother you? What was "hard to hear"?
   3. What did you not understand about what you read?
      Did something confuse you or not make sense? Who can you chat with about this or where can you go to get clarification?
   4. What did you learn about God or the Kingdom of God?
      How are God's ways different than our ways? How is Kingdom living different than living outside of the Kingdom? How is your "image of God" different than it was before?
   5. What is God calling you to do and what are you going to do about it?
      Is there something for you to do? Is there a misdeed to confess, repent of, and make amends for? Do you have an addiction God is prompting you to release? Do you have an attitude that needs an adjustment? How will you move from thought to action?
   6. What verse, phrase, word, or thought do you want to take away with you?
      What do you want to remember through your day? Is there something you want to tuck away into the back of your mind and muse over? What part of the reading will make a difference in the way you live today?

Approach each of the questions both prayerfully and thoughtfully, allowing the Spirit to nudge your heart as you write. On the other hand, you could probably write volumes for some of the questions if you put your mind to it. It's important to remember that even though the discovery questions have a cognitive component, the purpose of the exercise is to infuse the scriptures *through* you, to apply what the Divine has spoken, and to become a more authentic reflection of Jesus Christ.

Small Group Study

We should not practice all spiritual habits alone. Indeed, some *can't* be practiced without others. The spiritual habit of study can be practiced either way: on your own or with a group. When I speak with very busy people, they often tell me they don't have time to be part of a small group. There's too much responsibility, it takes too much time, or the cost-benefit ratio is too low.

I had the privilege to interview a number of *very* busy Christians when I was doing the research for this book. I interviewed Christian business people from around the nation in fields as varied as investments to communications, from nonprofit to high-profit. There were CEOs and publishers, scientists and top-level managers. As you might expect, their spiritual practices were as varied as their positions. However, there was one particular theme I heard surprisingly often: their dependence on a small Bible study group for their spiritual growth. As busy as these people were, they made it a point to attend their small group as often as they could, which is to say, as often as they were in town (many of those I interviewed traveled extensively).

One of the key differences between small group study and the devotionals described earlier in this chapter is that most small groups meet weekly. For those who practiced the habit of small group study, they found that it was often easier to make a once-a-week appointment than to try and carve out significant time for the practice of study on a daily basis. On the other hand, their small group participation regularly stimulated their devotional study time during the week.

There are all kinds of small groups, but most Christians are more familiar with the ones associated with the local church. A designated leader or a teacher leads many of these. Being a small group leader/teacher can be a powerful spiritual habit.

But there's another kind of small group I want to introduce first. When a small group of peers get together for nearly any reason in the church, you'll find the potential for a genuine small group experience. This is especially true for programs such as Sunday school, Bible study groups, and many of the fellowship groups that get together. It can also be true of choir practice, committee meetings, and even the board meeting.

The key phrase in that last paragraph is *genuine small group experience.* Defining a genuine small group experience is bit like trying to describe what being in love feels like to someone who's never been there. It's nearly impossible to get them to understand, but there's no question about it–they'll know it when they experience it. A genuine small group experience happens after the group has "clicked." The members are comfortable with each other, they truly like and trust each other, and there's an electricity that silently crackles when they're together. A genuine small group experience is almost like spiritual epoxy. Once the group experiences it, even though they may stop meeting together, the group never disbands. They will be there for each other the rest of their lives.

To have a genuine small group experience, the group has to be more than just a dozen people in a room; it must be an *effective small peer group*. Effective small peer groups share six specific characteristics. For one, they're small. Though researchers disagree on the exact numbers, most agree an effective small peer group has between three and fifteen members. Second, the members of an effective small peer group have something in common. Typically, this needs to be more than just being the same age, the same gender, or even members of the same church. Members need to be peers. Peer groups generally have like interests, but even more importantly, peer groups have like values. For instance, if the group has middle-class values and you've embraced the spiritual value of poverty, then you're not likely to fit. It's difficult to build deep and meaningful relationships with people who don't share your interests, and especially if they don't share your values. Third, the members make the effort to get to know and trust each other. Many small groups in the church get together weekly, but they don't take the opportunity to build significant relationships with each other. Fourth, an effective small peer group is participatory; that is, all the members of the group have the opportunity and willingness to share their input. Fifth, as small peer group members get to know and trust each other, they become open, transparent, and vulnerable to the group. Of course, this doesn't happen during the first several weeks. Indeed, vulnerability can take quite a while to develop, but this characteristic is *consistently* present in effective small groups. Finally, an effective small peer group has a common purpose for coming together other than it's Sunday morning at 9:45. Whether they gather for Bible study, choir practice, or prayer, everyone knows why they are there.

Only when a small group reflects these characteristics is there *any* chance that the members will bond and share a genuine small group experience.

Of course, the local church doesn't corner the market for effective small groups. Indeed, some researchers are suggesting that relationships between individual Christians are replacing people's dependence on the local church. Campus Crusade for Christ, YWAM, Bible Study Fellowship, and other parachurch organizations have long sponsored small groups in a variety of settings. Further, individual Christians are simply choosing to put together small peer groups of their friends for Bible study or prayer.

Small Peer Group Study

Bob Gandrud was the President and CEO of the Lutheran Brotherhood, a Fortune 500 company that sold life and health insurance and investment products.[5] The company managed over thirty billion dollars in investments in order to underwrite outreach products for the Lutheran church and their communities. As you can imagine, Bob was a very busy man as the leader of the Minneapolis-based company, but he was also a Practicing Christian.

I had the opportunity to chat with Bob about the spiritual habits he practiced while he served as CEO. Though Bob practiced a number of spiritual disciplines, the one that seems to have most influenced his faithfulness was being a participant in a small peer group study. Bob got involved in a weekly study just after he became CEO of the Brotherhood. Invited by Norman, the CEO of the Metropolitan Federal Bank, Bob offered to host the study at the Lutheran Brotherhood Headquarters.

> We'd have breakfast together at seven and then read a chapter of the Bible. We'd discuss it and then share a prayer time with one another and we'd get done about 8:15. We talked about a lot of personal things, business, and all kinds of issues. We had lawyers, and investment people, presidents, and CEOs. There were about fifteen of us and we came from many different faiths. We would have anywhere from three to four to sometimes all of us there on any given week.
>
> We'd read a chapter a week and then read the same chapter the next week. We did the same chapter twice because that's a busy group of people and we were traveling all over the place and so we'd miss something. It's interesting…we'd have one group of ten people talk about the chapter, then the next week we'd add two or three others who weren't there the week before and we'd get a whole different bent on the same chapter of the Bible.[6]

Bob was fortunate enough to be a part of an effective small peer group that provided him with a genuine small group experience. This weekly practice made a real difference in his Christian life. "That Bible study group was extremely important to me when I was CEO. I really loved Wednesday mornings."[7]

But the small group affected Bob more than on just Wednesdays. During the week he would take the time to read and study whatever chapter the group would be covering. The effect of this once-a-week study group had a lasting impact throughout Bob's week in a variety of ways, not the least that it helped hold him accountable as a Practicing Christian. (For more information on the spiritual habit of accountability, see chapter 8.)

Although there's been a rise in the number of Christians who are attending small groups, many haven't had a genuine small group experience. Unfortunately, most folks who regularly attend church don't participate in any small groups, let alone in an effective small peer group. If you're one of the many, consider adding a weekly appointment and getting involved in an effective small group.

There are really only three tasks when it comes to participating in an effective small peer group: Get into a group; fit into the group; and commit to the group.

1. GET INTO A GROUP. Probably the most difficult task is actually finding an effective small group. Bob was fortunate enough to have been invited into an emerging small group with others he had much in common with. *Finding* such a group can be challenging. If you are a member of a church that sponsors home fellowship groups, this may be an avenue to explore. But as you explore even these groups, remember that to have a small group experience you will need to have something in common with the membership of the group *besides* the fact that you all go to the same church. You will need to be peers.

On the other hand, if you can't find an effective small peer group, consider *starting* one. Although there are lots of books about how to start and lead small groups, the fact is, if you invite a couple of good friends together and agree to model the six characteristics of an effective small group, the only thing left to add is a Bible study method. You could follow the example of Bob's group by reading a chapter of the Bible each week, discussing it (consider using the Discovery Devotion questions as a guide), and then spending time sharing and praying for each other. It really is that simple.

2. FIT INTO THE GROUP. If you find an existing small group you can join, you will want to carefully explore your "fit" with the existing members. Don't make a rash commitment to the group before you've visited a number of times. You should immediately feel welcomed, even though you should recognize you will be an "outsider" for six weeks or more (it takes time to build trust–and as nice as you might be, trust isn't automatically extended). As you visit, watch the interactions of the group. Does it exhibit the characteristics of effectiveness? Are the members genuine friends, or just friendly acquaintances? Have you been included, not only in the Bible study, but in conversation and chat? Do you have similar values? And do you have something in common? Once you're comfortable with the group and you've found a fit, you're ready to move to the final step.

3. COMMIT TO THE GROUP. Making a commitment to an effective small peer group means more than just joining. It means doing your part to be an effective small group member. This means the group can count on you to attend regularly. But attendance is only a tiny commitment compared to the rest. You'll also need to extend trust to the members of the group and take the initiative to be transparent and vulnerable in your sharing. Be intentional in building relationships with group members, and do so beyond the group time. You can get to know them better by "doing" lunch or having coffee together and listening to their stories. Finally, make it a point not only to pray for them regularly by name, but also to ask specifically *how* you can pray for them.

The last question I asked Bob before we parted company was if he had a last piece of advice for a busy person who wanted to make a powerful connection with God. He responded, "I'd say go find friends like them [the members of his small group] and try to meet with them regularly. Everyone should have a Norman in their life to help them formulate a Bible study group and really get people together."

Small Group Teaching

A leader is defined as someone with followers. Someone who doesn't have any followers, no matter what that person says, is not a leader. However, there are many different kinds of leaders. An effective small *peer* group leader is first and foremost a fellow member of the small group. In Bob's group, Norman was the "leader," but primarily because he was the founding member of the group. He didn't teach nor did he dictate. Small peer group leaders aren't those kind of leaders. At most, they facilitate the discussion and help navigate to keep the ship on course—but they're not the captains. And because they are with peers, there is a commonality between them and the rest of the members of the group.

On the other hand, a teacher typically has a *different* relationship with the group. First, though teachers may have a lot in common with their students, the fact is, they're the teachers and everybody else is a student. The teacher may even be a peer with the students most of the time, but when the small group gets together for Bible study, the teacher is still the teacher.

Second, a teacher tends to be the captain. He or she decides where the ship is going by developing the lesson and choosing what to teach. Certainly, the group may have jointly decided the topic of study, but ultimately the teacher dispenses the information *about* the topic and steers the course.

For all of these reasons, Sunday school classes are seldom small peer groups. Even adult classes are typically (though not always) teacher-led small groups rather than effective small peer groups.

This isn't to say that Sunday school and other small Bible study groups (or any other small group for that matter) are somehow inferior to small peer groups. An effective Sunday school class–a small group–is one that achieves its objective, which in most cases is to teach the Bible. And there's nothing inferior about that. The church *needs* good small group teachers; it's an important spiritual discipline.

Jim Martin was one of those good small group teachers. When I spoke with him and asked him about his spiritual habits, he was quick to tell me that being a Sunday school teacher was his primary spiritual discipline.

Jim was a senior research chemist for the Shell Oil Company.[8] Besides his heavy work schedule at Shell, he raised a family, returned to take classes at the university a number of times, and was heavily involved in church. Though he practiced a number of different spiritual habits over the years, it was his role as a Sunday school teacher that was responsible for his spiritual development.

> When I was seventeen, just out of high school, a lady in the church asked me to teach a boys' Junior Sunday school class and I didn't have sense enough to say no. That was my first teaching assignment and I didn't teach again until after I went to work for Shell. I began teaching an adult class for a new church in Pasadena, Texas. Before I left that class I had sixty or seventy students on Sunday mornings.
>
> My spiritual development came from being a teacher and in getting ready to teach each week. My heart was in the teaching and I would come home on Sunday and read the lesson material for the coming week so I could ponder it in the early part of the week. But I found I was never free from thinking about the Sunday lesson and how I would get the material across to the class. Prayer accompanied my preparation time. I would pray to get through the next lesson and for help with my insights.
>
> I used to say I was kind of an "aha" Christian. I would be doing something else and all of a sudden I'd get a new insight. For instance, I would be cutting the grass or working in the yard and my thoughts would come back to the lesson for Sunday and all of a sudden I'd think, "Oh, yeah!" and a light would turn on.[9]

Why would a really busy person want to become a small group teacher? Because, like being a member of a small peer group, the primary set-aside time commitment is limited. It's sometimes easier to make a standing weekly appointment than to try and squeeze some of the other spiritual habits into your day. If you can make a place for that appointment, the rewards for teaching include an increasing reliance on the whispering of the Spirit, a deepening knowledge and understanding of the scriptures, as well as having an opportunity to be a spiritual mentor.

Besides being "too busy" to teach, one of the chief objections to teaching a small group is a confessed lack of knowledge: "I don't know the Bible well enough to teach." Well, I've got good news and bad news. The bad news is, though that may be true, most of the people who come to church know as little or less than you. Certainly there are people you know who seem to really know the Bible well, but think about the majority of the folks you know. They probably know very little about the Bible. The good news is that if you decide to teach, you only have to stay one step ahead of your students—and the best way to learn the Bible is to teach it.

It's beyond the scope of this book to instruct you how to teach a Sunday school class or a small group. (For leading a small peer group, reread the section on "Small Peer Group Study.") Most of the time, teachers use a curriculum of some sort as their primary teaching tool, and virtually all curriculums come with a teacher's guide that will walk you through the process. However, there are some general guidelines I'd like to share if you're going to add teaching to your repertoire in the spiritual habit of study.

These three steps to teaching will ensure you enhance your spiritual journey: prepare; offer a prayer; and share.

1. Prepare. Effective preparation is like a fine wine. It takes time to ferment. Although whatever curriculum you use will have specific instructions for preparation, if you read the materials early in the week, as Jim did, the Spirit has the opportunity to stir, mix, and ferment what you've read. Indeed, if you prepare early, you'll regularly find you're experiencing Jim's "aha!" Christianity. Another advantage of preparing early is that as you muse over the material, even subconsciously, there will be times during your week when what you've read will apply to your life. A decision to make? Perhaps the parables about counting the cost may float through your mind. A bridge to build? The Lord's Prayer, "Forgive us our sins as we forgive those who sin against us," may spur you on. When you prepare in advance, you give the Divine an opportunity to plug-in with you during the week.

2. Offer a Prayer. Although Paul reminds us to approach everything in prayer (Phil. 4:6), this is never truer than when it comes to teaching. During the week as your teaching engagement approaches, spend some spare moments praying for insights into your teaching and for your students. Make it a habit to learn your students' name so you can pray for each specifically. As you practice these spiritual habits you'll find that, like Jim, your heart will be in teaching and your mind will seldom stray far from the Divine Presence.

3. Share. If all you ever did was prepare for teaching and pray about it, you'd still have a very rewarding spiritual life. However, the real joy of being a teacher is found in the sharing. Whether you're sitting before a semicircle of wide-eyed elementary school children, or with a small group—or even a large group—of adults, the opportunity to enrich others' lives is unmatched by almost any other experience. As you share what you've learned during your week's preparation, your commitment and your words will help shape the spiritual lives of those who call you Teacher. Everybody needs a mentor and everybody needs a hero. As a small group leader, you have the opportunity to be both.

The spiritual habit of study is probably the most important habit of all, except for prayer. Whether you practice the habit in your car, at your kitchen table, or in the presence of fifteen curious students, as the word of God sifts through your mind and infuses your life, your connection to the Divine Power Grid becomes more reliable. Your commitment to study, even if it's only ten minutes a couple of times a week, can become the catalyst for a power surge that will change your life forever.

SPARKS AND RESISTANCE

Questions for Discussion and Reflection

1. Technology marches on. What are some of the newest innovations that could be used in the spiritual habit of study? What are their advantages? Their disadvantages?
2. Have you ever kept a diary or a journal? How long did you keep at it? If you're not keeping one now, what caused you to stop?
3. Do you agree with the author that you can trust your imagination when you've entrusted it to the Spirit before practicing Imaging the Word? Why or why not?
4. Describe your "perfect" peer small group. Who would you include as members? Are they all church people? Is there anyone you would invite who isn't a church member or even a Christian? Why or why not?
5. List all the small groups in your church. Which ones are small Bible study groups led by teachers? Which ones are small peer groups? Do any of them meet the characteristics of an effective small peer group? What would need to change for those that aren't effective to meet all the criteria?

5

The Spiritual Habit of Worship

In the world of religion, crystals have come to play an important role. In several New Age practices, crystals are used in part because they generate, or respond to, a variety of wave frequencies. In the world of electrical engineering, this is called the piezoelectric effect, with the crystal either generating or filtering voltage depending on it's use. When a crystal is exposed to the "right" frequency, it can generate significant voltage. Alternatively, when it is exposed to the "wrong" frequency, it can effectively filter it out.

Because of a crystal's traits, it has become an important electronic component in several devices you have in your home. The quartz watch, quartz tuners, microphones, phonographs, and so on all use crystals because of their ability to resonate at particular frequencies and to produce voltage from that resonance. Indeed, a one-centimeter cube of quartz with five-hundred-foot pounds of force applied to it properly (with the right frequency) can produce 12,500 volts of electricity.[1] That's a lot of power generated from a little chunk of crystal.

How do crystals play an important part in *our* faith? In our *High-Voltage Spirituality* metaphor, each of us has a crystal integrated in our faith circuit and the practice of worship provides the input frequency. When worship produces the frequencies we need, our inner crystal comes to life and generates mega-volts of spiritual electricity—we literally glow from the connection with the Divine Power Grid.

Worship is an important practice in our spiritual journey. For many, worship connects them with God more surely than any other spiritual habit. Unfortunately, we live in a society that has largely undervalued worship because it has been confused with "going to church." And though worshiping in a local church is important, it isn't the only way to worship. In fact, it's only one of several worship practices.

In our North American culture we've tried to compartmentalize nearly every aspect of our lives. Life's opportunities for celebrating the wonders of God have been relegated, collected, and packed into the "High Holy Hour" at eleven o'clock on Sunday mornings. However, if we hope to experience an ongoing connection with the Divine Power Grid, we need a worship-*filled* life, not just a once-a-week prepackaged worship service. Worship is too important to be sacked, wrapped, sealed, boxed, and stored until next week. Our spiritual crystals need to resonate daily. When they don't, our connection with the Divine suffers. Worship was meant to be an integrated part of who we are and how we live because:

1. WE WERE CREATED WITH AN INNATE NEED TO WORSHIP. Anthropologists and sociologists alike have noted that there appears to be an innate need for worship. Blaise Pascal, the French mathematician, said that we have a God-shaped vacuum in our hearts.[2] That vacuum can *only* be satisfactorily filled with the Presence of God. Every tribe and every people-group on every continent has developed some sort of religion trying to fill that vacuum.

2. WORSHIP OPENS THE DOOR TO THE DIVINE PRESENCE. Worship does more for us than you might imagine. Like the magical words, "Open sesame," in *Arabian Nights*, worship mystically opens the door to the spiritual realm. It was while Isaiah was in worship that he was visited by angelic visions. It was while Jesus was in prayer atop a mountain that he donned his heavenly body for a time and communed in the presence of Moses and Elijah. Whether the spiritual realm is another reality or a fourth dimension, we can be assured that it exists. We can also be sure that we have access to it through worship.

3. WORSHIP DE-COMPARTMENTALIZES OUR LIFE. Compartmentalism has been one of the side effects of our scientific age of reason. We've sliced up life's pie and put each piece in an airtight freezer container. On Mondays, we remove the container labeled *Work,* open it, and live with it for most of the day. At five o'clock we reseal it, put it back in the freezer, and snag the one labeled *Leisure* for the evening. If we're particularly "good," we may remember to briefly open the container marked *Religion* to pray before our meals, but for most of us, after the prayer, *Religion* is resealed and returned to the fridge until tomorrow's dinner. On the other hand, when we engage in a worshipful life, all those sealed compartments are opened, the contents gently folded together, and the Divine Presence infuses every aspect of our lives. As the Presence seasons our whole being, we discover the power in God's leavening. We begin to rise and to shine, empowered by the Spirit, realizing we've been plugged into the Divine Power Grid. We experience what can only be described as a *High-Voltage Spirituality.*

But if a spiritual wanderer asks about worship in North America, most of the time he or she will get an answer that mentions something about

Sunday at eleven. On the other hand, if a minister asks why a golfer wasn't in church, the minister might well hear, "Well Pastor, I can worship in the beauty of the great outdoors on the fairway as well as I can at church." And though the golfer's answer sounds like a limp excuse, the answer is at least more expansive than limiting worship to Sunday mornings in a local church. Indeed, worship is much more than singing majestic hymns to the polyphony of a pipe organ, or the raised, clapping hands of a joyful congregation singing and dancing to praise choruses pounded out by a thumping band. And worship is also much less. From the still, small voice of God in the wilderness, to the flood of indescribable emotions that overwhelm you at the sight of a sublime sunset, worship is simplicity to the nth degree.

Worship comes in all sorts of different packages and has a variety of flavors. There's something for everyone, because each of us has a crystal that longs to resonate. The frequency that unlocks *my* inner resonance, however, may raise your *angst,* hurt your ears, or even offend your sensibilities. That's why each of us needs to discover worship practices that fine-tune our inner spirit to God's "yoddaHertz"–the broad spectrum of frequencies the Divine transmits on.

As we look at the spiritual habit of worship, you'll discover there are two broad practices: intentional worship and incidental worship. Intentional worship is the practice of scheduled worship. Congregational worship, small group worship, and devotional worship are intentional opportunities you can put on your calendar. On the other hand, incidental worship includes practices that I call add-ons. They are lifestyle habits that are sometimes specific practices and sometimes more like an attitude adjustment. I recommend adding a sprinkling of both into your busy schedule.

Intentional Worship

In the midst of being grilled by Satan, Jesus rebuked him and said, "It is written, 'Worship the Lord your God and serve him only'" (Lk. 4:8). When we think of worshiping God, most of us initially think "church services." Church attendance and worship is one of the long-standing traditions in the Christian faith and it is the predominant spiritual habit in North America.

Church Worship

There are many reasons every Christian ought to be an active participant in a local church,[3] but worship is certainly one of them.

Various churches define and practice worship differently. Some churches define worship as everything that happens between the opening chords of the organ and the "Go in peace" benediction. Others define worship as the music and prayer portion of the service. Neither is precisely correct. Authentic worship is any act that proclaims the worthiness of God. Does church music do that? Does the praying do that? Does the sermon do that? The question should be asked of everything that goes on in a church service from the invocation to the recessional. Scripture readings, communion, recited creeds, responsive readings, baptisms, skits, dramas, video clips, choir anthems, the offering, and musical specials all may or may not be worship. The litany of announcements is about the only event in the worship service that is virtually impossible to turn into worship in some way.

Authentic worship in the church is participatory, meaning everyone has an opportunity to express the worthiness of God in some way. That's why we sing together and recite the Lord's Prayer aloud together. It's the reason responsive readings are presented, and prayers are occasionally offered as litanies. It's also why the sermon is often dismissed as a worship opportunity. Let's face it, most sermons *aren't* participatory, and they generally do more to instruct us than to extol God's glory. But just because there are opportunities for everyone to worship, doesn't mean worship happens for everyone. For worship to be personally authentic it has to resonate with your spiritual crystal.

My wife and I are involved in the North American House Church Movement. For us, that means we "go to church" in our home. We have a number of friends who join us each week for worship. Music, communion, offering, prayers, and Bible study all play their respective parts. I love the small group worship–it *resonates* with my soul. On the other hand, even though my wife enjoys home worship, it seldom gets her spiritual crystal resonating. So on a regular basis, she visits one of two or three churches in the area that offer what *she* considers really great worship. Her preference is to worship with a larger crowd and to sing contemporary Christian songs while a praise band leads with guitars, drums, and keyboards. On the Sunday mornings she visits one of these churches, she will return home with a joyful countenance and a slight bounce in her step. It's just the right frequency applied to her soul, and it connects her with the Divine Power Grid.

All that's to say that if the worship service isn't resonating with you in the church you attend, you will want to find an alternative. *However,* there is a caveat. No church exists to feed your preferences. In fact, the church doesn't exist to feed *you* at all. Every week, the pastor and whoever does your worship planning and production work hard to produce a worship service that will provide food for the spiritually hungry and drink for the spiritually parched. They try to provide a variety of worship courses, from appetizers to desserts, and each week they set a table and invite the congregation and guests to come and dine.

Unfortunately, many who show up at the dinner table sit at their seats with their arms folded across their chests and wait for someone to pick up a spoon and feed them. Church leaders hear it all the time from disgruntled members, "The worship just isn't feeding me." What that normally means is that these people need their diapers changed, bibs tied around their necks, and their bottles warmed as well. Paul was pretty adamant about Christian maturity and expected the church to raise self-feeding adults. Spiritual milk and milkshakes are for infants and juveniles. As adults, our diet is supposed to be the meatier, more difficult to digest kinds of spirituality—the kind of practices that take discipline and practice. It also means we're expected to feed ourselves.

Getting the Most Out of Church Worship

There are two things we can control when it comes to church worship: our attitude and our application. There's an axiom that says, "You reap whatever you sow" (Gal. 6:7, NRSV). That's no less true of worship than any other investment opportunity, and it all begins with our attitude. If we attend a worship service with the expectation we're going to be fed and we sit back and wait for it to happen, we'll leave the table hungry. On the other hand, if you walk into the church with the expectation you're going to seek God until you find him, then your worship will find the Divine frequency that resonates within you and you'll leave the table both satiated and hungry for more.

Our attitude about church worship can be affected by a variety of events and thoughts, some good and some not-so-good. Here's a checklist to review that may be helpful in getting and keeping your go-to-church-worship attitude in the positive.

- Don't stress about getting to church on time—if you're late, you're late. No big deal. You won't be the only one, and if people are going to look down their noses at you for coming in late, you probably need to (a) confront those who do; (b) decide and internalize that it just doesn't matter to you *what* they think; or (c) find a new worship service, and perhaps a later one if it's difficult getting to this one on time.
- If you're angry or perturbed at someone at the church, make it right. Remember, no forgiveness is received unless forgiveness is extended (Mt. 6:14–15).
- If you have baggage from your week or your life that's dragging you down, make sure you bundle it up in a sturdy suitcase and take it with you. But as you do, go with an attitude that you're going to church both for worship and to get rid of it.
- If the worship service doesn't resonate with you because the music style, order of service, or the formality/lack of formality gets in the way, find a different worship service.

Finding a worship service that resonates may or may not involve leaving the church you're currently affiliated with. Sometimes a church that has been ineffective in reaching out to the community will change their worship style in order to reach the spiritual wanderers. The music style and repertoire may shift and the order of service transformed. In these cases, your continued support and participation in the life of the congregation could be critical to the success of the church's mission. Remember, the church does not exist to meet your needs, it exists for the sole purpose of extending the gospel to those who are strangers to grace. Remaining active in a church that's attempting to be faithful may be a sacrifice, but remember that giving up something in the name of the Lord is an effective spiritual habit as well.[4] Hang tough with the church and give it your full support, even if the worship isn't generating any spiritual electricity for you. If your church offers multiple services, see if one of those can resonate. If not, consider worshiping occasionally elsewhere—as my wife does, even though she is quite involved in our house church.

Although the attitude you arrive with will largely determine whether or not you'll leave hungry, you also need to apply the fullness of your senses. Worship is meant to be a multisensory experience. We weren't created with just one or two senses, but with six. God is worthy to be worshiped with the whole of our being. To get the most out of worship, plan on utilizing as many of your senses as you can.

HEARING. In most churches today, this is the most used sense. We listen to the music, listen to the prayers, and listen to the sermon. There isn't much I can say about how best to employ this sense, since almost everything in a church worship service is about listening. Just do it.

SIGHT. This is the second most used sense in a worship service, although its value in worship depreciated with the age of the Enlightenment. For the first fifteen hundred years, the sense of sight was as important in worship as the sense of hearing. The church didn't use stained-glass windows simply as decorations, but as teaching tools for the many who couldn't read or understand Latin. The "pomp and circumstance" of the worship service attempted to portray the majesty of the Godhead. Crosses, crucifixes, candles, icons, statuary, and architecture all demanded the attention of the eye with the aim of evoking thoughtfulness and awe. However, the Reformation embraced austerity and emphasized the cognitive and the logical, thus diminishing the grandeur of the visual.

Today, there is a trend in worship to return some of the prominence to the sense of sight. Video clips are used as illustrative devices. Candles, religious artworks, other religious décor, and even architecture are once again being used in worship in all sizes and styles of churches.

Nonetheless, even if you attend one of the "austere" churches, you can enhance your worship experience by taking the time to "see" your surroundings. Look for the religious symbols in your church's worship space. During the service, take time to focus your sight and your thoughts on one or two of them. Meditate on what the symbols are telling you about God.

One of the advantages to worshiping in a local church is the presence of others engaged in worship. A synergy develops when Christians worship together. Indeed, some worship spaces are being designed to enhance this synergy by arranging the seating so people can see each other during worship. This configuration creates a sense of unity among many instead of provoking the notion that worship is a personal and private affair. Whether or not your worship space is in the round or the pews are regimented in straight-ahead rows, look up from your hymnbook while you worship to smile at those around you. You're not alone in the crowd; you're a part of the congregation.

SMELL. Smell is the keeper of memories and emotions. When we walk into our childhood homes, the scents can take us back faster and more effectively than even a conversation with a long-lost friend. Years ago, scents were an important part of worship. In the Jewish temple, incense was burned to represent the prayers of the people (as well as to mask the smells of the sacrifices). The sight of the smoke and the scents of the incense were powerful triggers of sacred memory. Later, incense was used in the church to indicate prayer as well as to provide a reminder of the herbs and spices the women brought to Jesus' tomb on Easter morning.

Today, incense is used in only a few churches and in only a few services. However, every church has particular scents. As you worship, take the time to smell the coffee…or the old, worn leather, musty books, or whatever scents are there. Over time, awareness of these scents will become associated in your memory with worship and can help propel you into the Divine Presence.

TOUCH. Church worship hasn't put much emphasis on the sense of touch, but there are a number of ways in which you can enhance your worship experience through touch. The Roman Catholic Church has long used rosary beads, though the use of beads or knots for counting prayers predates the church. You can use beads to count repeated prayers or simply as a manipulative to help focus your mind by occupying physical energy in a repetitive task. Some people take a journal and pen to church to write their prayers or to take notes. Both of these practices can augment the sense of worship, especially for those who have a heightened awareness of their tactile senses.[5]

TASTE. For most of us, unless we take a cup of coffee into the worship space, the sense of taste is mostly ignored in worship. Chewing gum or nibbling on hard candy simply doesn't tend to do much to improve worship. Indeed, the only corporate worship practice I'm aware of that uses the sense of taste is the practice of communion. In some churches, communion is a regular part of the order of worship, while others serve communion infrequently. In any event, if you have the opportunity to receive communion, take the time to be fully mindful of the flavor.

SPIRITUAL. This is the sixth sense. It's the one that gets little attention, since we don't count it as one of our "real" senses. Nonetheless, this is probably *the* most important sense we have, especially when it comes to practicing the spiritual habits.

To experience worship in its fullness, like any of the spiritual habits, begin with centering prayer. In many church worship services, the order of service begins with an introit (an instrumental overture of sorts). This presents the perfect opportunity for getting centered and ready for worship. Once you've reached your center, concentrate on maintaining that centered place in the Divine Presence. Worship is, in its essence, a form of prayer that ascribes and extols the worthiness of God; it's not about us. When we're in the Presence and engaged in authentic worship, our spiritual crystal resonates and we experience a powerful connection into the Divine Power Grid.

The attitude you bring to church worship and the practices you apply largely determine whether you'll be going home charged with spiritual energy or going home feeling empty and disappointed.

Small Group Worship

The small group movement in North America has been gaining momentum for a couple of decades now. Although there have been small groups in churches for centuries, most of them have been task-focused. Sunday school classes are dedicated to education. Bible study groups are focused on, well, the obvious. Choirs sing, prayer groups pray, fellowship groups eat (most of the time), and committees commit. But recently, especially with the growth of cell churches, house churches, and even some home fellowship groups, the small group movement has been diversifying and adding a worship component to the agenda.

Busy people sometimes discover they can make time for a small group easier than trying to fit church worship into their schedule, especially if you don't have Sunday off. Small groups, like the one Bob Gandrud was in,[6] may be exactly the opportunity you need for corporate worship.

Virtually any small group can add worship to their agenda. It simply takes a decision to set aside some time, adding intentional acts of worship, and encouraging and promoting a worshipful attitude. Much of what was said of church worship is true of small group worship, except that spontaneity and informality tend to be more prevalent in small groups. Here are some intentional worship acts that are easily added to most small group gatherings:

SINGING. If you don't have an instrumentalist, you could sing *a cappella* or sing along with an audiotape, CD, or DVD. In fact, there are new resources for living room worship being released regularly—check your local Christian bookstore for ideas.

PRAYER. Most Christian small groups offer at least a perfunctory prayer, but the addition of prayer as an act of worship means that it is participatory and provides an opportunity to connect with the Divine.

SILENCE. Although practicing silence is primarily an opportunity for prayer, I list it separately because silence in *not* what we tend to think of as prayer. This quiet time of meditation can be especially useful when employed immediately after a scripture reading. Silence can be enhanced with the use of sacred objects, especially with candles and icons.

RESPONSIVE AND UNISON READINGS. Responsive readings aren't used in the church as often as they used to be, but they can still be powerful tools for worship. Many hymnbooks provide ready-to-use responsive readings; however, a responsive reading can be fashioned from any psalm or scripture passage. Have one person read a line or a verse and the rest respond by reading the next line or the next verse. Again, allow some time of silence afterward for reflection and meditation.

COMMUNION. There is something special about the celebration of communion in a small group. Perhaps it's the intimacy of being among close friends, but sharing a common loaf and cup can be a powerful connection to the Divine. Though there are several different ways to serve communion, one of the most popular in small group worship is to practice intinction. One person "breaks the bread" (tears it in half) and reminds the group that Jesus broke the bread with his closest friends and said that it was his body. Then a person presents a cup of wine or juice and reminds the group that Jesus shared the cup with his friends and said that it was his blood. Then the presenter holds the bread while a group member tears a piece off, dips it into the cup, and eats the juice-soaked bread. The presenter then gives both the bread and cup to the group member who in turn, offers it to whomever is sitting next to him or her. Participants pass on the bread and cup, repeating the process until everyone has had an opportunity to serve and to be served.

Virtually any worship act used in larger congregational worship can be adapted and practiced in a small group. The difference is primarily found in the intimacy of the setting.

If you're a part of a small group that isn't doing worship, consider adding it. When you do, the benefits will be twofold. First, you'll have an opportunity to worship—which is one of the most efficient ways to get plugged into the Divine. And second, whatever the small group task at hand, whether Bible study or a personnel committee discussion, the group will operate from a spiritual center generated by their resonating spiritual crystals.

Quiet Worship Time

 The last of the intentional worship opportunities is the practice of adding a quiet time of worship to your devotional practices. Although the chapter on the spiritual habit of study covers the basics for practicing devotionals, adding a worship component to your devotional time can generate a significant power boost.

Many church worship practices can be adapted for your personal quiet time. Again, worship is the combination of attitude and application, and this is no less true in your personal worship time. If you're in a hurry and feel the pressure to rush, then trying to add worship to your quiet time will be an exercise in frustration. On the other hand, if you find your centered place and invoke the presence of the Spirit, you've already begun the process for a rewarding worship time.

Here are some tips I've discovered that may be helpful in adding worship to your own quiet time.

CENTERING PRAYER. The first step of every spiritual habit.

CREATE A WORSHIPFUL ATMOSPHERE. Intentional worship opportunities are seldom multitask friendly. When you're going to engage in a personal quiet time with the Divine, turn off the cell phone, take the phone off the hook, and mute your computer's instant messaging notification. If you're at work, you may need to remove papers or projects from your desk that could distract you. If you're at home, turn off the television and find someplace where you can't see dirty dishes, laundry, or clutter that clamors for your attention.

This brings us to the subject of space. If you have the opportunity to practice your quiet time consistently in the same space, you may find you can enter your center more easily than if you regularly relocate your worship space. Familiarity is a friend to habits and can enhance your awareness of the Divine Presence. If you have control of your space, consider adding sacred objects into your line of sight that have meaning to you. Ever since the movie *Brother Sun, Sister Moon,* I've been inspired by the life of Saint Francis, so I've added the San Damiano crucifix to my worship space. By meditating on the image, I'm drawn into an introspective attitude through which I feel enfolded in the Divine Presence.

You might find the addition of candles, icons, crosses, crucifixes, small statues, or other religious objects helpful invitations to an attitude of worship. Some burn incense to enhance their sense of worship. I have a friend who uses a "prayer pillow" to sit on when she begins her quiet time. Others don a prayer shawl or even a yarmulke as they enter into worship. The point of the exercise is to help create a setting that will enhance your quiet worship time.

SILENCE. Silence is one of the most powerful acts of worship. However, worshipful silence is different than meditative silence. Remember that the point of worship is to extol the worthiness of God; therefore, silent worship is about exuding an attitude of wonder and awe in the presence of God. Some achieve this state by pondering the works of the Creator. Others experience it in the mystery of the cross-resurrection event. Whether these, or some other image takes you there, a worshipful silence is centered in the majesty of the Divine.

MUSIC. I play guitar. Not really well, but well enough to accompany myself when I'm feeling worshipful and I want to express myself to the Lord. When I'm not on the road doing workshops, researching, or writing, I occasionally spend a few moments of my "quiet time" singing. My wife often approaches her personal worship time by putting on a praise CD and singing along with it. If you're so inclined, music can be a gratifying way to express yourself in personal worship.

READING THE PSALMS. The book of Psalms is one of the most comprehensive hymnbooks in the faith. As already mentioned in previous chapters, the Psalms reflect every human emotion, but many of them are particularly awe-inspiring and useful in personal worship. Read a psalm as your personal prayer. Let the psalmist's words be your words as you offer sentiments of praise. You may want to read the words slowly and ponder them line-by-line as you ascribe the attributes to the Lord. Though there are a number of great Psalms, you may want to begin with these classics: Psalms 8; 29 (my personal favorite); 97; 120; and 134.

COMMUNION. Most of us consider the celebration of communion as a community event. However, communion is ultimately a commemorative and worshipful act that needn't be limited to the local church or to small group worship. John Wesley practiced communion every day, whether he was in the presence of others or not. To practice communion in your own quiet time, simply provide bread and cup (juice or wine), break and eat the bread and drink from the cup as you contemplate the death of Jesus.

Intentionally adding worship to your spiritual habit of study, or taking the time for personal worship is a powerful practice for your spiritual repertoire. However, intentional worship opportunities are only a small part of the spiritual habit of worship.

Incidental Worship

In ancient times, expressions of worship came virtually unsolicited as the wonders of nature unfolded around unscientific minds. Those events we now consider natural phenomena, the ancients ascribed to the gods. The sun came up at the beckoning of some divine will. The rains fell, or not, at the whims of the powerful deities. In Old Testament times everything that happened for good or for bad was attributed to the will and the control of God (e.g., Job 1:21). Since the faithful believed God was *actually* in control of everything, reverence and worship were part and parcel of every waking moment.

What would it be like if you believed your health was literally in the hands of God, or that the ability to conceive a child was based on Divine choice alone? The fact is, you might take worship more seriously. We all would. But Copernicus and Galileo, Pasteur and Mendel brought natural law into the fore and put God on the sidelines of the equation. Ultimately, we may *say* we believe the Divine is "in charge," but mostly we expect the God of order to be revealed through the orderly laws of science. So we know the sun will rise because the Earth is orbiting as it should; the rains fall when the condensation in the clouds becomes too heavy to remain suspended in the atmosphere; and we'll get a cold if someone sneezes and doesn't cover their mouth. God may be at work, but we seldom give the Divine any credit (or blame). So worship becomes a scheduled act instead of a spontaneous response to the wonders of the world. We compartmentalize it like any other appointment, since we know that appeasing God isn't really necessary—we figure weekly worship is *more* than enough.

I have a good friend who is a professional mechanic who reminds me that no one becomes an automobile technician by standing in a garage an hour a week. Depending on a weekly church worship service to get connected into the Divine Power Grid is perhaps one of the reasons Christianity seems to be a powerless faith to most North American practitioners. It takes more than going to church for an hour each week to become an effective, faithful Practicing Christian.

An incidental worship opportunity is a "chance" occasion to offer an act of worship. These opportunities present themselves throughout the day, although most of the time the pressures and the bustle of life hasten us on and we miss them. One of the keys to developing a worship-full life is to increase our awareness of these incidental worship opportunities and to take advantage of them. Developing a lifestyle that includes incidental worship opportunities is instrumental in experiencing a powerful Christian life.

Worship at Mealtimes

 Both in the practice of the Jewish faith and the early Christian faith, worship and religious education were centered around the meal. With the ongoing erosion of the family in North America, the opportunity for worship during mealtimes cannot be overstated. In the Jewish faith, the lighting of candles marks the beginning of the family worship time. With prayers, singing,

and words of remembrance, meals have long been one of the key foci of worship.

In the North American culture, it can be difficult to change our habits and make the mealtime sacred. Today few families actually sit around a table every night to eat, choosing instead to spend their time "together" in the living room watching a sitcom, a movie, or the news. Changing the evening rituals can be challenging and even agonizing, yet there is plenty of evidence that the family that eats around the table together grows closer. Additionally, families that manage to routinely make the mealtime a sacred event can expect to experience increased spiritual interest, as well as to hone the moral compass and ethical practices of each family member.

There are any number of ways to make the mealtime a sacred event. However, if you've not been in the habit of making the mealtime sacred, you should realize that it will take a while before the practice becomes routine and feels "right." Until then, the practice might seem affected, contrite, and even insincere.

Add Ritual to the Meal

Over the past several years, ritual has gotten a bad rap. However, ritual is one of the most important ways we internalize the faith. Like learning the multiplication tables, repetition is the clue to internalization. Here are a number of rituals to consider adding to transform your mealtime to sacred time:

CANDLE LIGHTING. Begin each meal by "kindling the candles," thus designating the mealtime as a sacred event. In the Jewish faith, the kindling of the candles takes place only in preparation of the Sabbath (eighteen minutes before sundown on Friday evening) and on other special holiday occasions. The woman of the family lights the candles–one for her, one for her husband, and one for each child. In some homes, as the children get old enough to pray aloud, they learn to light their own candles. In any case, you can certainly establish your own traditions. As you light the candles, some sort of a blessing or prayer should be pronounced in order to offer the time at the table to the Lord. Consider something like this, modeled on a Jewish candle lighting prayer: "Blessed are you, O God of the universe, who called forth light from darkness, gave your Son as the Light of the World, and call us to take his light to our family, to our neighbors, and to the nations. Amen."

PRAYERS. In the Christian tradition, grace is generally offered before the meal. Consider adding the Jewish tradition of closing the meal with prayer as well. The closing prayer could be a general thanksgiving for the provisions of the Lord, or it could include prayers for others based on the mealtime conversation. In any event, by marking the opening and the closing of the meal with prayer, a sense of holiness will emerge that bathes the family time with a spiritual awareness.

RECITATION. A great way to internalize the faith is to practice recitation. For instance, if you are able to embrace the ancient creeds or statements of faith, consider beginning each meal by reciting it as a family. Alternatively, an effective way to hide God's word in the hearts of the family is to practice reciting a scripture passage at every meal. Perhaps before the family begins to eat, but after gracing the meal, a "verse of the week" could be recited. By reciting a verse—especially a short verse—seven times during the week, most family members will be able to memorize it or at least be very familiar with it.

BIBLE READINGS OR FAMILY DEVOTIONS. In the Old Testament the parents were expected to teach the faith to their children:

> Fix these words of mine in your hearts and minds; tie them as symbols on your hands and bind them on your foreheads. Teach them to your children, talking about them when you sit at home and when you walk along the road, when you lie down and when you get up. Write them on the doorframes of your houses and on your gates, so that your days and the days of your children may be many in the land that the LORD swore to give your forefathers, as many as the days that the heavens are above the earth. (Deut. 11:18–21)

Although there has been a tendency in our culture to count on our community's institutions to educate and instill a moral compass in our children, the fact is, Christian parents are ultimately responsible for their children's faith development. Bible readings and family devotions are excellent ways to build a strong faith foundation. (A consistent Christian behavioral example by the parents is, of course, the most important way to impart faith to our children.)

There are a number of ways to lead a family devotion. You may want to use one of the many family devotional books that are available. Consider choosing one that will interest the youngest member of the family at the dinner table—the mealtime is not an appropriate venue to teach advanced theology to your seven-year-old.

On the other hand, a simple Bible study using the six Discovery Questions may be the best model to use for family devotions. To use this method, choose a complete passage of scripture, such as one of Jesus' parables or some other complete story or thought, and then ask the family these questions—allowing everyone to share:

- What did you like about this reading?
- What did you *not* like?
- What did you not understand?
- What did you learn about God from the reading?
- What is God calling you to do about it?
- What verse, phrase, word, or though do you want to take away with you?

The beauty of the Discovery Questions is that everyone can share on their own level.

COMMUNION. When Jesus said, "Whenever you eat this bread and drink this cup, do it in remembrance of me,"[7] there are plenty of us who believe he meant that *every time* we sit down to eat we should do it in remembrance. Therefore, consider offering communion as a standard part of your meal. There are a number of ways to do so, but one of the easiest ways is to ensure that each meal has bread and a beverage. (You may use any beverage of choice, but there is something "special" about serving wine or grape juice, either in individual juice glasses or in a chalice.) During the meal, break the bread and give each person a portion, reminding them, "This is the body of Jesus." Then lift the chalice or have everyone lift their individual glasses (as if making a toast) and remind them, "This is the blood of Jesus."

Another way of doing communion at the meal is to offer the bread at the beginning of the meal and then closing the meal with the cup. This is actually closer to the way Jesus practiced the first communion with his disciples, and it encloses the meal with a spiritual presence that is unmatched by any other practice.

There are probably as many ways to make your meals sacred as there are days of the year. If you are single or without your family for a time, the potential for raising the spiritual climate of the meal is without equal. Most of the rituals can be adopted and adapted to suit whatever situation you find yourself in, including when you are eating out. A friend of mine regularly eats out with both churched and unchurched acquaintances. When he does, he begins the mealtime by taking whatever bread is available on the table, such as a dinner role or a cracker, and then saying something like this: "You know, this bread reminds me of something Jesus said to his friends," and then he proceeds to briefly introduce the Lord's supper. Then he shares communion with those at the table. If done sensitively, this is an excellent way not only to raise the spiritual intensity, but to usher in a conversation about the faith.

Because eating is such an important and regular event in our lives, it provides an ideal opportunity for incidental worship. So clear the table, turn off the TV, and find your place in the presence of God.

Worship at Work

 Most adults will spend approximately two thousand hours each year at their workplace. Though you may not be aware of them, the workplace offers many incidental worship opportunities. With just a little forethought and a commitment to engage in these practices, you may find the tenor of your day completely changed.

The first step to practicing incidental worship at work is to develop an appropriate attitude about your vocation. For many Christians, there is little connection between their faith and their workplace; however, the Bible makes it clear that our attitudes and behaviors at work are direct reflections of our faith. Paul wrote to the Christians in Colossae that they were to approach their work differently than other workers:.

> Whatever you do, work at it with all your heart, as working for the Lord, not for human masters, since you know that you will receive an inheritance from the Lord as a reward. It is the Lord Christ you are serving. (Col. 3:23–24, TNIV)

Bear in mind this particular passage wasn't addressed to folks who had dedicated their lives to pursuing professional ministry or even to those who believed they were engaged in a Godly secular profession. No, these words were written to *slaves.* If these are the instructions to forced laborers, imagine how much more we will be held responsible for faithfulness in our work environment.

Whether you're in a vocation you consider your God-called ministry or working at a job you're "stuck with" so you can pay bills, the attitude you carry will either facilitate or hinder your ability to enter into incidental worship.

Once our vocational attitudes are aligned with the Lord, we can begin to participate in worship as we work. Here are a couple incidental worship opportunities that may present themselves at your workplace.

CELEBRATIONS. In every day there are opportunities that are celebration worthy. For instance, whenever you complete a task—especially when you've completed a difficult or onerous task—you have a chance to celebrate. Take a moment to share the joy with the Lord.

There are several ways to practice celebration as incidental worship. For instance, consider picking up a pocket New Testament and Psalms and quietly reading and praying one of the praise psalms as an act of worship. Another way to worship may simply be to sit back for a moment and bask in the joy of accomplishment with the Lord, whispering a prayer of praise in your heart.

THANKSGIVING. We have multiple daily opportunities for profound gratefulness, no matter what our circumstances. This is no less true even when we're stuck in a nine-to-five rut at a dead-end job. There is always *something* in our day that can evoke a spirit of thanksgiving from our heart and our lips.

For instance, consider the fact that you're still employed. The unemployment rate in North America is low when compared to the rest of the world and, the fact is, there are millions who are without work who would gladly trade places with you.

Or consider the moments when everything seems to be going wrong. This might not seem like the appropriate time to turn to the Lord and whisper a "thank you." But recall what James, the brother of Jesus, wrote:

> Consider it pure joy, my brothers and sisters, whenever you face trials of many kinds, because you know that the testing of your faith develops perseverance. Let perseverance finish its work so that you may be mature and complete, not lacking anything. (Jas. 1:2–4, TNIV)

These are amazing words when you consider what his brother went through—and how the church in Jerusalem was experiencing severe persecution. It is in these difficult times that we should be the most grateful, since we only grow and mature when we face times of trial and difficulties. So even in the worst of times, take a moment to embrace a spirit of gratefulness for the growth you are experiencing.

Most of the time, however, you won't have to look behind the dark clouds to discover glimmers of gratefulness. In every day there are many reasons for offering thanks to the Lord: when an onerous task is complete; when someone offers a compliment or a word of praise; when you encounter a friend; when you hear good news; when an unexpected boon comes your way (you open your drawer and discover that special pen you thought you'd lost); and there's always one of the most important reasons people offer thanks each workday—when it's time to go home!

No matter what your circumstances, begin to develop a habit of offering moments of profound gratefulness as often as you can during the day. As you do, you'll discover your spirit elevated into the Divine Presence and your heart filled with a worshipful attitude.

Worship on the Go

Most of us commute. Whether we commute from the suburbs to the city, from the house to the classroom, or from the bedroom to the laundry room, we tend to spend time driving, riding, or walking from one place to another. For many people, when they're on the move they discover that incidental worship is eager to emerge from their hearts, and often their lips.

In most cities across North America, the average commute is more than twenty minutes.[8] Although public transportation is available in virtually every metropolis, most choose to drive a car to work. The sanctuary of our vehicles may very well be the most popular "church building" in North America. Even those who refuse to "go to church" may find themselves participating in a worship service on the way to work.

Although there are many ways to worship, as we've already seen, the most common practice of worship revolves around music. The advantage of worshiping in our cars while we commute is that whether we have the voice of an angel or can't carry a radio (let alone a tune), we can unapologetically let loose in full voice. John Wesley, the founder of the Methodist church, wrote that when we sing in worship we should sing "lustily and with a good courage. Beware of singing as if you were half dead, or half asleep; but lift up your voice with strength."[9] When we're in our automobile we have one of the best opportunities to follow his instructions without undue self-consciousness.

To enter into worship in your car, tune your radio to a Christian music station, put a favorite Christian CD or audiocassette tape in your player, or choose your favorite Christian playlist from your MP3 player and let the music play. As it does, let the words and the melody or beat (whichever one sends your pulse racing) flow over and through you. Before you join in, take a moment to center yourself in prayer and offer the commute to the Lord. Then let loose with full heart, soul, and voice. One of the joys of worshipful singing while you drive is that no one is listening to you; further, in a society in which half of the drivers are singing to the tunes in their cars and the other half are on their cell phones, no one is likely to take any notice of you. So sing out!

But suppose you're one of those disciples of Jesus who takes the biblical commands to be good stewards of our earth and possessions seriously enough to let them influence your lifestyle. And so you take advantage of environmentally friendly public transportation. Although, as Cat Stevens once wrote, "When you want to sing out, sing out,"[10] you may realize that if you do, you're going to get a few odd looks. What then? How do you worship on the bus, the commuter train (or plane, for that matter), or in the carpool lane with a van full of officemates?

Music is, of course, still an option, though you will probably need to use a personal player with headphones, and you won't want to join in with much more than a low hum. Nonetheless, you can still enter into a worshipful place by listening to the music and releasing your heart to join in the heavenly chorus.

Alternatively, consider taking a page from those in microchurches, that is, house churches that don't meet in homes, but in other public places where congregational singing may be less than appropriate. Since worship is an attitude and act that ascribes worthiness to the Divine, music is simply one tactic to achieve that attitude. There are many other ways to enter the realm of worship. For instance, instead of listening to music, consider getting a copy of the Bible on CD, audiocassette tape, or MP3 files and listening to the Psalms, especially those that extol God's majesty, and pray along in the beauty of holiness.

Of course, any of these worship practices are adaptable even if your longest commute is from kitchen to living room. In your home you can crank up the volume of the stereo for worship or put an MP3 player on your hip. When you do the soccer mom (or dad) thing, leading worship with your children is not only a good use of time, but it instills a high value for the spiritual and for worship in their impressionable hearts and minds.

There is no question that worship is one of the most important spiritual habits. If you will avail yourself of picking up a couple of these practices, especially the incidental worship practices, you will find your spiritual crystal resonating with the Divine frequency and generating a power unequaled in your heart.

SPARKS AND RESISTANCE

Questions for Discussion and Reflection

1. In what ways have you experienced worship in the past?
2. What worship practices have caused your spiritual crystal to resonate within you?
3. Have you ever left a worship service feeling unfulfilled? What happened that deflated your spiritual fervor? What could you do to make sure this doesn't happen again?
4. What do you need to do to ensure you are "fed" when you attend a church worship service?
5. What incidental worship practices have you experienced?
6. Which worship practices seem inviting to you? How will you add them to your busy schedule?

6

The Spiritual Habit of Giving Up

The Divine Power Grid pulses with the power of the Spirit, but, as I shared in chapter 3, if we made a direct connection into God's seven billion yottavolts, well, let's just say it wouldn't be a pretty sight. Thankfully, God provided us a step-down transformer in the person of Jesus Christ. Our connection through him via prayer is what allows the Divine Power to flow through us. That Power lights up our lives, keeps our spiritual back-up batteries charged, and gives us the energy for living as Practicing Christians. Those who have experienced a solid connection with the Divine are both satiated and left wanting more. I guess you could say that God's Power is addicting.

When I bring up the spiritual habit of "giving up," you might be feeling just a bit uncomfortable. Sacrifice, denial, abstinence, surrender, and submission are terms generally considered four-letter words and antithetical to North American values. It's one thing to embrace the notion of being *willing* to give up everything for the sake of the gospel; it's quite another to *actually* give up anything.

Several years ago Jim Furry, a videographer and one of the best church comedic scriptwriters I've met, produced an offering video for our worship service. In a spoof of old family sitcoms, he and his family "starred" in an episode that left the congregation both thoughtful and in stitches. The scene, filmed in black-and-white, opened in the Furry Family living room. The family–Mom, Dad, the son, and daughter–are relaxing and watching the television. Suddenly the cable went out and the television screen was nothing but snow.

"Did you pay the cable bill?" Mom asks Dad.

"I thought you were going to." Both roll their eyes.

The daughter furrows her brow and wonders aloud, "Who pays the bills at church?"

"I think Marcia the treasurer does," answers Dad.

With wide eyes, she whistles, "Wow! She must be rich."

"No, no," laughs Dad, "She pays the bills with the money people give in their tithes and offerings."

"How much do we give?" asks the son.

"This year we're trying to tithe," Mom says.

"What's a tithe?" asks the daughter.

"The Bible teaches that it's 10 percent of our income."

"Wow, that's a *lot.* Aren't there any other payment plans in the Bible?" asks the son.

Dad grins and replies, "Well, *Jesus* said we're supposed to give *everything* we've got."

"Wow, 10 percent is sounding pretty good!" the son exclaims.

Suddenly all the lights go out. "Honey, did you remember to pay the power bill?"

"I thought you..." [roll credits and theme].

You might think it's odd, but literally everyone I've known who were committed to tithing have told me they wouldn't give it up because of what it does for them. The same goes for the spiritual giants I've met who intentionally engage in any of the "giving-up" habits. On the other hand, those who haven't tried intentional serious sacrifice just shake their heads in wonder—mostly wondering when the staff from the local sanitarium is going to show up with the long-sleeved white jacket. They figure the committed have got to be getting *something* out of it, but they can't imagine what.

The answer lies in the Divine Power Grid and our built-in, personal, step-down sacrifice-transformer.

The way a step-down transformer works (see the illustration) is that electricity flows through the input side of the transformer and passes through a series of coils, creating a magnetic field. (Remember wrapping wire around a nail in grade school to make a magnet? Same concept.) The output side of the transformer has a series of coils, but there are fewer of them. As electricity passes through the input side, the magnetic field it creates reaches across to the output coils and generates electricity, except it produces *less* voltage because there are fewer coils responding to the magnetic field. But here's the amazing thing: although the voltage drops, the power (amps) actually increases because

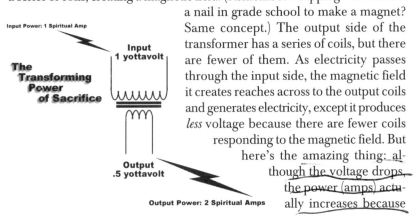

the power flowing through the input coils transfers the full amount of it's energy into a smaller package.

The spiritual habit of giving up uses the same principle as a step-down transformer. Whenever we make a real sacrifice for the sake of the Kingdom, we are giving up something. When you give up something, there is a loss, a step-down of your personal voltage so to speak. That leaves you with less of something, but, like the transformer, when you step-down your personal voltage, your spiritual power increases proportionately.

Increasing your spiritual energy is what the spiritual habit of giving up is all about. In fact, the more you give up, the more spiritual energy is available to you.

Besides the benefits of increasing our own spiritual energy, there is another reason for practicing the spiritual habit of giving up: our addiction to privilege.

Bill Easum—pastor, writer, and church consultant—is fond of asking, "What are you willing to give up for the sake of the gospel?" He poses that question primarily to those who have been in the conventional church for decades and who have embraced a gospel of preference, that is, a belief that membership has its privileges. These people believe their personal preferences should set the standard for the whole church, including their preferences of worship music, dress style, level of formality, Bible translation, and so on.

Bill offers a corrective for these folks—becoming a disciple of Jesus. Committed followers of Jesus aren't offered a life of preference, but a life of sacrifice. Jesus reminds us that no one can be his disciple if they don't leave all they have in order to follow him (Lk. 14:33). The fact is, the life of a Practicing Christian is about giving up, not about privilege or preference. Paul reminded his readers that he would do anything that wasn't immoral in order to effectively share the gospel:

> Though I am free and belong to no man, I make myself a slave to everyone, to win as many as possible. To the Jews I became like a Jew, to win the Jews. To those under the law I became like one under the law (though I myself am not under the law), so as to win those under the law. To those not having the law I became like one not having the law (though I am not free from God's law but am under Christ's law), so as to win those not having the law. To the weak I became weak, to win the weak. I have become all things to all men so that by all possible means I might save some. I do all this for the sake of the gospel, that I may share in its blessings. (1 Cor. 9:19–23)

The old America Express motto, "Membership has its privileges," is untenable to those who count Jesus as their master and leader. Jesus' motto is, "Membership is about sacrifice."

The spiritual habit of giving up is an important practice for at least three reasons. First, Jesus taught that his followers could expect to experience sacrifice and loss. The early church encouraged personal sacrifice—and sometimes overzealous Christians exhibited rather extreme sacrifices, such as living atop a pole, whipping themselves, or standing in cold water for days on end. As extreme as these seem to be, however, they pale in comparison to the sacrifice many were both willing and required to make...the offering of their lives. Offer them they did, and gladly. (For example, consider the story of Perpetua and Felicity, martyrs in 203 C.E.[1])

A second reason the spiritual habit of giving up in important is because it helps us learn to say "No!" There's an axiom that says, "If you want to get something done, ask a busy person to do it." I think that proverb began in the church. In North America, our churches are filled with busy people who are busy because they're pleasers. We think it would be nice if we could make everybody happy, so whenever somebody asks us to do something, we say "Yes." It doesn't matter if our plates are full. It doesn't matter that we're going to have to lose sleep or neglect our family to get it done. It doesn't even matter if we're going to sacrifice our own spiritual well-being to make you happy; we still say "Yes." Of course, there's a widening credibility gap for some of us, because our "Yes" really means, "If I can get around to it, I'll do it, but don't count on it." In the end, much of what we committed to do either doesn't get done, or what we do is mediocre at best.

The vaccination for "Yes" is a healthy dose of "No!" The spiritual habit of giving up provides that inoculation when we faithfully practice fasting in its various forms and fashions. Jesus said our yes should mean yes, and our no should mean no (Mt. 5:37). The spiritual habit of giving up helps us get there.

And, finally, the spiritual habit of giving up is important because nearly every North American "suffers" from an addiction to stuff. The fact is, we're addicted to consumerism, possessions, and the accumulation of either wealth or things. Unfortunately, this addiction has affected North American Christianity as well. It is one of our most prevalent sins. Indeed, writing about tithing, offerings, and/or sacrificial giving is the one topic guaranteed to raise objections in the church. Many confessing Christians in North America are guilty of offering at least some homage to the idol named *Money*. The evidence that we worship *Money* can be seen by how we sacrifice large portions of our lives to making it so we can get more "Stuff" that we could do without. Sadly, we actually believe we *need* most of the Stuff we've accumulated. What would your life be like if you did away with, say, television? computer games? microwave ovens? PDAs? pleasure or fishing boats? a second (or third) car? stereos? guns? or even pets? I'm pretty sure somewhere on that list your spirit took a sharp intake of breath in abject horror.

The god of *Money* has blinded most of North America. We've been conditioned to believe we *need* and *deserve* more than we actually do. The truth is, most of us could make do without most of what we have—including most of our furniture. Consider those who are Practicing Christians in China, Africa, India, and in other parts of the world. They get by with very little.

Paul had a rather different view of Stuff than we do in North America:

> If anyone teaches false doctrines and does not agree to the sound instruction of our Lord Jesus Christ and to godly teaching, he is conceited and understands nothing. He has an unhealthy interest in controversies and arguments that result in envy, quarreling, malicious talk, evil suspicions and constant friction between men of corrupt mind, who have been robbed of the truth and who think that godliness is a means to financial gain.
>
> But godliness with contentment is great gain. For we brought nothing into the world, and we can take nothing out of it. But if we have food and clothing, we will be content with that. People who want to get rich fall into temptation and a trap and into many foolish and harmful desires that plunge men into ruin and destruction. For the love of money is a root of all kinds of evil. Some people, eager for money, have wandered from the faith and pierced themselves with many griefs.
>
> But you, man of God, flee from all this, and pursue righteousness, godliness, faith, love, endurance and gentleness. (1 Tim. 6:3–11)

The line in that passage that strikes me is, "*Some people, eager for money, have wandered from the faith...*" I've known many very busy people who over-commit to their job, or even take on second and third jobs, so they can have more Stuff. It's one thing if we work that hard to meet basic needs; it's something else again when we believe we need all that Stuff, or that we're *entitled* to accumulate more Stuff because we work so hard.

I realize I've just stepped on a lot of toes—and probably on yours. The truth is we're all guilty of the sin of Stuff (unless you've taken and embraced a vow of poverty). There's a very real paradox between what Jesus taught and our understanding of God's material blessing upon North America. I have to confess I'm not sure what the answer is, but before we move on and look at some of the particular habits of giving up, I want to share a passage from Juan Ortiz in his book *Disciple*. The passage follows a section on what it means to give up everything in the name of the Lord.

> When we first began to preach this message of discipleship in Buenos Aires, our congregations were very willing to obey. Many of our members were bringing their homes and apartments to give to the church. (In my country, inflation is so bad that you don't put money in the bank, because you will only fall behind. Instead

you buy something–anything–that has a value that will rise with the inflation. Our apartments are our life savings.)

We didn't know what to do with these properties. The pastors met together. One said, "Maybe we should sell all these and use the money to build a big church in the city."

But others said, "No, no, that's not the will of the Lord."

After six months of prayer, the Lord showed us what to do. We called the people together and said, "We are going to return everyone's real estate. The Lord has showed us that He doesn't want your empty houses. He wants a house with you inside taking care of it. He wants the carpets and heating and the air conditioning and the lights and the food and everything ready–for Him. He also wants your car, with you as the driver.

"Just remember, though, that it all still belongs to Him."

So now all the houses are open. When visitors come to our congregation, we don't say, "Who can take these brothers to your house?"

Instead, we say to someone, "You, brother, you're going to take these people to your house." We don't ask; we command because the house is already given to the Lord. And the people thank the Lord that He lets them live in His house.[2]

Radical? Certainly. Biblical? Assuredly.

The spiritual habit of giving up is especially needed by North American Christians where we have been given much, but are generally unwilling to give up much. Breaking the spiritual noose of privilege, preference, and Stuff is one of the most important steps to a fulfilling, faithful, and power-full life in Christ.

Fasting

 Busy people often have difficulty adding anything additional to their schedules, such as a formalized worship service or even a regularly scheduled prayer time. On the other hand, the spiritual habit of giving up won't make a dent in your schedule–it may even free up some time so you can add other spiritual habits.

Fasting, the practice of depriving ourselves in the name of spiritual nourishment, has been a part of the Judeo-Christian faith almost from its inception. From giving up chocolate for a day to abstaining from food, water, or other needs and desires for a period of time, fasting has long been a mark both of repentance and of deep devotion to the Lord. However, the practice of fasting has all but disappeared from the Western church. Sure, there are a few who still practice it today, but there were times in the distant past when the larger church and even whole nations fasted.

There are actually no commandments in the Bible that require us to fast. On the other hand, it is also clear that fasting was an expected practice for the early Christians. For instance, several times Jesus gave instructions about fasting to his disciples:

"When you fast…" (Mt. 6:16)

"But this kind does not go out except by prayer and fasting." (Mt. 17:21)

"In those days they will fast." (Lk. 5:35)

Further, the early church practiced fasting, especially when they were seeking direction from the Lord in prayer. (See Acts 13:2–3; 14:23.) Abstinence was a regular part of the spiritual life.

The standard practice of yesterday's Christianity is a far cry from our practices today. In our culture, we maintain a high value on self and comfort. The contemporary proverb, "If it feels good, do it," has its counterpoint, "If it doesn't feel good, avoid it." In the past there were devoted men and women who intentionally chose to live on bread, salt, and water alone—and not for a limited period of time, but for their whole adult lives. They would regularly deprive themselves of sleep for days on end in order to spend additional time in prayer and meditation. They would give up the comfort of a bed for the austerity of the floor, and so on. In today's culture, the notion of giving up anything at all for the sake of the Kingdom is considered radical, ill-advised, and odd. And yet, the practice of fasting can be one of the most effective spiritual habits in a Christian's arsenal.

Because fasting is so seldom practiced today, there is a lack of understanding of what fasting is, why we should fast, and how to practice it. So let's shed some light on the subject.

What Is Fasting?

Fasting is the practice of giving something up for a specific period of time. Most of the time, fasting has been associated with the voluntary giving up of eating and/or drinking. However, the practice of fasting is broader than that. For centuries, the Roman Catholic Church practiced a fast from meat on Fridays. Paul suggests that married couples may choose to fast from having intimate relations for a *brief* period of time now and again in order to pray (1 Cor. 7:5). There were, and are, many different ways to fast, and things to fast from.

Why Fast?

There are a couple of traditional reasons for fasting. Initially, fasting was a sign of sorrow. This may have started when someone noticed that people sometimes lose their appetites when they experience grief. After the death, resurrection, and ascension of Jesus, fasting became an act whereby a Christian could, in some way, share in the suffering that Jesus endured on the cross—it became a way to make a connection with Jesus in concrete ways. Others practiced fasting as an indication of repentance or as penance (self-punishment) for their sins. Later, Christians began to fast as a spiritual habit specifically to "tune in" so they could hear from God.

Of course, all of these reasons are valid today. However, the underlying reasoning for *all* of these fasts is to make a connection with the Divine through time given to prayer.

How Do I Fast?

There are a number of different ways to practice fasting. How you fast primarily depends on what you're planning on giving up and for how long. However, regardless of which fast you decide to practice, your time should begin with centering prayer and move from there. Whether you're fasting for an hour or for a week, be intentional during the fast about connecting and reconnecting with the Divine. It's only by practicing a fast and making the effort to connect with God that our spiritual transformer will generate more energy.

Next, let's look at several different kinds of fasts. First, we'll explore the two kinds of fasts found in the Bible, and then look at a few contemporary fasts that are especially meaningful today.

Food

Abstaining from food (or beverages) is the most commonly practiced fast. Exactly how you do it depends on how long you intend to not eat. If you've never fasted before, I don't suggest fasting for any longer than three days, and you should probably start with a one-day fast. However, you can start the spiritual habit of fasting by giving up one meal rather than all of your daily meals and snacks. You can also fast by giving up foods such as meat, alcohol, soda, chocolate, and so on.

To fast for a brief period of time, simply make a commitment not to eat for that period. Most busy people will have no trouble finding something "important" to do to fill up the time during which they would otherwise be eating. However, resist the temptation to read another report or make another phone call during your "lunch break." Instead, devote that time to prayer or to one of the other spiritual habits, such as study or intentional worship.

If you've opted to fast from a particular food, you may not have that extra ten minutes that you'd have had if you skipped lunch. (Short lunches are an unfortunate reality for many too-busy people.) However, to use this fast as a connection to the Divine Power Grid, take a few moments, however brief they may be, to practice a centering prayer and remind both yourself and God that you've given up this indulgence as an offering to the Divine.

The point is not to bask in an attitude of self-acclamation, but of humble quiet—after all, this (or any sacrifice we might make) isn't really all that much of a sacrifice when compared to the cross. Again, this whole offering might only last ten or fifteen seconds, but humbly and honestly making any sacrifice in the name of the Lord is a pleasing and acceptable gift.

If you decide to practice a full fast, that is, if you give up all foods, increase your intake of water or other liquids in order to stave off dehydration, because food provides much of our hydration needs.[3] And if you choose to fast for a longer period of time, say three or more days, add fruit and vegetable juices to your liquid intake.[4] As you fast, spend time in prayer or another spiritual habit—and make sure you're listening to hear the voice of God.

Intimacy

The second biblically mentioned fast is a fast from sexual intimacy. This fast is limited to married couples—abstinence is the *expectation* for all other Practicing Christians. Paul wrote of this kind of fast when he addressed the church in Corinth. He wrote:

> Now for the matters you wrote about: It is good for a man not to marry. But since there is so much immorality, each man should have his own wife, and each woman her own husband. The husband should fulfill his marital duty to his wife, and likewise the wife to her husband. The wife's body does not belong to her alone but also to her husband. In the same way, the husband's body does not belong to him alone but also to his wife. Do not deprive each other except by mutual consent and for a time, so that you may devote yourselves to prayer. Then come together again so that Satan will not tempt you because of your lack of self-control. (1 Cor. 7:1–5)

Notice the scope of this fast—it is limited in time, mutually agreed on, and for the purpose of prayer. It is inappropriate to impose this fast unilaterally on one's spouse.

Abstaining from food and intimacy are the two traditional fasts recorded in the Bible; however, a variety of others have since been introduced and adopted. In ancient times, abstaining from food and intimacy served to heighten awareness of the Presence of the Holy—food and intimacy were the two main "luxuries" in the average person's life. For most of us in North America, food is almost an afterthought (unless we have food addictions). Though giving up food is undoubtedly a real sacrifice, we might be better off giving up something else altogether—perhaps something more meaningful and more apt to free our spirits for communing with the Divine. Consider surrendering something a little more challenging: television, work, or leisure.

Television

A friend of mine suggested that the most effective fast we could practice today would be abstinence from the television. Although this might seem somewhat trivial, many find it difficult to turn off the TV in order to spend the time in prayer or with another spiritual habit instead. Considering that the average person in the U.S. watches four hours of television each day,[5] this could well be one of the reasons we're so busy the *rest* of the time! If missing *Monday Night Football* or MTV seems like a sacrifice to you, fasting from television may be an excellent spiritual habit to take up. Simply make a commitment to leave the television off and spend the time with God instead.

Although there are lots of great reasons for turning off the television and doing something else, remember that the purpose of a *fast* is to enhance your connection with the Divine. Claiming that you're fasting from television one night a week, but then spending the evening with the family or reading a good book may result in an improved life, but it's not going to result in a deeper, more vibrant spirituality. So instead, turn the TV off *two* nights a week. Spend one of them with your loved ones and spend the other one in prayer. You'll improve your *whole* life that way.

By the way, if you *really* want to engage in this fast as a meaningful sacrifice, schedule your fast for the evening you would normally watch your favorite show. And then *don't* record it. That would be an opportunity to actually give something up rather than deferring a luxury or desire to another time.

Work

Chris Black directs a religious publishing house. I've known him for several years and I would characterize him as one of the "busy" people. He is also a Practicing Christian, and I had an opportunity to chat with him one afternoon. He was explaining what he does for a living and the hours he puts in:

> I don't keep excessive office hours. A typical week I'm in the office at eight and out of the office by five. On the other hand, the nature of what I do means that I'm always "at work." I'm in a situation that is entrepreneurial, that is, based on innovation and creativity, so I'm thinking about what's next all the time.[6]

Chris's confession that he's "always at work" may ring true with many reading this book. As an entrepreneurial pastor and a writer, I can relate to the "always at work" syndrome. From the CEO of a Fortune 500 company, to the CEO of a household of kids, some of us don't seem ever to get a break. For some, homework didn't end with high school, college, or grad school. Briefs or proposals need to be written, or customers give us a jingle on our cell phones while we're at home. For others, it's not the homework that gets us, it's the brain that never quite shuts off from work, sort of like what Chris described.

Now as I said, Chris is a Practicing Christian and he's learned a few things about being "on" all the time. In fact, he's learned to shut it off:

> To take Sabbath from working and thinking about work, to step away from work, is a discipline in itself. It's setting aside some time to be present to whatever I'm doing–of being present to where I am and the people I am with in that time. So when I'm with my wife, I'm to be present to her. When I'm with my daughter, then I'm present with my daughter, and not thinking about something that's going on at the office or about some new development I want to do.[7]

Time off is an all but vanished luxury in our busy lives. Americans work more hours per week than those in any other affluent nation.[8] Though there are many reasons for this, including the near-insatiable appetite for more Stuff, the result is we have less time for family, for leisure, and for God. Fasting from work is an idea whose time has come.

However, unless you're working more than one job, you probably already get a day or two off each week. Now I don't know about you, but I sometimes find my "day off" is less relaxing than being at work. There's always something that needs to be done, especially if you're a homeowner. The yard needs attention, the fence needs to be painted, and there's a never-ending mound of laundry, dishes, or clutter that demands our time.

That's why God decreed a Sabbath. You may remember that *no one* was allowed to work on the Sabbath, and that included doing yard work, home repairs, or running errands (all of which tend to claim my days off). At the risk of being redundant, *fasting from work is an idea whose time has come.*

Fasting from work takes a bit of planning and a bit of discipline–it isn't going to start on its own. First, you'll need to schedule it. Even if you intend to adopt this spiritual habit on a weekly basis, putting it on your calendar needs to be a priority. There's no reason you have to schedule a full day for this fast. You can schedule it for a Saturday afternoon, an evening after work, or an hour in the morning. Any time you set aside for prayer or another spiritual habit during which you would have normally worked is a fast.

Second, you'll need to disconnect. As I write this chapter, I'm in a hotel room overlooking the Rocky Mountains in Denver. Though I'm nearly fourteen hundred miles from home, in some ways it's like I've never left. My cell phone is on and I'm getting e-mail notes every ten minutes. As a busy person, I develop anxiety if I'm not wired-in and available. This, when I think about it, is just plain silly. I'm not irreplaceable or indispensable, and there's no need to be available 24/7. And, most likely, neither are you.

When you're going to fast from work, take your phone off the hook, turn off the cell phone (putting it on vibrate doesn't count—we *both* know that just because it doesn't ring doesn't mean you won't check the number when it buzzes, just in case), and turn off your computer.

Third, go someplace where you won't be interrupted. That may mean you have to leave your kids in the care of your spouse or a babysitter. Go ahead and do it. It may mean you have to leave home—it generally does for me. Take a walk, a ride, or a drive to some secluded spot (someone's empty office, a park, the woods, the beach, or your own backyard) so you can find some solitude.

And, finally, spend the time in prayer or another spiritual discipline. Remember, this is a fast. It means giving up something in order to connect with God.

Leisure

Giving up leisure is like giving up work, only in reverse. According to the U.S. Department of Labor, those who are employed full-time still manage to spend an average of about four hours each day in some sort of leisure activity, with the vast majority of those hours spent in front of the television.[9]

Much of what has been said about giving up television can be applied to giving up leisure. You may choose to give up an hour of television, or forgo a night at the movies or theater, a round of golf, your monthly guys' or gals' night out, or any of hundreds of other leisure activities. Whichever you willingly give up as a gift to God, surrender that time to the Lord, and connect your spiritual transformer up to the Divine Power Grid by spending the time in prayer or another spiritual habit.

Cheerful Giving

Thinking back on the introduction of this chapter, you may have felt pretty bruised and banged up by what I had to say about sacrifice, especially about giving money. I promise, this section will be gentler.

The practice of giving financially stems back to the Old Testament. Most Christians today are familiar with the tithe, which literally means tenth (in fact, the word is the Old English ordinal for tenth: eighth, ninth, tithe). In the Old Testament, the Israelites were required initially to give a tenth of their increase, i.e., the harvest, for the support of the religion. The money went directly to support the priesthood.

But there were other giving requirements than just the tithe. The Israelites were also required to give additional offerings including first fruits, a half-shekel temple tax, contributions into the sacrificial system, and so on. I'm not sure about the math, but some scholars say the sum of the tithe, the first fruits, and the half-shekel came to about 23 percent of a family's annual income—and that's *before* the cost of the sacrificial system.

However, as many Christians are wont to say, "We're not under law, we're under grace. Tithing is *Old* Testament law." True.

The spiritual habit of cheerful giving is an important practice nonetheless. Many Practicing Christians have decided, Old Testament law or not, that the tithe is a pretty good place to start. I asked Chris Black what particular spiritual habits he practiced and he began telling me about tithing:

> Things I think of as spiritual practices, things I do intentionally that cause me to focus on my relationship with God, on other people, or to reorient my life are things like prayer every day and tithing. I started to tithe when an elder took me aside and told me a story about a man who took *him* aside when he was a young man and just married. He told me what tithing had meant to him and how he'd done it—and to start now while I was young and let it become a part of my lifestyle. This man was in his seventies, and he was taking me aside in my twenties and just telling me the story. I began tithing a little at a time, but now I'm at a place where it's a regular part of my life. When I think about what's been entrusted to me and how I use it, I think I'm almost at a place where I'll be ready to tell that story to somebody coming up.[10]

I can honestly say that those whom I know who have started tithing haven't stopped—they feel a profound sense of blessing they aren't willing to give up. Remember, it's that step-down transformer principle: we give up something, but when we do, the spiritual power proportionately makes up for it.

The spiritual habit of cheerful giving is about giving up. It's about sacrifice. If you're well-to-do and tithing isn't really an issue, then giving 10 percent, although a nice offering, isn't practicing the spiritual habit of giving up. On the other hand, if giving 5 percent of your income means you have to forgo desserts this week, then *that's* a spiritual habit worth practicing.

Finally, there are two words in cheerful giving—*giving* and *cheerful.* If you aren't at a place to practice this (or any other) spiritual habit with a joyous heart, then don't.

Centricity

I've practiced all of the fasts above, plus a number of others, at sometime in my life. I can testify that each is a helpful tool in making a solid connection with the Divine Power Grid. I've been energized and revitalized through all of these practices. However, though giving up food, intimacy, television, work, or leisure are great tools in a spiritual toolbox, it is really only when we practice the spiritual habit of giving up our centricity that the Spirit of God is fully enabled to work through our lives.

We are egocentric. It's a fact of biology; we have a built-in survival instinct designed to protect us. As we are raised, our culture molds our centricity for better or for worse. Some societies are family-centric, some are tribal-centric, and so on. Those growing up in these cultures learn to sacrifice their own personal comfort for the sake of others. The North American culture, however, places a high value on individualism and independence. Self-determination and self-actualization are our keystones. Unfortunately, that means we are likely to have a difficult time becoming aligned with the expectations of biblical Christianity. Consider the following instructions from Jesus:

> "So the last will be first, and the first will be last." (Mt. 20:16)

> "Whoever loves father or mother more than me is not worthy of me; and whoever loves son or daughter more than me is not worthy of me; and whoever does not take up the cross and follow me is not worthy of me." (Mt. 10:37–38, NRSV)

> Then Jesus told his disciples, "If any want to become my followers, let them deny themselves and take up their cross and follow me." (Mt. 16:24, NRSV)

In the North American context, we've had a tendency to brush over his words, to ignore them, or to rationalize them away. However, getting our "self" out of our center is the most important "giving up" we can do. It's more important than fasting and more important than cheerful giving. It's also happens to be the most difficult thing you can do.

When I look back over my personal history, I can clearly identify the times when I was in the driver's seat of my life. Sometimes it *looked* like I was doing all right, but I realize that those were the times when I *felt* particularly empty or uneasy. I knew something wasn't right. But whenever I've been in the driver's seat on the road of life, it's only been a matter of time before I smash into a guardrail or worse. Today, when I get into the driver's seat–and I'm not going to lie, I still climb in on the wrong side of the car now and then–it isn't long before I'm asking myself Dr. Phil's famous question, "How's that working for you?" and I offer to change seats with God.

You know, you can practice all of the spiritual habits and still be sitting in the driver's seat. Until you understand, embrace, and *complete* the Alcoholics Anonymous third step, the spiritual power to be an effective Practicing Christian is going to elude you: "3. Made a decision to turn your will and your life over to the care of God."

There are many ways to put this step into practice. But this is a book for busy people, so I want to offer three practices that will help you to remove yourself from the center.

Centering Prayer

You've read about this prayer in virtually every chapter and in nearly every section of this book. But centering prayer is effective because it starts where we are, in the awareness of our own centricity, and then invites us to displace ourselves and allow the Divine Presence to be our center. When God is the center of our lives, we can't help but experience the power of the Divine.

Listen More than Talk

I don't remember if my grandma ever said it, but if she didn't, she would have, given half-a-chance: "God gave you two ears and one mouth, to use in those proportions."

Most of us love the sound of our own voices. We love to tell our stories and to share our experiences. Many of us have no problems making decisions, solving problems, and giving direction without listening as well as we could. The book of Proverbs addresses the issue: "Plans fail for lack of counsel, / but with many advisers they succeed" (Prov. 15:22). Listening is an important practice for busy people.

Some of you who are reading this are probably natural listeners, so this may not be a particularly helpful spiritual habit for decentralizing yourself. But for the rest of us, let me offer a couple of tips for giving this practice a whirl. When someone is speaking to you, even at work:

- Practice looking at their face and maintain your focus without speaking until they are finished.
- Intentionally refrain from formulating a response while the other is speaking. Some of us have developed a habit of listening to about a third of what someone is saying, then we tend to lose our focus because we're formulating a response. When people speak, they don't often get to the important part of a story or to the problem until very near the end. Wait until they've finished the *last* two-thirds of the conversation.
- Draw them out. Practice drawing people out by inviting them to "go on…" when appropriate. Paraphrasing what they say to help them elaborate is another drawing out method–and as a side benefit, you'll ensure you've understood what they're trying to say. Paraphrase what they've said by starting out, "I hear you saying…," and then repeating what you think you heard them say in your own words.
- Focus on paying attention. If you'll surrender your centricity and work on putting the other person first, it becomes easier.

Be Loving Rather than Right

I'm exactly like Popeye, sort of. Whereas Popeye says, "I am what I am," I regularly think to myself, "I know what I know." And I stick by what I know. When I was in church camp as a young teenager, my mom sent me a card with Lucy Van Pelt telling Charlie Brown, "If you can't be right, *be wrong in a loud voice!*" Be that as it may, what I "know" can change pretty regularly. For instance, I'll get into a "discussion" with my loving and brilliant wife about a decision needing to be made and I'll defend my position come hell-or-high-water. Bless her heart; she's learned to almost always let me think I'm right. How is it she concedes that I'm right so often, you may ask? Because she knows that by the morrow I'll have processed her alternative and, nine-times-out-of-ten, I'll figure out her was suggestion better, so I adopt it.

Being right is not a Christian virtue. Being loving is.

Paul wrote to the Roman church and told them to "Honor one another above yourselves" (Rom. 12:10b). Putting others first is one of the keys to decentralizing ourselves, and one important way to do this is to decide what's worth fighting for and what isn't. Frankly, most battles just don't matter that much in life.

At first thought, we tend to assume everyone thinks like we do, so we think if they were intelligent people at all, they'd draw the same conclusions as we do. If someone doesn't agree with us, we assume they just don't understand. So we try to explain it to them again, knowing if they just *understood* our position, they'd see the error of their ways. If that doesn't work, we assume they think *we're* the dense ones, so our defenses go up, the battle lines are drawn, and we draw our swords.

When I was being apprenticed as a child therapist, my mentor would regularly remind me, "Bill, pick your battles." She meant two things by this, and I pass her wisdom on to you.

First, consider whether the issue is worth risking the relationship over. Some things are. If you're a supervisor of a warehouse and the forklift driver has decided it's too hot to wear a hardhat, you will need to risk the relationship both for the driver's safety and your liability. However, few issues are worth risking a relationship over. Your way *may* be easier, but it may not be worth going to the mat for.

Second, before going to war, decide whether it's a battle you can win or not. In the case of the forklift driver, if the hat doesn't go on, you're going to fire them. It's black and white; you're not going to lose. But if I disagree with someone's politics, even if I feel strongly about the issue, I probably have no business engaging in a debate because I probably can't win. I may have more statistics and quotes on my side, I might even be able to dazzle them with my brilliance, but most political discussions are opinion and emotion based. *No* one wins in that case.

Practicing being loving more than being right is a discipline that honors others over yourself. Listening more than talking also honors others. Whenever you practice these disciplines, you're developing a habit of not being the center—you're practicing a Christlike attitude. Giving up your center, letting God have control of the steering wheel of your life, loving others in the same way Jesus loved others (he wasn't just *willing* to die for them, he *did* die for them) is the ultimate spiritual habit.

It may be paradoxical that you gain spiritual power when you practice giving up, but the power of paradox has been a Divine attribute from the very beginning. Joyful sacrifice is probably the most difficult, and I suspect the least popular, of the spiritual habits. Yet, it is the most prominent spiritual habit that Jesus practiced:

> The reason my Father loves me is that I lay down my life—only to take it up again. No one takes it from me, but I lay it down of my own accord. I have authority to lay it down and authority to take it up again. This command I received from my Father." (Jn. 10:17–18)

SPARKS AND RESISTANCE

Questions for Discussion and Reflection

1. What is the most you've ever given up for someone else? For the church? For your faith?
2. What are you willing to give up for the sake of the gospel? Would you give up your position on the board (or as pastor, elder, deacon, teacher, etc.)? Would you give up your church music preference? If it meant listening to rap (if you're over 40) or pipe-organ hymns (if you're under forty)? Would you give up your job? Your car? Your home?
3. Which of the fasts in this chapter would be the most difficult for you to practice? What does that tell you about yourself?
4. It's been said that Jesus talked more about money, treasure, and wealth than any other topic. Why do you think that is? Do you know anybody who tithes? Invite them to share their experience with you.
5. Look back at your personal history. Can you identify a time when God was firmly in the driver's seat of your life? What was that like? Can you identify a time when you were in the driver's seat? How did that work for you?
6. What spiritual practice do you think would be the most helpful in surrendering your centricity?

7

The Spiritual Habit of Taking On

The last chapter covered the habit of giving up. This chapter deals with the opposite. Jesus said to take up our cross daily and to follow him. Most of the time, his commandment conjures visions of what we must give up—mostly our centricity. However, there's another side to the command: Taking on. There is an expectation that we're taking something on even while we're letting go of something else.

Have you ever noticed when you do something really nice for someone else, something totally unexpected, there's an accompanying charge in your internal battery that fills you with a sense of well-being? That is what happens when you practice the spiritual habit of taking on. Your spiritual battery gets recharged.

Rechargeable batteries work because of an electrochemical reaction that takes place between two different metals when they are immersed in a catalyst. (Really, it's not as complicated as it sounds.)

Electricity is the flow of electrons. Figure 1 is of a NiCad battery being used in a small flashlight that, at the moment, is switched off. Cadmium is a metal that collects electrons for a hobby and hoards them. On the other hand, Nickel has a scarcity of electrons—but the Nickel in our battery has always coveted them. In our NiCad flashlight illustration, the two metals are encased in a catalyst, which in this case is an electrolyte paste. The electrolyte paste serves two

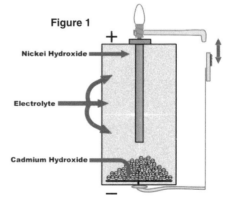

Figure 1

+

Nickel Hydroxide

Electrolyte

Cadmium Hydroxide

−

functions. First, it's an insulator that separates two metals; however, it is also a medium that facilitates the chemical reaction between the metals and creates electricity.

When you slide the switch to turn on the flashlight, you "close" the circuit. (See figure 2.)

As soon as you do, the Nickel "sees" its opportunity to attract the hoarded electrons from the Cadmium through the connection. As the electrons flow through the circuit, they light the bulb and the Nickel begins to hoard the electrons itself. Unless you turn the flashlight off by "opening" the circuit, the Nickel will continue to attract Cadmium's electrons and the flow will continue for some time, so your flashlight may be bright for a couple of hours. But as the Cadmium's electron hoard is depleted, the flow of electrons slows to a trickle and you know it's time to recharge the battery because the light begins to dim.

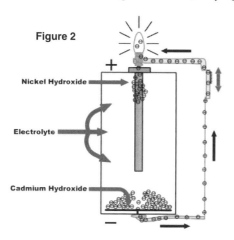

Figure 2

Nickel Hydroxide

Electrolyte

Cadmium Hydroxide

Recharging a NiCad battery is a simple matter of connecting it to a recharger.

The recharger applies just the right amount of voltage to the battery so that it robs the Nickel of its electrons and returns them to Cadmium's hoard. When the process is complete, the battery is ready to be put back into our flashlight to await the next power outage.

In a Practicing Christian's life, the spiritual batteries regularly give up their power during the course of a busy week. Temptations drain it. Being unplugged from the Divine Power Grid drains it. And difficult circumstances or difficult people—especially—drain it.

The good news is, like the NiCad, our spiritual batteries

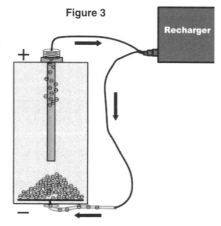

Figure 3

Recharger

recharge whenever we plug into the Divine Recharger—in this case, when we practice the spiritual habit of taking on.

The Spiritual Habit of Taking On

It's been said by many that North American Christianity has historically been known for what it's against, rather than what it's for. Various Christian groups have been known for abstaining from dancing; card playing; alcohol consumption; males with long hair; and females wearing jeans, make-up, or jewelry. Although these churches also engaged in helping the poor, building hospitals, and sending missionaries, that isn't what gets noticed.

The trend that North American Christianity is known for what it's against continues right up the present day. Many know about Christianity as the vocal opponent to: homosexuality, abortion, and more recently same-gender marriage. But ask an unchurched person what Christianity is *for* and you'll get blank looks. We're still better known for our negatives than our positives. Perhaps it's time to change that.

But the spiritual habit of taking on is more than a demonstration to the world that faithful Christians are *for* something. Taking on is a habit that builds our spiritual maturity by encouraging us to reach beyond ourselves. We grow as we pour our lives into others by practicing a variety of good works. And though these good works help us mature, they also have a positive physiological effect on us. According to Dr. Hans Selye, who was a pioneer in stress research, "One of the greatest buffers against the ravages of future stress is to spread good-will in the lives of other people."[1] Practicing the spiritual habit of taking on accomplishes a great deal of good, both for those who receive our acts of kindness and for us.

Serve in Your Gift-Ability

What are your spiritual gifts, your talents, your skills, and your passions? If you can rattle them all off, congratulations! You know your "gift-ability" and you're miles ahead of most Christians. Several years ago, my wife and I developed what we call the *Personal Ministry Assessment* (PMA). We created the tool when we discovered, to our dismay, that there were people in our budding congregation who didn't know—or worse, didn't believe—they had anything to offer that God could use. For one, they didn't know God had graced them with spiritual gifts for the good of the Kingdom. Not only that, they had no conception that God could use the talents or skills they had.[2] Some weren't sure what they were actually passionate about. However, once they took the PMA and we had taken the time to go over the assessments together, they were excited to discover that not only did they have gifts, talents, and skills, but that there were ways to practice their passions in the name of Jesus both inside and outside of the church.

The Divine Master Plan seems to demand virtually every different gift, talent, and skill in order to achieve God's purpose; therefore, everyone has something to offer. The first question to be answered is, "What do I have to offer?" The second is, "How does God want me to use the gifts, talents, and skills I have?"

It's beyond the scope of this book to delve deeply into how to discover your spiritual gifts. (It is my hope that you already know what skills, training, and expertise you've developed.) There are, however, a number of books, resources, and spiritual gifts inventories available at your local Christian bookstore, as well as online.[2]

If you don't already know what your God-given talents are, probably the best way to discover them is simply to ask. Begin by asking God–and then taking the necessary time to listen. (See chapter 3 for how to hear the voice of God). You could be amazed by what the Spirit whispers into your soul. Only after you've sought a word from God should you go to the next step. That's when you ask for input from your family, friends, coworkers, teachers, and others who know you well or who have worked alongside you. Listen openly, but weigh what they say carefully. Sometimes our humility, whether real or false, will cause us to doubt the truth of their observations. At other times, hurtful voices from our past may echo through our minds and create doubts. Getting past our own humility and any hurtful recordings is critical in order to hear those who know us. When they speak, they may recognize talents we hadn't considered.

On the other hand, you will need to pass what is said through a flattery-filter lest you find yourself committed to deliver more than you're capable of. For instance, I play guitar. I enjoy it and I'm not bad at it. My ever-loving and supportive wife will tell you I have talent and that I'm a gifted musician. I have a skill. I took guitar lessons for three years and I spent a lot of time as a teenager practicing. So long as the song only demands that I strum, and I have access to a chord chart, *and* I don't have to make a bar-chord, I do all right. Beyond that, I'm a rank amateur. Like I said, skill, not talent.

Okay, you've identified your gifts, talents, and skills. Now what? Before you launch out into the deep, consider what you're passionate about. Do you want to work within a church's programs, or out in the community? Do you want to serve Christians, or are you more interested in being a Christian witness? All these are important questions to consider.

Taking On: The Church or Not?

Once you know your gift-ability, the next big question is deciding where you will practice the spiritual habit of taking on. It used to be that Christians simply expected to use their gifts inside the church, but more and more Christians are taking their gift-abilities and taking on services in the wider community.

Why are so many leaving the church to do service in the community? There are two reasons. First, in many churches the service that "needs" to be done within the church is being on some committee or another. People go to meetings and talk about, but seldom actually *do,* ministry–other than writing a check. On the other hand, there are many agencies that offer opportunities to serve the one-anothers and the everyone-elses beyond the walls of the church. Many, if not most, of these opportunities involve doing hands-on ministries that change people's lives. Although most of these organizations are not specifically "Christian," the fact that someone like *you,* a Practicing Christian, gets involved elevates that ministry as a Christian witness. Let's face it. What makes a ministry a "Christian ministry"? When a Christian is doing the ministering.

There's a second reason Christians are opting to do ministry outside of the local church. It used to be that the church was the community's chief social service agency. People used to turn to the church not only for spiritual needs, but for help with their emotional, financial, educational, physical, and social needs. But times have changed and the government has taken over most of the roles the church used to fill. The church abdicated much of its responsibility for reaching into the community. Ministries no longer needed were abandoned and the church turned its focus primarily on Christian education and worship. Though some large churches have reintroduced a variety of social programs, the fact is, relatively few people turn to the church when they discover they're in need.

Because there are a limited variety of ministries available within a local church, there is a tendency by many church leaders to place people into in-house ministries in which they simply don't fit. The prevailing attitude in many churches is that there's a job to do, and *somebody* needs to do it. If you're an available body, then you'll do fine. Far too little consideration is given to the fact that effective ministries are only effective when passionately skilled, talented, and gifted people are engaged in what God has called them to do. Take the story of Sarah, a budding Practicing Christian in a local church.

Sarah was the comptroller of a major accounting firm in the city. She was married, raised a family, and stayed very busy. She also attended, but didn't do much else in, her local church. However, by-and-by, her children grew into fine adults and left home. Sarah was grateful to her church for the nurture and support she'd always received, so she decided to practice the spiritual habit of taking on. Unfortunately, so she didn't know how to avoid what follows.

Sarah went to the pastor saying she wanted to serve the church in some way, though she didn't know how. What did he suggest she could do? It turns out that the junior high Sunday school class didn't have a teacher, so the pastor asked her to step into that position. She was a little perplexed by the request, but trusting that the pastor knew how best she could help the church, she agreed.

Have you ever taught a dozen twelve- to fourteen-year-olds? Unless you have the gifts of teaching and patience, coupled with a healthy dose of creative energy, don't. The kids will eat you alive! They're not *bad* kids, but this is the time in their lives when they are stepping out of childhood and becoming young adults. Their hormones rage, their need to test their independence begins to bloom, and they can sniff fear and/or incompetence from forty paces away. Sarah tried. She went to workshops to figure it out. She used the best curriculum she could get her hands on. But in the end, it was a train wreck waiting to happen. In less than a year, under a cloud of frustration, Sarah quit. She quit teaching. She quit the church. And she just about quit the faith. Why? Because she was "placed" rather than "passioned." There was a slot to fill, and she was a warm, willing (and unsuspecting) body.

Talk about a mismatch! Sarah loved her job as a comptroller. She clearly had a gift of administration. She was talented in interpersonal skills. (You have to be if you're an effective comptroller). And she was skilled in number crunching in almost all of its manifestations. But instead of helping her discover what her gifts, talents, skills, or interests were, and then steering her into a place where she could experience the fulfillment of her God-given passions, she was asked to fill a slot.

The advice I'm offering is this: Make sure you know your gifts, your talents, and your skills; link them to your passion; and *then* find a task or a responsibility to take on. Perhaps there is an opportunity in your local church. And if you've got a passion for junior high kids, I know a church where they can use you.

Finding Your Niche to Practice In

Exactly where you turn to put your gifts to work should ultimately depend on what makes your heart ache, whether or not the opportunities are inside or outside of your local church. In the past several years, many have felt a desire to help the homeless. Working with victims of AIDS has made a claim with many. But these just scratch the surface. There are literally thousands of opportunities to serve in hundreds of areas as diverse as evangelism; ecology; battered women, children, and seniors; run-away children and youth; prison and hospital ministries; poverty prevention; children, youth, and adult literacy; disaster ministries; short-term overseas and local missions; after-school tutoring; etc.; the list could fill pages and pages. However, to find the one that matches your gift-abilities, let me offer a couple of specific suggestions.

1. FIRST, ASK YOUR PASTOR. If you're involved in a local church, asking your pastor really *is* a good idea. To begin with, there may be an opportunity within your local church to take on a ministry that will charge your spiritual batteries to overflowing. However, don't ask the pastor to try to make a match on a Sunday morning as you walk out of the church building with the rest of the congregation–if the pastor shoots from the hip you'll end up filling the most urgent need instead of the most important. Make an appointment and share your gifts, talents, skills, and passions with your pastor. If you feel like you're being slotted, don't take the position suggested. Instead, be honest about your passion—or lack thereof—and ask about other possibilities.

2. ASK AROUND. Many taking on opportunities come by word-of-mouth. Ask other Practicing Christians who have similar interests about opportunities they know of. One reason many people are so busy is because they've made commitments to organizations that are making a positive difference in people's lives. Those are opportunities worth investing in.

There are a couple of other resources besides Christians that that you should access. First, your public library will have a number of resources that list community volunteer opportunities. Second, local colleges and universities often carry listings of organizations, both on and off campus, that are looking for help. If you live in a town or city with megachurches (churches with an attendance of more than two thousand), they are also likely sources of information on volunteer opportunities.

3. OTHER RESOURCES. There are a number of other resources you can consult to discover opportunities within your gift-ability.

- If your church is in a denomination, your denominational offices will have a wealth of opportunities to serve within the larger church, some locally and some even overseas.
- The United Way probably has the nation's largest listing of agencies that are looking for people willing to share their gifts, talents, skills, and passions (www.unitedway.org). I did a search for opportunities within my zip code and got 333 different possibilities, ranging from popping popcorn to building Web sites, from teaching English as a second language to providing employment counseling to the disabled.
- Most cities have listings of volunteer resources, as does the federal government. Currently, there are two U.S. government sites of note. The www.volunteer.gov/gov site was developed in partnership with over a dozen different federal agencies, including the National Parks Service and the USDA. The second site, www.usafreedomcorps.gov, is particularly noteworthy because it allows you to search by interest, including your interest in volunteering with a faith-based organization.

Now it's time to turn to some specifics. What is it you can take on to get your spiritual batteries recharged? Let me introduce you to three opportunities.

Take On: Another Spiritual Habit

You might be thinking, "Unfair!" but the fact is, taking on an additional spiritual habit can make a significant difference in your spiritual life. The more spiritual habits you take on, including the habit of serving others, the deeper your spirituality will grow. The deeper your spirituality grows, the more connected you will be with God. And the more connected you are with God, the bigger the difference you will make in the world. Though there are a number of other things you can take on, I simply want to remind you of the most important:

1. The Spiritual Habit of Projection and Reflection
2. The Spiritual Habit of Prayer
3. The Spiritual Habit of Study
4. The Spiritual Habit of Worship
5. The Spiritual Habit of Giving Up
6. The Spiritual Habit of Taking On
7. The Spiritual Habit of Accountability
8. The Spiritual Habit of Faith Sharing

Whenever you experience a Spiritual Power Shortage, taking on an additional spiritual habit is the most effective way to ensure the Divine Power Grid recharges your batteries.

Take On Serving Passionately

I had an opportunity to speak to Marcia Holland Risch while researching this book. Marcia has served as the CEO for several nonprofit organizations and is known for her effective lobbying efforts for their causes. She's also a faithful Practicing Christian who chose the path she's on because of her faith. She is an excellent model of someone who practiced the spiritual habit of taking on, but she did so because of her passion.

> I was five years old when the World War II war criminals were being tried and we began seeing the terrible images from the holocaust. I remember being horrified and deciding then—as a five-year-old girl—that I would say "No" to evil. That shaped who I was for the rest of my life. I still choose to say "No!" to evil. It's why I became a lobbyist.[3]

Marcia is a passionate woman and is known as a fierce lobbyist, an effective leader, and a committed Practicing Christian. Her spiritual habits don't just recharge her life, they energize it and give her both meaning and purpose.

As you saw earlier, you don't help anyone well by serving outside of your gift-ability and your passions. When you use your gift-ability in passionate leadership, as Marcia did, great things can happen. On the other hand, if God is calling you to a more humble role, the role of a servant like Mother Teresa, great things can happen in this role as well. Deciding where you're being led is a matter of prayer, but it's also a matter of understanding the difference between passionate leadership and humble service.

Take On Passionate Leadership

Want to make a significant difference in the lives of others? Interested in seeing your faith facilitating life changes in a practical way? Then practice the spiritual habit of taking on by using your gift-ability in leadership.

Remember Sarah the comptroller? Imagine the difference it would have made in her life if she had devoted the gift of her time and skills to some endeavor she was passionate about.

As a church leader, I know how badly we need to fill the ministry "positions" we have open–like the junior high Sunday school class. And the two unfilled deacons' positions. And the evangelism chair. And... and...and...But we do a terrible disservice to the Kingdom of God whenever we "use" people while disregarding their gifts, talents, skills, and passions. Further, there's a tendency to be provincial and keep the gifts within the local congregation. Yet, the Kingdom of God is bigger than a local church. It's even bigger than our own community. We owe it to those who seek to serve, as well as to God, to take the "living stones" (1 Pet. 2:5) we come across and "fit" them where they can be most effective. People are most effective when they serve within their gift-ability and their passions.

Where would *you* suggest Sarah use her gifts? Consider the following possibilities:

- Comptroller of a local Christian parachurch ministry
- Raising funds for a local mission project
- Helping local churches learn to manage their finances
- Arranging financial aid for new churches and/or ministries
- Serving on the board of the county hospital
- Teaching financial ethics to business professionals

You may have noticed that the last two suggestions have little to do with serving a Christian ministry. Why would I suggest that? Surely there's a Christian hospital or a group of Christian professionals who could use her help. Though that's true, a Practicing Christian can often make a more dramatic difference for the Kingdom by working in a non-Christian environment. Not only would Sarah bring a Christian perspective to these tasks, she would also be a billboard for her faith. Further, by working with either of these rather powerful groups, she has an opportunity to keep her ears to the ground for particular needs the church might be well-equipped to offer in the name of Jesus, needs that would otherwise have gone unnoticed and unmet by the church.

What gifts, talents, skills, and passions do you bring? You may have to think outside the box, but no matter what gifts you have, God can use them to make a difference in the Kingdom of God–and as a battery recharger in your life.

Take On Humble Service

Want to make a significant difference in the lives of others? Interested in seeing your faith facilitating life changes in a practical way? Then practice the spiritual habit of taking on a humble service.

Let's revisit Sarah the comptroller's story one more time. Even a brief conversation with her would reveal that not only does she love her job, but that she has a real heart for girls born without privilege. And though she enjoys number crunching, she might like to do something completely different...She might like to do something where she can just serve and not have to lead.

Where would you suggest she use her passion? Big Brothers and Sisters? Tutoring in a local school?

Who's to say where the Divine could use Sarah most effectively? Just because she's a talented and skilled comptroller doesn't mean God can't use her elsewhere to accomplish a great purpose—or perhaps to help Sarah learn something about herself. After all, Jesus washed his disciples' feet. You can't get more humble than that.

Finding a place to take on humble service can be very easy. There are literally hundreds of ministries and agencies that depend on those who give of their time and talents, and most of them will even accept any treasure you'd like to share. Further, your local church most likely has ways you can take on humble service. I remember years and years ago joyfully scrubbing a hardwood floor in a Sunday school classroom on my hands and knees. There was something so fulfilling in doing that menial task that my spiritual batteries stayed charged for weeks. You just never know.

However, it is still important to consider your gift-ability before you take on a particular task. There are some acts of service that aren't appropriate for all of us. For instance, I'm a kid at heart, so I was asked to do a stint at a summer church camp with high school students. It was a *disaster*. High school kids, it turns out, aren't interested in forty-year-old guys being one of the kids. On the other hand, several years later, I was asked to serve at another summer camp, this time with nine- to twelve-year-olds. Wow! What a difference. I had a great time, the kids seemed to soak in what I had to offer, and I returned as a counselor to that camp for several years. So a word of caution: If your heart isn't in it, then your heart is probably trying to tell you something.

Desperately Needed Take Ons

The previous section of the chapter emphasized a number of opportunities outside of the church, though certainly there are a number of opportunities to serve within the church. Nonetheless, the widest number of possibilities for practicing the spiritual habit of taking on, whether in passionate leadership or humble service, are found outside the local church. However, in this section, I want to invite you to consider three particular take ons that are desperately needed *within* the Christian faith.

Take Ons for the "One-Anothers"

"Love one another as I have loved you."
"Be devoted to one another."
"Be at peace with one another."

It is commonly thought and often taught that all those commands about the one-anothers must be applied to everyone. I'll be the last person to suggest that a non-Christian should be accorded anything less than lavish respect. Indeed, Jesus himself, our ultimate model, was a "friend of sinners" and taught that we should love everyone across the continuum, from the one-anothers to our enemies. However, the New Testament actually makes a distinction between the "one-anothers" and "everyone else."

The difference between the "one-anothers" and "everyone elses" is most clearly seen in Paul's letters to the Thessalonians: "Make sure that nobody pays back wrong for wrong, but always try to be kind to each other and to everyone else" (1 Thess. 5:15; see also 1 Thess. 3:12). In this verse, Paul teaches that Christians should not *just* be kind to one another (fellow Christians), but to everyone else as well, i.e., the non-Christians. Paul clearly differentiates between the two.

There are over forty references to "one-anothers" in the New Testament. Most people I speak to tell me that when they went to Sunday school, they were taught–as I was–that *everyone* was a one-another. However, if you peruse the list of commands for the one-anothers, it becomes clear that several don't make sense when applied outside of the faith community. (See Appendix D for a list of the New Testament one-anothers.)

> Greet one another with a holy kiss. All the churches of Christ send greetings. (Rom. 16:16)

This command only makes sense when practiced within the bounds of the church.

> Let the word of Christ dwell in you richly as you teach and admonish one another with all wisdom... (Col. 3:16a)

Paul would find it inappropriate to appoint unbelievers to instruct and admonish the Colossian church, or *any* church for that matter.

> Therefore confess your sins to one another, and pray for one another, so that you may be healed. The prayer of the righteous is powerful and effective. (Jas. 5:16, NRSV)

This time it is James who instructs his readers, but he'd hardly be telling them to confess their sins and expect healing from someone outside of the faith.

> I myself feel confident about you, my brothers and sisters, that
> you yourselves are full of goodness, filled with all knowledge, and
> able to instruct one another. (Rom. 15:14, NRSV)

And finally, in this verse Paul actually *names* the one-anothers—the brothers
and sisters of the faith are the one-anothers.

Again, this doesn't change the mandate that we are to love those outside
of the faith, nor is it permission to treat them with disrespect in any way.
Practicing Christians live with the commission to be Jesus for the world.

On the other hand, take a moment to reflect on how Christians treat
fellow-Christians in the church. Of course it doesn't happen in *every* church,
but there's enough anecdotal evidence to show that we don't live up to the
ideal of the one-anothers. Indeed, our community *doesn't* "know we are
Christians by our love." Unfortunately, many of North America's "unchurched" are actually the church's carnage; people who have been
wounded by the very people to whom they turned to (or ran from) in their
time of darkest need. I've long maintained that if the church treated one
another as the New Testament mandates, churches would have lines of
unchurched people trying to get through their doors.

Which is exactly the take on we need both in the church and in the
faith. Taking on the spiritual habit of practicing the "one-anothers" can
make a tremendous difference in your own life as the Spirit empowers
you, but it will also make an incredible difference in the world around us.
If enough Practicing Christians take up the habit, we could perhaps even
change North American Christianity's sullied reputation.

Although an extensive list of the one-anothers can be found in appendix
D, here are few to help get you started.

> Bear with each other and forgive whatever grievances you may
> have against one another. Forgive as the Lord forgave you. (Col.
> 3:13)

Forgiveness is always the first order of business for Practicing Christians. Do
a quick inventory of your life. Do you need to forgive someone? If so, start
the one-another process there—be the better person and go make it right.

> Encourage one another daily... (Heb. 3:13a)

Take on the habit of offering encouragement to another Christian *every*
day. Send a card, or an e-card, of encouragement. Make a phone call and
share an encouraging thought. Stop by their desk—or their house—and pray
with them. Whatever it takes, be an encourager today.

> And let us consider how we may spur one another on toward love
> and good deeds. (Heb. 10:24)

Take a moment to consider how you could spur another Christian on to
take on a good deed. Perhaps you could do some good deed together.

> Let us not give up meeting together, as some are in the habit of doing, but let us encourage one another—and all the more as you see the Day approaching. (Heb. 10:25)

I've heard this verse quoted as if it means "Go to church on Sunday." The early Christians didn't just meet on Sundays—they actually hung out together almost every day. Not *all* of them in one place—they hung out with their friends who just so happened to be Christians. What did they do when they hung out? Ate. Prayed. Laughed. Cried. Talked business, especially how they could be an influence with their Christian lives. And they prayed some more. They weren't "holier-than-thou," they just lived their faith. They were *Practicing* Christians.

There are lots more one-anothers, but imagine the impact you would have on somebody's life if you called them a couple of times a week to encourage them, if you spurred them on toward love and to do good deeds, and if you spent time with them. It could revolutionize their world—and yours.

Take On Mentoring

 Everyone needs a mentor, someone more mature and wiser than us, to help guide us on the path of life. On the other side of that coin is the truth that every Practicing Christian needs to *be* a mentor.

One of the true deficits in North American Christianity is the lack of intentional discipling relationships. Assuming Jesus provides us with an ideal model of what a mature Practicing Christian should look like, we have much to learn from him about mentoring.

At first glance, we might be tempted to assume Jesus mentored all of his apostles. Though it is true that he *trained* twelve, in actual fact, he only mentored three of them.

> When he arrived at the house of Jairus, he did not let anyone go in with him except Peter, John and James, and the child's father and mother. (Lk. 8:51)

> About eight days after Jesus said this, he took Peter, John and James with him and went up onto a mountain to pray. (Lk. 9:28)

Repeatedly, Jesus expended extra time and attention on these three in order to prepare them to continue the work he'd begun. Indeed, Jesus intended for these three to become the pillars of the emerging church. James would go on to become the initial pastor of the Jerusalem Church. Peter and John served as the initial spokespersons for the faith, but would become more involved in overseeing the affairs of the church after James was arrested and killed (Acts 12:1–2). The church largely exists today because Peter, John, and James had been carefully trained *and* mentored by Jesus.

In my conversation with Chris Black, he recalled the first time someone intentionally mentored him:

> When I was in my early twenties and working for a college, something I said in a casual conversation prompted the dean to tell me about centering prayer and the writings of Merton, Pennington, and Thomas Keating. He lent me some of his books and audiotapes to explore on my own. This was powerful to me because it was the first time someone who wasn't a parent or an adult in my church recognized a spiritual quest in me and shared his own journey. It validated me as an adult, as a young man. That was a huge moment.[4]

Not a long-term mentoring commitment, just a short encounter with a bit of follow-up. And it helped a young man along his spiritual journey.

There are many ways to mentor someone, but no matter how you do it, it will take an intentional investment of your time. But any investment you make can reap bushels of results in terms of the spiritual future of your community, your church, and your nation.

Although chapter 8 deals with a different styles of mentoring, especially in terms of accountability, let me offer a few thoughts to get you started. An effective mentoring arrangement is a mutual agreement between two people. To be a mentor in the faith you must first be active on your spiritual journey–you must be taking personal responsibility for your own spiritual progress. The fact you're reading this book is a pretty good sign you're serious about it, so you most likely "pass" the first requirement. A mentee–that is, the person to be mentored–must be serious about being mentored. Don't waste your time with someone who takes the relationship lightly–there are many Christians who really *want* to connect to the Divine Power Grid.

Mentoring is more than a teaching assignment. It's more than a training assignment. Mentoring means pouring yourself, your heart, your knowledge, and all that you are into another person. The best mentoring relationships tend to be both vocational (or avocational) and spiritual. Jesus mentored Peter, John, and James to become, in a sense, *him*. He poured himself into them, taught them what they needed to know–and probably even a bit more–so that they could continue the "business" when he left. Helping others make sense of their Christian lives, learning how to apply it to the everyday decisions they must make, is what a good mentoring relationship is all about. Whether it's one homemaker mentoring another in how to pray while cleaning the upholstery, one CEO mentoring another how to make decisions based on their faith, or one fire fighter mentoring another how to maintain a spiritually focused family life even when on seventy-two hour duty, I hope–and pray–you will consider being a mentor for the one-anothers.

Take On Investment

The last take on I want to introduce to you arises out of a need I see developing in the North American church, especially in the U.S.

Let me begin by sharing that I'm involved in a house church network rather than what would commonly be called a local church. A house church meets in homes or in other informal places. They tend to have a very limited "membership," typically between three to a dozen in attendance. The house church movement around the world is multiplying fast enough that many believe it is one of the key reasons Christianity is growing at a global rate of about 90,000 new converts each day.[5] However, the house church in North America is just getting a toehold. Those of us working with the movement are praying and studying and tweaking in order to help this movement begin multiplying rapidly here. Many of us believe the house church, and other forms of small fellowships (sometimes called "Marketplace Ministries"), offer tools for reaching the growing unchurched population.

As I've traveled across North America and spoken with pastors, both in the house church movement and outside of it, one of the clear messages I'm hearing is that the day of the seminary-trained, full-time pastor is waning. Recently I was at a convention–a very *small* convention–and spoke to no less than a dozen trained pastors who were in transition; transition as in total life-change. Each of these seminary-trained pastors had been serving established churches for some time and had come to the conclusion that a career as a local church pastor was no longer viable. These men and women were committed to remain in the ministry, but they knew that they were going to have to make a living outside of the church.

A change of careers is hardly a novel concept in North America. People do it all the time. However, one of the rude awakenings each of these pastors had experienced when they went out to find a job was this: virtually nobody wanted to hire someone *because* he or she has a Master's Degree in Divinity. Although these former pastors have incredible skills in recruiting, training, administration, human resources, volunteer retention, budgeting, as well as entrepreneurial skills, their degrees didn't help them get jobs, and their experience in the church was often held against them. This problem is going to get increasingly worse over the next fifteen to twenty years.

There is a solution, however. Some of you are business owners, managers, CEOs, human resources personnel, and so on. In other words, you have the opportunity to make decisions about who you and/or your company hires. The church needs men and women like you to occasionally take one of these former pastors under your wing and train them. They are not looking for charity or a handout, but there is a need to provide an alternative funding option for these folks so they can continue in ministry, but ministry as an avocation–as a lifestyle–rather than as a career.

Lest you think an entry-level job will do, consider that most of these men and women have a bachelor's degree and a master's degree, along with an average of over $25,000 in student debt.[6] Additionally, most are married and have children. Further, some have incurred an additional debt load as they made the transition from career pastor to whatever they are doing today. (This often means being unemployed and largely unemployable.) No one's surviving financially on just over minimum wage in those circumstances.

Here is how to practice this spiritual habit: Find some of these men or women who are actively seeking jobs, and talk with them. Interview them. Don't just look at M.Div. and six years church experience and dismiss them as religious fanatics. Sit down with them. Listen to them. If they're not the right fabric, then try again.

You can find these folks by picking up the phone and calling your denominational offices–or another denominational office if needed. (Last time I checked, we're all on the same team.) Or talk to your pastor, or to someone involved in a house church, or another alternative ministry. Believe me, you'll find them.

The spiritual habit of taking on is one of only a few spiritual practices that have a direct effect on those beyond your own walls. Some of the practices have the potential to change your community. All the practices will change you. As you practice any or all of them, you'll discover that warmth that comes when you do something nice for someone else. It will be the warmth that accompanies the power surge as your spiritual batteries are recharged.

SPARKS AND RESISTANCE

Questions for Discussion and Reflection

1. What are your spiritual gifts? your talents? your skills? your passion(s)?
2. How can someone in your church discover their gift-abilities if they are unsure of what they are?
3. How could you use your gift-ability in passionate leadership? in humble service?
4. Do you agree with the author that the active presence of a Christian makes a social agency a Christian ministry? why or why not?
5. Which of the one-anothers have you seen practiced well in the church? Which have you not practiced so well?
6. Who is your mentor? Who could you be a mentor to?

8

The Spiritual Habit of Accountability

There are a lot of reasons why busy people experience spiritual power shortages. Some don't have *any* working connection with the spiritual realm. For these, God is mostly a word to be invoked when someone cuts them off is traffic, or to call on when they've experienced some tragedy. They don't even know their lights are out and there's a spiritual power crisis, though they may wonder why they feel so empty. Some busy people have made a connection to the Divine Power Grid in the past, but they've not taken the time to maintain their circuits. Indeed, they may be so busy they're not aware their inner light is but an intermittent flicker now and again. For these, God is mostly an afterthought. And then there are those busy folks who've made a connection with God, and the Divine Power flows through them, but they're too busy for maintenance. It is for these that this chapter is primarily written.

You may remember the East Coast blackout in 2003–chapter 2 covered the details. Do you remember what caused the power outage? Untrimmed trees. Branches that literally caught the attention of an Ohio high-voltage transmission line created a tremendous short. The sudden drop in power shut down a Cleveland generating plant and launched a cascading failure that affected over forty million people. Though the U.S.–Canada Power System Outage Task Force uncovered several issues that allowed the cascading failure, the bottom line was the failure on the part of several utility companies to maintain their infrastructure.

Maintenance of our spiritual circuits is crucial. Like the utility company that didn't keep the trees trimmed, they weren't even aware they had a problem until it was too late. The company *did* trim the trees above the power lines; they just didn't do it often enough to ensure ongoing power delivery. It wasn't a priority. Other daily activities got in the way, and maintenance was one of those tasks that could be put off until tomorrow.

Silently, unobtrusively, even sneakily, a couple of branches grew a slight quarter-inch each day. They were innocuous and insidious until they got the attention they deserved. They became the first domino in the largest power outage in North America.

In our own busy lives, we often don't recognize our own need for spiritual maintenance. Unhealthy habits, unintended misdeeds, and bad choices need to be pruned, but we may not realize their potential for destruction. Our thoughts, beliefs, or practices may need refurbishing, but we may not even be aware our batteries are corroding or that a circuit is overheating until a fuse snaps and we begin a spiritual meltdown.

Those too busy to maintain their spiritual circuits risk a cascading failure in their own lives. Pastors are particularly susceptible, and accordingly about fifteen hundred pastors burn out every month.[1] Pastors aren't the only ones in peril. Laypeople are burning out at similar rates. In North America, the exodus from the church has hovered unabated at the rate of over a million people per year for the last several years. Indeed, according to Martin Marty, there is a spiritual ice-belt stretching from Western Europe through Canada, the United States, and including Japan. Here, Christianity as a religion is reportedly losing some three thousand people to other religions, or to no religion, every day.[2] Spiritual power outages and cascading failures are much more common than perhaps we'd care to admit–and you may well be at risk.

I suspect if a maintenance crew had been driving down the utility road in Ohio and saw the encroaching branches, they would have immediately recognized the threat and dealt with it. But the fact is, no one was looking. So often, that's the case in our own spiritual lives. We're so busy we don't take the time to look for potential problems. At other times, it can be difficult to recognize potential problems. Let's face it, how can you tell at a glance that an electronic circuit board is about to "pop"? The truth is, most of the time, you can't. Not at first glance. But the right tools in the hands of an experienced technician can reveal a failing part long before it malfunctions.

We need to probe our spirit, mind, and soul to find areas in need of maintenance. We need to regularly run diagnostics to discover where we have weak parts. However, when it comes to probing and diagnosing, the fact is, we can't do it ourselves–we're too close to the issues. We need a technician to help. I call those technicians "accountability partners."

Accountability Defined

Accountability has become a catchall word in both business and the church. Indeed, the whole accountability group idea has been so watered down that it often has little or no substance. Twelve-step meetings are commonly considered accountability groups. Home fellowship groups are said to be accountability groups by some. Unfortunately, many have tried the accountability route but came away with the *Been There...Done*

That…Only Got a T-Shirt experience—it didn't make a real difference in their lives. Most of the time those wearing the "I Did Accountability" logos didn't engage in a meaningful accountability relationship.

Buck Jacobs, the founder of C12 Groups, an accountability cluster of Christian business owners, realizes there's a difference between meaningful and superficial accountability:

> It's important to practice the discipline of accountability (this is part of the reason I created The C12 Group). I know, I know. It's almost trite to say that accountability is essential, but guess what: *accountability* is essential, both with friends and with God. And I'm not referring to some superficial accountability, but to intimate, *meaningful* accountability. Our thoughts, not just our actions, need to be brought into the light and evaluated by both wise, mature Christian friends and by God Himself.[3]

There's another reason the practice of accountability has lost its luster. Some have abused their role as an accountability partner and used their relationship to manipulate and overpower those who fall under their abusive spell.

Meaningful accountability, however, makes a *huge* difference in people's lives and it is the polar opposite of abuse—indeed, it is one of the most loving and empowering practices of all the spiritual habits.

In the workplace, being held accountable typically means knowing it is *your* head that rolls if you don't meet your objectives, whatever they may be. Accountability, in those terms, means being held responsible, but it also means that someone holds power over you. When it comes to spiritual accountability, however, the only one who holds power over you is God. Nobody else gets to do that—nobody else *can.* Ultimately, you are responsible for your own spiritual development. Your parents can't do it. The church can't do it. And your accountability partner can't do it. One day you'll stand before God and have to answer for what you've done with your life, for better or worse. It's God who will do the "judging" because God is the only one who holds any power over your spiritual life.

What does the spiritual practice of accountability look like? First, let's take a peek at the definition of the word *accountable.* According to *Dictionary.com,* *accountable* means you're "liable to being called to account; answerable." Let's look at these two accountability definitions: "called to account" and "answerable."

Being "answerable" describes the accountability level I share with my bike-riding partner. Skip is a friend of mine who is a bicycle enthusiast. At best, I'm a hobbyist at two-wheeled transportation, but I volunteered to ride the STP with him this summer. The STP is a two-day ride from Seattle to Portland, just over a two hundred mile ride. Now the last time I had been on a bicycle and rode over a mile was when I was fifteen—which was rather a long time ago. Skip was my accountability partner in our training. He regularly called me and asked when I was "up for a ride." We'd make an appointment and I'd put it on my calendar. I became "answerable" to Skip for riding as soon as I hung up the phone. He held me accountable for *one* thing in my life–bicycle riding. I was answerable to him for this, and this only. I call this level of accountability *Accountability Lite*.

"Called to account" describes a level of accountability well beyond just being answerable. As we saw, the *Dictionary.com* definition of account-ability means we're "liable to being called to account." "Liable" means to owe someone. "Being called to account" is literally to give or offer an accounting. It almost sounds like a synonym for the word *confession*. According to this definition of accountability, we "owe an accounting." I call this level *Spiritual Accountability,* not because *Accountability Lite* isn't spiritual, but to differentiate between the two.

When Skip calls to ask about going for a ride, that's pretty much the only thing I'm accountable to him for. In *Accountability Lite,* an accountability partner doesn't need to be either a spiritual mentor or even a close friend.

On the other hand, at the level of *Spiritual Accountability,* an accounta-bility partner is someone you've given permission to speak into your life, or, more accurately, someone you've given permission to *inquire* about your life. Whereas my *Accountability Lite* partner can pretty much be anyone, when my whole spiritual life is laid open, I need an accountability partner who is more involved in my life. That accountability partner is someone you can trust enough to tell the truth to. And you *will* tell the truth, because, otherwise, why bother being in an accountability relationship at all? Besides, your accountability partner becomes your spiritual circuit technician and diagnostician–and your circuit tech can't effectively probe for malfunc-tioning parts if you're evasive or deceptive.

The rest of this chapter explores the two different levels of account-ability. Please don't get the impression that *Accountability Lite* is inferior in any way to *Spiritual Accountability*. Both have their places, and both can and will have a positive impact on your life. And perhaps the practices will keep you from experiencing a spiritual power outage.

The Habit of Accountability Lite

Accountability Lite isn't a spiritual habit that's light on results. Indeed, this habit will have a profound impact on your spiritual life for a couple of reasons. When *Accountability Lite* partners hold you accountable for the practice of a spiritual habit that you're developing, the effectiveness of that habit nearly doubles. It takes some time to internalize a spiritual habit, but since you're going to be held accountable for practicing it, you'll pick it up quickly. The second reason *Accountability Lite* will have a profound effect on you is because there are great gains in spirituality whenever you practice with a partner.

You will need two things to practice the spiritual habit of *Accountability Lite*. First, for most of the practices below you'll want a committed companion. Because you will be sharing only one particular aspect of your spiritual life, this companion need not be one of your closest friends; neither does this person need to be a spiritual giant. In fact, the only requirement you'll need in choosing an *Accountability Lite* companion is that this person will commit with you to participate in one of the spiritual habits in order to help hold you accountable.[4]

The second thing you need to decide is which of the spiritual habits you and your partner want to practice. The reality is, virtually any of the spiritual habits can be adapted and adopted for *Accountability Lite*. However, let me introduce you to two specific habits.

Shared Prayer

I have a confession to make. Though my wife and I both strive to be faithful Practicing Christians, until recently we haven't spent much time in prayer together. Table grace? Sure. Prayer together in our house church? No problem. But morning or evening prayers spent wrestling or pleading with God? Praying for each other together? It didn't happen.

It's not like we didn't try. Several times we committed ourselves to praying with each other, but after a day or two we'd stop. There were several reasons for this, not the least of which is I don't sit still well and my wife is a contemplative who can sit for hours. It just seemed like we weren't compatible...until I learned how Chris Black and his wife pray together:

> We both travel and are frequently apart. When we *are* together, part of our prayer practice is to use a small bell. We learned about this on a retreat at a monastery. We ring the bell to call ourselves into prayer and to create a sacred time and space. Then one of us reads scripture aloud and we ring the bell again. Then we'll pray in silence together for twenty or thirty minutes. At the end of that, one of us rings the bell again to call ourselves out. This happens everyday when we're together. When we're not together, I call her on the phone and let it ring a couple of times and then hang up. That's the signal that calls us into prayer together. Then at the end of the time, I ring again and we'll talk for a few minutes just to be in connection with each other, and then we go about our days.[5]

My wife and I adapted this practice and we've been praying together ever since. It's literally revolutionized my own spiritual life as we begin each morning in prayer "together." The beauty of this habit is its adaptability for anyone who wants to have a prayer companion. As Chris and his wife demonstrated, you don't have to be together in order to effectively pray as a partnership. Instead, it simply takes a commitment to a time set aside for prayer and for a couple of phone calls. With the number of cell phones that now include free long distance coverage within their payment plans, the practice means you can maintain a faithful prayer practice with someone anywhere in the nation–just make sure you make allowance for the changing time zones!

The 10:2b Virus

You may wonder why I'm suggesting you get a virus, but my fondest hope is that this is a prayer practice that catches on across our nation–it already has a foothold in certain circles. The 10:2b Virus comes from the Gospel of Luke, chapter 10, verse 2.

> He told them, "The harvest is plentiful, but the workers are few. Ask the Lord of the harvest, therefore, to send out workers into his harvest field." (Lk. 10:2)

The part "B" is the key to the virus: "Ask the Lord of the harvest, therefore, to send out workers into his harvest field." This is one of the few things Jesus instructed his disciples to specifically pray for: Pray for workers.

In North America, the harvest fields are particularly wide open. As I mentioned previously, the church has been losing over a million members a year for several years. The fastest growing "church" in North America is the church of the unchurched. Many of these people have left the church because they have restless souls who desire to be effective Practicing Christians, but have discovered the local church didn't offer the "discipling" they sought. They were *taught* rather than trained; they were invited to meetings rather than to do ministry; they were given programs rather than power; and they experienced authority rather than accountability. So they went looking elsewhere–and in many cases there was no *elsewhere* to be found. All that's to say that they are ripe and ready for working harvesters who are willing to train them to practice the spiritual habits, teach them to pray, and walk alongside them as spiritual companions on their journey.

But we need workers who are willing to intentionally enter the harvest field. We need them badly–Jesus said *he* needs them badly. There is a shortage of faithful Practicing Christians in North America. There are relatively few who are practicing the spiritual habits, praying and listening to God, and who are making literally all of their decisions with an abiding awareness of the Divine Presence and a commitment to "*Thy will be done*" in every aspect of their lives. These are the people for whom we need to be praying, that God will raise them up and send them into the harvest fields.

There are pockets of faithful prayer partners across North America who are engaged in praying Luke 10:2b. Those who have committed to practice it report they've seen tangible results as people feel called to enter into Marketplace Ministry (leading Bible studies at work, doing hands-on ministry in the name of Jesus, and so on) and into other ministries that result in people getting connected with Jesus and being plugged into the Divine Power Grid. Those who have been praying and seeing these results have told others about it and it's been catching on as others begin to pray and in turn see their prayers answered, hence the 10:2b *Virus*.

Even the busiest of people can engage in this important spiritual practice. You only need a partner who's willing to pray *with* you as close to every day as possible. Then, covenant to touch base once a day by phone or in person to pray together and ask the Lord to send workers into the harvest, just as Jesus asked. This practice needn't take long, perhaps as briefly as two or three minutes. However, consistency is the key. Remember the parable of the widow who nagged the judge in Luke 18:1–8? In the story, the judge grants the widow justice because of her incessant nagging. Through the story, Jesus reminded his disciples that God hears those who pray and that we should pray and not give up. And don't forget, the Luke 10:2b prayer is a prayer God *wants* to answer. Imagine what the results could be when we pray continually for what God already wants!

Those of us practicing this habit have discovered there are some "secrets" to the prayer.

1. PRAY CONSISTENTLY. Pray as close to every day as possible. If you or your prayer companion is out of town, pray onto their answering machine–remember, your partner will hear it when he or she returns, and God heard it when you prayed it the first time. There is something particularly powerful when we commit to pray and then pray incessantly.

2. PRAY SPECIFICALLY. Pray as specifically as possible. My wife and I have a map of the Seattle area, complete with all ninety-seven neighborhoods identified. So we pray for the different neighborhoods and ask God to raise up harvesters in each. When we discover an answer to the prayer, we mark the neighborhood in thanksgiving. You may choose to pray for a nation, region, state, county, city, neighborhood, or even for those on a specific street. You might also want to pray that God will move particular people to work in the harvest fields, particularly if you know Christians who aren't engaged in the harvest, but may have identifiable gifts.

3. PRAY EXPECTANTLY. We pray expecting God to answer our prayers. James told his readers to pray believing without doubt, "for the doubter, being double–minded and unstable in every way, must not expect to receive anything from the Lord" (Jas. 1:8, NRSV). As God does answer your prayers, you may find that people begin to call you for some direction in the harvest field. Be ready to point these folks in a helpful direction or be ready to mentor them yourself.

4. PRAY OPENLY. When you pray this prayer, you should expect God to answer the prayer, but you should also be aware of the verse immediately following Luke 10:2b. Jesus looked at his disciples and informed them, "Go! I am sending you…" Know that as you pray, the Spirit may well begin to stir in *your* heart. Be open to what the Spirit says and where the Divine is leading. There really is a huge, ripe harvest waiting for workers.

Informal Accountability

 There is another practice of accountability that is in some ways even lighter than the *Accountability Lite* opportunities I just shared, but it has so much potential that I couldn't leave it out. *Informal Accountability* is different that *Accountability Lite* because it is really a combination of mentoring, *Spiritual Accountability*, and *Accountability Lite*.

Very few Christians experience any form of accountability at all. They may have been good, church-going Christians for many years, but no one ever asked them how their faith journey was going. There is a myth that the practice of our Christianity is a personal and private matter, that it's really nobody else's business. But the "one-anothers"[6] clearly indicate that our faith is meant to be encouraged and nurtured by one another. But, mostly, it just doesn't happen. As one businessman put it:

> In the almost thirty years of my professional career, my church has never once suggested that there be any type of accounting of my on-the-job ministry to others. My church has never once offered to improve those skills which could make me a better minister, nor has it ever asked if I needed any kind of support in what I was doing. There has never been an inquiry into the types of ethical decisions I must face, or whether I seek to communicate the faith to my coworkers. I have never been in a congregation where there was any type of public affirmation of a ministry in my career. In short, I must conclude that my church really doesn't have the least interest in whether or how I minister in my daily work.[7]

As a Practicing Christian, you have a unique opportunity to encourage faith practices in Christians like the businessman in the example above. The practice of *Informal Accountability* can make a forever-difference in the lives of those who are seeking to be faithful, but who may be struggling to make a significant connection with the Divine.

The practice of *Informal Accountability* takes practically no time, even though it has the potential to make a tremendous difference. However, it will take a concerted effort on your part to be consistent. You will need to practice the habit repeatedly until it becomes a natural part of your repertoire.

There are only two steps to the process: Ask a gentle, probing question, and then listen.

The practice begins by making a connection, typically in person, with another Christian. Because this process takes very little time, you actually *can* ask a gentle, probing question almost anywhere and at almost any time. However, be sensitive and don't ask in the company of others. This is a one-on-one question.

Let's say you're standing at the water cooler, or you've bumped into a Christian friend in the drugstore, and you decide this may be a Divine appointment. To practice *Informal Accountability*, you simply ask one of the following gentle, probing questions and then listen.

Gentle Probing Questions

- How's your walk with Jesus these days?
- How are you and God doing?
- What have you been reading in the Bible lately?
- How's your prayer life?
- What are you hearing from God?
- How has God been faithful in your life lately?
- For what in your life are you counting on God?

Ask one of these questions and then take a few minutes to listen. You may be surprised at the answers you'll get. Many, if not most, Christians really *want* to be faithful, but either don't know how or simply don't think about their faith outside of their local church's worship hour. As you listen, you'll regularly hear stories of pain or frustration. And you'll hear lots of excuses for why they're *not* practicing these disciplines. Don't give into the temptation to offer advice or suggestions. Your job is to *listen,* not to pass judgment, rebuke, advise, or even comment. Just listen. They haven't given you permission to *speak* into their lives just because they responded to your question. They've simply offered you a modicum of trust by sharing their hearts.[8] It has *never* happened to me, but there are conceivably times when you might ask a gentle, probing question and get a rather terse, "That's none of your business," as a response. In those cases, simply apologize for overstepping their boundaries and file their "Do Not Ask Until Invited" memorandum into your brain's filing cabinet. Make a note that you've overstepped a boundary *they* have set up; don't lose sight of the fact that the biblical one-anothers encourage inquiries such as these. So don't let one person's discomfort discourage you. The vast majority of Christians welcome the opportunity to grow in their faith.

I make it a habit to ask gentle, probing questions regularly. However, *regularly* doesn't mean everyday. I tend to ask my Christian buddies one of the questions about once a month or so, typically tucked into a spiritual conversation we're having. Ask different questions at different times. For instance, I asked my neighbor recently what he'd been reading in the Bible lately. But a month or so ago, I asked what he was praying for. By asking a variety of these gentle, probing questions, my Christian friends are encouraged to practice a variety of the spiritual habits. Though they may not jump into them right away, the act of gently asking one of these questions reminds them of the essential Christian practices.

The Habit of Spiritual Accountability

There is a distinct difference between *Accountability Lite* and the habit of *Spiritual Accountability*. In *Accountability Lite*, as you've seen, the level of accountability is limited to a single specific practice. Even the habit of *Informal Accountability* is unlikely to elicit deep confessions. However, the practice of *Spiritual Accountability* probes deep into the soul—it covers the full spectrum of our behaviors so we can effectively practice our faith. The practice of *Spiritual Accountability* has the potential to change our lives, starting with our innermost core, and thus facilitates significant change in our thoughts, words, deeds, and attitudes. When practiced, *Spiritual Accountability* infuses our whole life with the Spirit's influence. Our accountability companion and the whisperings of God become the technicians and diagnosticians who help ensure we don't suffer from a cascading failure.

When you enter into a *Spiritual Accountability* partnership, you're giving your companion permission to ask the tough questions—*any* of the tough questions. We won't experience a spiritual maturing if we won't allow our partner to ask which Web sites we've visited this week, what we did yesterday to show we were available to our children, or what we've read in the Bible this week. On the other hand, when entering into a *Spiritual Accountability* partnership, you *haven't* given anyone permission to correct, rebuke, nag, judge, or offer either verbal or nonverbal comments to whatever you might share. Ultimately, *you* are responsible for your own spiritual growth, and God is the only one with the power (or permission) to hold you responsible. When you start an accountability partnership, make sure this is understood and agreed on.

There are a number of accountability plans out there, but what follows is the one that I've used for several years and have come to appreciate because I've seen the lives that have changed when it has been used.

Journey Group Partnership

A Journey Group Partnership will cut into your time about a half-hour a day, with the addition of a weekly face-to-face that will last up to an hour.[9] You can certainly do the weekly meeting over lunch or breakfast, and you can actually break up the half-hour daily commitment into two halves. No matter how you choose to practice it, the fact is, if you will make this practice a priority, it will change your life. I promise.

Before we explore the details of Journey Group Partnerships, let's step back and view the big picture.

The "C" Word

The power of a Journey Group Partnership is in the way it connects us into the Divine Power Grid. There is a reality about the power that God generates that I've waited to introduce until now. The power of God is a power so potent and pure that it vaporizes anything and everything associated with the "s" word.

With the renunciation of the Roman Catholic Church by the church reformers of the Protestant Reformation, the Protestants have pretty well concluded that sin is a personal and private matter that's between just "me and God." Never mind that our sin has a wide circle of influence, from those we sin against, to those who watch us sin and therefore think less of our Christianity. Never mind what sin does to our own sense of worth and integrity.

And forgiveness? That's even more a personal and private matter. In fact, don't *even* mention the "C" word: *confession.* It carries a lot of baggage in the Protestant church. Because of abuses by the Roman Catholic Church in the Dark Ages, the confession of sin of one to another has been banished from common practice among Protestants—never mind that it is an important biblical commandment (Jas. 5:16).

However, confessing sins to one another was a common practice in the early church, long before Popes and even long before church buildings.[10] For instance, when John the Baptist and the apostles performed baptisms, they insisted upon confession and repentance (Mt. 3:5–8; Acts 2:38). Later, in Acts 19, we see Christians making *public* confessions of their sins (19:17–20). But public and one-on-one confession didn't stop at the end of the first century. It was a common practice in the church for the next several centuries as well. We can read the letters of Cyprian of the church in Carthage, who wrote to the churches in about 250 C.E. and repeatedly admonished the faithful to confess their sins to one another.[11]

If confession is biblically commanded and was practiced in the early church, why did Martin Luther in 1517 launch such a vehement attack against the practice?

He had three reasons. First, the Roman Catholic Church was profiting from confessions by collecting funds to *ensure* the forgiveness of sins. This practice stirred Luther's ire more than perhaps any other. Second, the Roman Catholic rite of confession implied that the priesthood carried the authority to forgive sins. Only the Divine can forgive sin. And, finally, the sacrament of confession in the Roman Catholic Church included the rite of penance. Penance is a form of punishment imposed on those who have made their confession. However, Jesus already endured the punishment for sin. Adding additional punishment was tantamount to saying Jesus hadn't done enough. And so, for all these reasons, Luther and the other church reformers banished the practice of confession from the church.[12]

So why am I suggesting you practice this spiritual habit? Because the biblical practice of confession isn't about a confessor granting forgiveness. It isn't about doing penance. And it certainly isn't about lining the coffers of the church. Instead, biblical confession is about accountability–both positive and, well, positive.

The Good Confession

When Jesus asked the disciples who they believed he was, Peter got the credit for making the "Great Confession" (Mt. 16:16). The church adopted this confession and it became known as the Good Confession. The Good Confession became the verbal profession of the Christian faith; however, it also became an invitation for persecution. Indeed, it became the death confession for thousands of Christian martyrs in the early church– and it still is in some nations.

Nonetheless, we are called to make the Good Confession in every aspect of our life. We're called to obey the commandments of Jesus–including the ones about being fruitful and making disciples. We're called to be ambassadors for Jesus and the Kingdom of God. We're called to be witnesses–that is, those who *testify* about Jesus Christ–at home, in our community, and globally. Indeed, Jesus made a rather stark statement about this very issue:

> Everyone therefore who acknowledges me before others, I also will acknowledge before my Father in heaven; but whoever denies me before others, I also will deny before my Father in heaven. (Mt. 10:32–33, NRSV)

We disown Jesus whenever (1) we have an opportunity to share our faith and choose not to; or (2) we disgrace Jesus or the body of Christ (the church). On the other hand, we acknowledge Jesus whenever (1) we take the opportunity to share our faith; or (2) we bring honor to Jesus or the body of Christ.

The spiritual habit of confession includes making the Good Confession as a regular habit. We'll talk about this more in a few moments.

Confession of Sin

When James, the brother of Jesus, wrote his letter to Jewish Christians throughout the Roman Empire, he didn't mince words about the behaviors of a follower of Jesus. Besides reminding his readers that "faith without works is dead," he insisted on the confession of sins to one another.

Therefore confess your sins to one another, and pray for one another, so that you may be healed. The prayer of the righteous is powerful and effective. Elijah was a human being like us, and he prayed fervently that it might not rain, and for three years and six months it did not rain on the earth. Then he prayed again, and the heaven gave rain and the earth yielded its harvest.

My brothers and sisters, if anyone among you wanders from the truth and is brought back by another, you should know that whoever brings back a sinner from wandering will save the sinner's soul from death and will cover a multitude of sins. (Jas 5:16–20, NRSV)

Notice the two reasons why James says confession is important. First, confession of sin may lead to healing–in this case, James is talking about physical healing. Second, confession of sin is meant to help those wandering from the truth to turn from the errors of their way. There's nothing here about the pronouncement of forgiveness. Instead, confession is meant to bring about a change in heart. In other words, confession means holding one another accountable to the faith, which is exactly why we need to be in an accountability partnership!

Practicing the Journey Group Partnership

There are three components to an effective Journey Group Partnership: Bible reading, prayer, and face-to-face accountability. Each component is interrelated with the other two–they come as a package deal. If you eliminate any one of them, you will miss the life-changing experience that comes with this practice. A removable Journey Group Bookmark is included in the back of this book; the scriptures and questions are also listed in appendix E. You will want to remove the bookmark now so you can refer to it as you read the next section. We'll look first at the three components and then take a look at who makes a good Journey Group partner.

1. DAILY BIBLE READING. There are plenty of reasons to spend time in the Word, many of which were covered in chapter 4. In your Journey Group Partnership, you will read a portion of scripture for a set period of time each day. Begin by committing to read your Bible just ten minutes each day. Although, as a busy person, you may find it tough at first to follow through with this commitment, stick with it. As the relationship with your accountability partner grows, your ability to finish your study time will become more consistent.

After you (and your partner) have become comfortable with a ten-minute study time, increase your daily reading time by five minutes. Give yourselves a couple of weeks practice and, when you've become comfortable with this commitment, add *another* five minutes. Do this until you reach a reading time of at least thirty minutes each day. If you find that you've finished reading the selected scriptures before the end of the week, begin rereading them over again. You will discover the scriptures become especially meaningful as you become intimate with a particular book in the Bible. Additionally, to enhance your study time, review chapter 4 on the spiritual habit of study and consider taking up journaling at least a couple of times each week.

Notice that the suggested scripture readings include an opportunity for you and your partner to choose whichever Bible book you want to read once every four weeks. You may decide to read a book from the *Additional Reading* list, or you may choose to read or reread any other book of the Bible. This allows you to complete a book you couldn't finish, to read a book not covered in the normal cycle, or to reread a particularly meaningful book, such as one of the gospels or Acts.

There is a second option for your Bible reading selections. Again, start by deciding how long each day you are going spend reading. Then, mutually select one of the books of the Bible to read, rather than using the suggested readings. If you finish the book before the end of the week, reread the book during the remaining time. If either of you didn't complete the full reading time, then both of you would reread the same book again. This provides an excellent way to hold each other accountable for your reading time, as well as helping you to become more familiar with a particular book the Bible—which is not a bad thing!

2. PRAYER. Although you were introduced to a number of different prayer models in chapter 2, prayer in a Journey Group Partnership is devoted to a single purpose—to pray for those who have wandered away from the Divine. You are provided with three tools for this task. (See the included Journey Group Bookmark.)

First, use the *My Most Wanted List.* Fill in the blanks with the names of your friends, relatives, acquaintances, neighbors, and coworkers who are not Practicing Christians.

Second, use the following three prayer sentences to pray for each person on your list by name.

- Lord, prepare the heart of _____ to hear the gospel (Mt. 13:23).
- Lord, raise up a worker to bring the gospel to _____ (Lk. 10:2b).
- Lord, send me to be a witness to _____ (Isa. 6:8).

3. FACE-TO-FACE ACCOUNTABILITY. This is the key to the Journey Group Partnership, as well as for the practice of *Spiritual Accountability.* Make an appointment to meet with your accountability partner every week. You can meet virtually anywhere, such as a coffee shop, restaurant, pub, a home, or even in your car. The key is to meet *face-to-face* each week.

Plan on spending at least thirty minutes together in order to complete the accountability questions. When you get together, there should be no agenda except to ask and answer each of the accountability questions and to decide how much daily time to spend reading during the upcoming week. To practice the accountability partnership, ask the first question and wait for your partner's response. When he or she finishes, it is your turn to respond to the question. When you're finished, ask question two and repeat the process. There is no need to elaborate on any of the answers except where it's indicated, though you can if you'd like to. Neither of you should offer any comments or advice unless it is sought. Finally, rotate your roles as reader each week so that you take turns answering the accountability questions first.

1. Have you been a verbal witness to someone this week about the good news of Jesus Christ?
2. Have you exposed yourself, either accidentally or intentionally, to sexually alluring material, or have you entertained inappropriate sexual thoughts this week?
3. Have you lacked any financial integrity this week?
4. Have you been honoring, understanding, and generous in your important relationships this week?
5. Have you lied or shaded the truth to look better to others this week?
6. Have you given in to an addictive behavior this week? If so, explain.
7. Are you harboring anger, resentment, or bitterness toward someone?
8. Have you secretly wished for someone's misfortune?
9. Your personalized accountability question goes here.
10. Were you faithful in your reading and praying, and did you hear from God? What will you do about it?
11. During this conversation, have you lied, left out parts of the truth, or left a mis-impression with me that needs to be cleared up?

Notice that question number nine is a personal accountability question. This question should concern an issue that the Spirit has convicted you of. For instance, my personal question is, "Have you put off an important task that needs to be accomplished?" because I have a tendency to procrastinate on tasks I find distasteful. In any event, your partner will ask you the question you develop for yourself each week in order to help you overcome whatever issue haunts you.

I've found that this accountability appointment is one of the highlights of my week. You will discover that the longer you are in this relationship, the deeper and more faithful your relationship with Jesus will become. You will find yourself better able to share your faith story with others, temptations that once plagued you will begin to lose their power over you, and you will find release from old addictions.

Study, prayer, and the face-to-face accountability appointments are the three interrelated components of the Journey Group Partnership. However, you can't practice them on your own—it takes a partner. As you may suspect by the nature of the questions, not just any partner will do. I suggest you begin your search with prayer. Ask the Spirit to begin stirring the heart of an acceptable partner. You may be rather surprised, however, at just how easy it is to find a partner. There are many "out there" who are desperately looking for a committed spiritual companion, and you are likely one of the few Practicing Christians in your neighborhood or workplace who has something as tangibly productive as the Journey Group Partnership to offer.

There are three characteristics/requirements when choosing a Journey Group Partner.

1. SAME GENDER. First, your accountability partner *must* be of the same gender. This is almost always the point I get the most push-back on, but there are very good and valid reasons why this is necessary. For one, if you want to stay married, don't do this with your spouse. Although I've had conversations with many husbands and wives who tell me they "have no secrets," the truth is, though they may not have any secrets today, if ever there comes an occasion to *have* a secret, and if their spouse is their accountability partner, they won't share it—even to the detriment and eventual dissolution of their marriage. Besides, who of us is going to be comfortable telling our spouse that we're struggling with temptation by the opposite gender? Even in very good and open relationships, it is difficult to maintain the needed level of absolute honesty, transparency, and vulnerability with a spouse over a long period of time. It's much easier—and more effective— to have someone who is more neutral to share your deepest yearnings with.

The second reason for the same-gender requirement is, if you want to stay married, don't do this with a member of the opposite gender who *isn't* your spouse. The level of intimacy you're going to build with your accountability partner has the potential to encourage transference. The process of sharing so intimately with your Journey Group companion can introduce serious temptations and relationship issues. This is also true for those who are *not* married. No one needs that kind of temptation, especially when seeking a deeper spiritual relationship with the Divine. So when you look for a Journey Group partner, look for one of your buddies.

2. TRUSTWORTHY. Having a partner you can trust with the intimate details of your life is the second characteristic you need in an accountability partner. Partnering with a known gossip is probably not the best choice. On the other hand, remember that *both* of you will know the intimate details of each other's lives, so perhaps both of you will be cautious. Regardless, you're spiritual growth will be better served if you feel a modicum of trust with your companion.

3. WILLING PARTICIPATION. The success of a Journey Group Partnership requires full participation from both partners. Both of you must commit to daily Bible reading, prayer, and to the weekly face-to-face accountability meeting. I've found that if a Journey Group Partnership crumbles, it is almost always because one or both of the partners were unwilling to invest fully in the three components.

One final note about choosing a Journey Group Partner. Though it might seem counterintuitive, your Journey Group Partner does *not* necessarily need to be a Christian. Because Journey Group Partnerships produce a transformed life, they are helpful to anyone experiencing a life crisis, and thus they are an excellent evangelism tool. The point is, people who are experiencing life's storms or who have hit rock bottom often have the right heart condition for sprouting the Word in their hearts. These people may be well-motivated for change and are probably open to the Spirit's touch in their lives.

Other Spiritual Accountability Groups

The Journey Group Partnership is not the only all-encompassing *Spiritual Accountability* process. In Neil Cole's book *Cultivating a Life for God,* he offers an excellent process involving "Life Transformation Groups" (LTGs).[13] LTGs use similar components to the Journey Group Partnership, though they have different accountability questions, a different Bible reading program, and different prayer questions.

However, *Spiritual Accountability* did not begin with Bill Tenny-Brittian, nor with Neil Cole. And it didn't begin with John Wesley either, but the process he used is probably the foundation for most contemporary accountability groups. Wesley would gather together about a dozen men or women (never coed) for a "class," and a leader would ask the following questions:

1. What known sins have you committed since our last meeting?
2. What temptations have you met with?
3. How were you delivered?
4. What have you thought, said, or done, of which you doubt whether it be sin or not?
5. Have you nothing you desire to keep secret?[14]

These questions have been expanded and used in many different accountability processes. If you peruse the Internet, you can find literally hundreds of other Christian accountability programs, and at least an equal number of accountability questions. I close this chapter with three Web sites of organizations that advocate and practice accountability.

- The C12 Group, www.thec12group.com: Buck Jacobs founded the C12 Group for Christian business owners. Membership is limited to business owners, though there are other restrictions as well. However, these groups are widely known for their effectiveness.

- Connecting Business Men to Christ, www.cbmc.com: Another Christian business organization, but with relaxed membership requirements—so long as your gender is male.
- Christian Business Women Association, www.cbwa-az.org: There appear to be limited resources for Christian Business Women, especially in terms of accountability. If you are interested in finding out about a local chapter of the CBWA, or in starting one yourself, touch base with the Arizona chapter to learn more.

SPARKS AND RESISTANCE

Questions for Discussion and Reflection

1. What have you done in the past to run "diagnostic tests" on your spiritual life? Were they effective? Why or why not?
2. What was your initial gut-reaction to the words *accountability* and *confession*? Have those feeling changed since finishing the chapter?
3. Who do you know who is "ripe" for the harvest? How can you tell? What can you do about it?
4. Has anyone ever asked you a "gentle, probing" accountability question? What was your response? Who will you be asking tomorrow?
5. Which of the Journey Group Partnership accountability questions will be the most difficult to face? Why?
6. Who are you planning on asking to be your accountability partner?

9

The Spiritual Habit of Faith Sharing

This chapter isn't last because it's the least important, but because my fondest dream is that this chapter will have the biggest impact on you. I believe that since Jesus' last words on Earth were about being witnesses and making disciples of all nations, he meant it. And not only did he "mean it," but this was the apex of what was important. I believe the most important mission we have on Earth is to share the gospel—beginning in our homes, our neighborhoods, our communities, our workplaces, and into the entire world.

Why do I believe sharing the gospel with others is so important?

Let's go back to our power grid metaphor, and specifically to the 2003 East Coast blackout for a final insight.

How is it that a couple of untrimmed branches in Ohio could shut down electricity to 9,300 square miles of power lines? Believe it or not, the answer is found in the redundant systems of the power grid.

Electricity doesn't only flow from generating plant to power lines and into the consumers' homes, businesses, and industries. Transmission lines carry electricity from generators to consumers, but they also carry it from power line to power line, forming what almost looks like a fishing net. (See illustration.) Of course, the *real* power grid is more complex than our illustration. The Northeast power grid has a variety of generating plants, transmission substations, power control stations, transformers, and the like. When

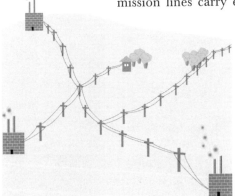

one power station or one section of the grid goes out, the redundant systems–
that is, the electricity flowing through the other parts of the grid–can be
rerouted so customers aren't left in the dark.

In 2003, when the Ohio power generating plant went off-line after
some branches shorted out a high voltage transmission line, other generating
plants took up the slack. But it was a hot summer's day in August, millions
of air conditioners were running, dinners were cooking, and the drain on
the grid was just too much. The utilities didn't have enough infrastructure
to handle the need. The redundant systems that were in place worked just
fine–they kicked in and rerouted power, trying to take up the slack. But
one after another began to fail; increasing demand on diminishing resources
created higher tension and stress; and in just a few hours millions of people
were without power.

Jesus left the gospel in the care of just eleven apostles. He knew if the
faith was going to survive, let alone accomplish its mission, they would
need "to build" additional infrastructure. "Therefore go and make disciples
of all nations," he told them (Mt. 28:19). "Ask the Lord…to send out workers
into his harvest field" (Lk. 10:2). And, "You will be my witnesses in
Jerusalem, and in all Judea and Samaria, and to the ends of the earth" (Acts
1:8). Peter would remind his readers that *they* were the infrastructure of the
church–they were the living stones being built into a spiritual house (1 Pet.
2:5). Even Paul would hearken to the need for building an infrastructure of
disciples (Eph. 2:21–22).

Today there are nearly seven billion people on Earth, and though
Christianity is doing well globally, here in North America our infrastructure
isn't keeping up with demand. In fact, there are more than a million fewer
folks in churches this year than there were last year–and the trend is showing
no signs of slowing. Further, though 82 percent of Americans claim to be
Christian,[1] the percentage of faithful Practicing Christians is *far* below that
number. The losses from the church alone put a strain on the existing
infrastructure of the faith. Fewer Practicing Christians are shouldering an
increasing responsibility for the mission and ministry of Jesus.

Jesus left the job of establishing an expanding infrastructure to his
apostles. The apostles left it in the hands of people like Timothy, Dorcas,
and Priscilla. They, in turn, left it in the hands of their families, neighbors,
and others with whom they shared the gospel. *They* left it in the hands of
those they shared it with, who left it in the hands of…all the way through
history until now. Today, expanding the infrastructure of the North
American faithful is in the hands of you and I, the Practicing Christians.

Faith Sharing Myths

Busy Christians, even busy Practicing Christians, regularly dismiss the
thought of faith sharing, claiming they don't have time and they're not
allowed to share their faith at work. Besides, isn't religion a personal issue?
In North America, we've come to believe that faith sharing is taboo at best,

and a rude intrusion at worst. These notions are based on misconceptions, misinformation, and socialization.

The Myth of Faith as Opinion

No matter where you may live, the prevailing culture has helped mold your worldview, sometimes blatantly, sometimes insidiously. North Americans, including North American Christians, have been socialized into a worldview that includes modernity and the Enlightenment. It all started, at least for the church, when René Descartes set the cornerstone of modern philosophy into place: *Cogito, ergo sum,* "I think, therefore I am." Reason rose to reality. Descartes' bumper-sticker philosophy promoted observation as the sole basis for science and the measure of fact. If something couldn't be measured in some way, then it was suspect. Faith, and even the existence of God, was called into serious question.

Religion needed a hero. Immanuel Kant rose to the challenge and responded by asserting that faith was not subject to empirical study. He was *trying* to say that matters of faith were beyond science's scrutiny, investigation, and even superseded reason.[2] He was hoping to communicate that truth is not equivalent to facts; that truth cannot be discovered and tested in a laboratory. But what he *communicated* was entirely different. Kant succeeded in removing religion and faith from analysis, at least by the hard sciences. However, in the process he effectively created a dual system of "truth": facts and opinions. Facts were those things you can "prove" through observation and analysis; opinions were like belly buttons: Everyone had one. It took a while to get there, but about fifty years ago or so we pushed and finally reached the logical conclusion of Descartes' and Kant's philosophies. Today, most people believe that religion is like a belly button, not only does everyone have one, but every belly button is pretty much as good as any other belly button. We don't just see religion as an opinion; we see religion as a personal, private matter. We wouldn't *dream* of sitting down with a chocolate ice cream lover to try and convince with them that Chunky Monkey is a superior ice cream, even if it is. In the same way, even faithful Practicing Christians believe they have no business sharing their faith with a Muslim, Buddhist, agnostic, or even a nonpracticing Christian because, after all, those other beliefs are A–OK. It's all just opinion.

Let's take a moment to think about this in another way. Suppose you met someone who had lived his or her whole life eating only rice. How would you share with them that there's a healthier way to eat? If you preached that their eating habits were evil and they needed to change their ways, you probably wouldn't get very far. If you pointed out all the deficits of their eating habits, they would probably get defensive. However, if you befriended them and they saw you eating now and again, if they could see the results of good nutrition by the way you lived your life, and if you shared about your healthy diet and the results you'd experienced without being negative about their diet, they might be interested in trying some of your foods, should you offer them. If they gave it a try and their health improved, they might just change their mind and embrace appropriate nutrition.

Now it is *not* an opinion that good nutrition is a key to health. Indeed, we send Peace Corp volunteers and support the United Nations so that healthy nutrition practices can be taught around the world. Similarly, it is also *not* an opinion that Christianity is the key to a vibrant spirituality. Indeed, anything else is like an all rice diet. In the end, it will kill you.

The Myth of Faithless Workplaces

I hear it all the time: "I can't take my faith to work," and I know what they mean. For one, it often means it's against company policy to proselytize on company time. You and I are paid to do a job and, of course, our employers expect us to do what we're being paid for.

Other times, when folks tell me they can't take their faith to work, they mean they don't want to be seen as a bigoted blowhard by their coworkers. And I'm right there with them. Christianity has plenty of distracters within its ranks—believers who have sullied the faith by their opportunistic bullying, holier-than-thou attitudes, and judgmental finger wagging. Though they say they are doing the Lord's work by pointing out sin and wickedness, for every one they get "saved," about ninety-eight have had their worst fears about Christianity confirmed. These may be lost from the faith forever.

However, I beg to differ with those who tell me they can't take their faith to work. Take a moment to consider what a faithless workplace might be like. Buck Jacobs, the founder of the C12 Group that brings Christian business owners together for mutual accountability, mused on this very topic:

> If it's true that we can't mix our faith with business, the implications are unlimited. For instance, what we call "sin" at church and at home may not be sin in business. There is no absolute standard— no absolute right and wrong—for how we treat people in business. We can do whatever we please with corporate money, confident of immunity from God's judgment. And on it goes.
>
> The truth, of course, is just the opposite: we cannot separate these dimensions of our lives without being a "hypocrite." When we as Christians use a different set of values in our work from those values we promote in our church, we deserve the ugly label. Bottom line: God has only one set of criteria that apply everywhere. He doesn't alter His his standards in the name of profit.[3]

Taking our faith into the workplace isn't about bullying or judging. It isn't about whipping out our Bible at every opportunity during work hours in order to proselytize. And it certainly isn't about judging the Wanderers (the "lost," strangers to grace, unbelievers, etc.). On the other hand, it *is* about being the light and salt to the world, even when we're at work.

The Myth of Time-consuming Faith Sharing

We use "too busy" as an excuse for a lot of things, though mostly for tasks and responsibilities we don't want to do anyway. I am often amazed that the same CEO who doesn't have time for fifteen minutes of prayer each morning can manage to "squeeze in" eighteen holes of golf, a night on the town, and a Friday afternoon baseball game–sometimes all in the same week! Being "too busy" for faith sharing either means we actually are just too busy, *or* it means we don't want to do it.

Let me confess that at times I'm too busy for faith sharing, too. I'm always too busy to go knocking door-to-door to share my faith in some community across town. I'm too busy to stop by the new guy's desk–so new I don't even know his name–to ask him if he knows for sure that if he died tonight, he'd go to heaven. And I'm too busy to lean around the wall of my cubicle to tell Sue that if she moves in with Carl outside of the bonds of marriage, she'll incur the wrath of God.

On the other hand, I'm *not* too busy to knock on my neighbor's door and invite them for dinner. And I'm not too busy to stop by the new guy's desk and introduce myself. I'm not even too busy to chat at an appropriate time with Sue about my great marriage and why I'd do it all over again– not to manipulate or manufacture her guilt, but to present an alternative.

The spiritual habit of sharing your faith, even sharing it at work, can effectively expand the Divine Power Grid's infrastructure without cramping your calendar or without decimating your coworkers' respect for either Christianity or you. And you can share your faith while maintaining the deepest respect for whatever faith "opinion" your friends, relatives, acquaintances, neighbors, or coworkers embrace.

The Spiritual Habit of Faith Sharing

There's a lot of discomfort when it comes to the spiritual habit of faith sharing. Fear raises its ugly head and says, "Boo!" Mostly we're afraid of losing the respect of those with whom we spend significant time. As you're going to see, however, there is no need for *any* discomfort or fear. Peter wrote a letter to some early Christians and advised them to be ready to give a reason for their hope, but to offer their reason with both gentleness and respect (1 Pet. 3:15). The implication is that Peter expected that people were going to ask about hope. So let me ask you, when was the last time someone sidled up to you and asked, "Why are you always so hopeful?" I suspect your answer is never. But it needn't be that way. There *are* ways to share your faith that will stimulate genuine faith questions from the Wanderers. It's about being light and salt (Mt. 5:13–16).

The Habit of Being Light

Jesus said he was the light of the world (Jn. 8:12). Most of us are pretty comfortable with that–there's no pressure for us to perform, just accept.

But then Jesus threw a wrench into the works. He told his followers that *they* were the light of the world. *That* pronouncement we're not so sure about:

> You are the light of the world. A city built on a hill cannot be hid. No one after lighting a lamp puts it under the bushel basket, but on the lampstand, and it gives light to all in the house. In the same way, let your light shine before others, so that they may see your good works and give glory to your Father in heaven. (Mt. 5:14–16, NRSV)

Now Jesus didn't just pick these two metaphors out of the blue, he chose salt and light because they represent the two ways Wanderers experience authentic Christianity. Salt has to do with taste; it's an intimate encounter. When you're salt, conversation is how others get a "taste" of your faith. On the other hand, light has to do with seeing from afar. In fact, when someone's in the dark, they can see a point of light from a long way away.

Many Christians tell me their faith-sharing tactic is to be a point of light in the world. These folks quietly go about their Christian lives in the hopes that Wanderers will seek them out demanding to know the secret of their faith. Actually, it's not bad tactic *if* they have such an exciting, fulfilling, and attractive Christian life that people are compelled to ask what makes them so deeply spiritual, holy, and God-connected. Unfortunately, I've yet to meet anyone claiming to use this tactic who has been asked at all, let alone regularly.

Light *and* salt: We don't get to choose which one we are. Jesus said we're both. We'll get to salt in a few minutes. But let's begin by focusing on how you can boost the lumens of your light so it shines so brightly that you might get questions.

The Light of Christian Ethics

 The spiritual habit of letting your light shine by practicing Christian ethics is probably the least time-consuming, and one of the most important, "billboards" for the faith. Busy Christians everywhere have no excuse to *not* practice this one. Unfortunately, many don't practice it, and these have seriously sullied Christianity's reputation.

Remember the CEOs mentioned in chapter 1? Those men who claimed to be Practicing Christians? Who would have ever guessed by their business practices? There's an old saying: "Charity begins at home." That saying has a corollary: "Ethics begin at work." Both the Old and New Testaments insist on our integrity and ethics as hallmarks of faithfulness.

> The LORD detests differing weights,
>   and dishonest scales do not please him. (Prov. 20:23)

"Simply let your 'Yes' be 'Yes,' and your 'No,' 'No'; anything beyond this comes from the evil one." (Mt. 5:37)

Differing weights and dishonest scales were used to defraud consumers in the marketplace, sort of like when the butcher puts a thumb on the scales when weighing out sliced ham. Be scrupulously honest. Letting your "yes" be "yes" means having integrity. Keep your promises–say what you mean and mean what you say.

I've rarely met a Christian in business who admits to being anything less than a Practicing Christian in dealings with others. Yet, I've also watched some of these same believers fudge figures, hedge on facts, and under-report earnings or over-report inventory. Again, Buck Jacobs comments:

> Often in business I have been tempted to lie or to shade the truth to gain what would appear to be a business advantage. Jesus wouldn't do that. Often I have been tempted to take advantage of my position to "lord it over" another. Jesus wouldn't do that. Often I have been tempted to compare myself to others, holding in subtle contempt those who have less and those who have accomplished less than I have. Jesus wouldn't do that. I still tend to look first at the temporal bottom line and only later to consider the eternal significance of what I have done. Jesus wouldn't do that. And I sometimes place importance on my job title and think that my value is demonstrated by it. Jesus wouldn't do that, either.[4]

Whenever we let our ethics slip, no matter how little, we tarnish Christianity's reputation and dishonor the name of Jesus. People are watching us, whether we like it or not. Gandhi is reported to have said, "I would be a Christian if not for the Christians I've met." If Christianity does nothing else, it should at least encourage us to be ethical. Our ethical light has got to start shining brighter.

It can be difficult to practice Christian ethics in the workplace. Not only is there a temptation to color the truth and bend the rules to make a profit, but in many fields unchristian practices are virtually expected. Jesus didn't say it would be easy–he just said it would be worth it.

The Light in Nonverbal Clues

If our Christian ethics are suspect, nothing else we do will have a positive impact. We'll be rightly labeled just another hypocrite. However, if ethical behavior is already your watchword, then letting your light shine through nonverbal clues can be an effective invitation to elicit Wanderers' questions.

Once upon a time, Christians traced the sign of the fish in the sand to communicate they were Christian. Later, they wore crosses and crucifixes as membership badges. Then came the bumper stickers and the silver fish on the back of cars.

Today, as stated earlier, 82 percent of Americans claim to be Christian. Crosses and crucifixes are so common as jewelry that they're no longer identification badges, except perhaps in the broadest possible meaning. Bumper stickers and silver fish are so cliché and so prevalent that they mean nothing.

For nonverbal clues of our faith to be effective, they must do two things. First, they must reflect a *positive* Christian lifestyle. Second, they can't be watered-down symbols that mean little to nothing. Think about it for a moment; the purpose of a good clue is to elicit investigation, to arouse curiosity. Think Sherlock Holmes, Hercule Poirot, Nero Wolfe, or Ben Matlock. What clues could you leave that would lead a detective, or, more importantly, a Wanderer, to inquire further?

Steve Necessary of Cox Communications intentionally leaves clues in his office, clues that serve both as an invitation for inquiry and as self-reminders of who he is and who he ultimately represents:

> In my office I have a Bible on my credenza. On the wall I have a neat picture that a coworker once gave me of a businessman sitting at his desk listening to Jesus talk to him. It serves as a reminder. I can look up and be reminded who I am and whose I am. It tempers some salty language that might come out of my mouth or those in my office—that tends to work pretty well. They are also there as an expression of what I believe to anyone who comes into my office and with whom I speak.[5]

Nonverbal clues are meant to be *clues*. Don't let them be so overstated that wanderers would need sunglasses to protect them from the neon lights you're shining. Instead, take note of Steve's clues: simplicity and subtlety lest you put people off.

In our home, we have a couple of decorations that serve as hints to our faith. For one, we have our marriage certificate hanging above our mantle. That gets lots of questions and comments, which gives us the opportunity to share something about our commitment not only to marriage, but to practicing our faith within our marriage. My wife collects communion chalices, and we have them displayed prominently on our mantle with a small sculpture of da Vinci's *Last Supper*. Subtle hints that elicit inquiries are sometimes the brightest light for a hilltop.

Just to get you started, here is a list of some nonverbal, *not*-in-your-face, clues you can incorporate in your home, office, or cubicle. Notice that some could even be used in your classroom if you're a teacher. Others would be appropriate to put into your toolbox if you're a mechanic or in a service field where you carry tools. Still others could find a place in your car.

- An open Bible (don't use an ostentatious family or pulpit Bible)
- Icons
- A cross or crucifix on the wall
- Prayer beads
- Small statuary, paintings, or reliefs
- Prayer candle(s)
- Chalice and paten
- A Christian magazine or book in your lobby or waiting room[6]
- Christian gift stores have literally hundreds of items that could serve you well

There is one more nonverbal clue story I'd like to share. I was chatting with Bert Knapp, who is a retired executive from the Gulf Oil Company. At one point in his career he was responsible for nearly eleven hundred employees and managed to take his faith with him into the workplace. One of the nonverbal clues Bert used was a tiny silver cross he carried in his pocket.

> I always carry a little silver cross in my pocket, not as a good luck charm, but as a reminder. And I lost it one day in the hallway in the Gulf building in Houston and didn't know where it was. Pretty soon a lady I didn't really know walked in with it and said, "I'll bet this is yours, isn't it?"[7]

It wasn't much. Bert didn't have to wear a banner or make a public announcement. It was enough that he practiced his faith where he worked. People notice the nonverbal clues; they often speak much louder than anything we could say.

The Light in Good Works

When Jesus taught his disciples about being the light of the world, he told them it was their good works that would offer the most convincing testimony of their faith. "Let your light shine before others, so that they may see your good works and give glory to your Father in heaven" (Mt. 5:16, NRSV). Good works speak much louder than good words. When Wanderers see someone doing a good work, especially something that is sacrificial in nature, their curiosity may be piqued enough to find out what's up.

Good Works Outside of the Church

Let me be blunt for a moment. If you're serious about practicing the spiritual habit of faith sharing, you'll have to go outside of the church. Truth be known, Wanderers are neither interested nor impressed with the good works you do at church. Nobody outside of the church cares if you're the

Sunday school superintendent or the mission's chair. If you happen to be a pastor, they're even *less* impressed by what you do at church, no matter *how* sacrificial it might be—let's face it, you're a *paid* Christian. The light you shine in church is pretty much light under a bushel basket—only a selected audience will see it.

A Christian doing good works at a Christian mission, such as the Salvation Army, or at a Christian food bank, thrift store, shelter, and so on, also casts a dim light. It's not that Christian missions aren't doing great things in the name of Jesus, but that's just it. Wanderers appreciate the ministry, but they *expect* to see Christians at a Christian mission. Further, they expect to hear the gospel there, so they're often prepared and come with a "hardened heart." The spiritual habit of taking on a Christian mission in the community is an important spiritual habit to be sure, but it is less effective for getting an opportunity to share your faith.

If you're going to practice the spiritual habit of faith sharing, do something beyond the church building and outside of an organized Christian community mission. When helping community volunteers clean up a local park, other volunteers may wonder (and ask) why a Practicing Christian is picking up broken glass under the swings rather than trimming the hedge on the church grounds.

If you work for a large company, there may be a number of volunteer opportunities organized by management and staff alike. Plugging your gift of service into these events may offer excellent faith sharing opportunities. If your company doesn't have anything like this going on, consider organizing something. It can be as simple as passing a hat for natural disaster relief, or as complex as coordinating with citywide poverty relief efforts. By practicing your works "before others" in concert with your workplace, your coworkers will "see your good works." And, who knows, they may be led to ask questions and eventually end up giving glory to God.

Servant Evangelism

 Remember the bumper sticker, "Practice random acts of kindness and senseless acts of beauty"? That's pretty much the crux of servant evangelism: doing random acts of kindness and beauty in the name of the Lord in such a way that God gets the credit.

Many churches today have taken up the banner of servant evangelism and have organized projects in their communities. You may have seen some of them: handing out free sodas on hot days to passing motorists, cleaning windshields or washing cars and *refusing* payment, or taking fresh doughnuts to a social services agency where the lines are long and the progress slow. Churches are practicing all these, and many more ideas, across North America. In most cases, they give the recipient a card or a flyer that lets them know the act was done in the name of the Lord—and, of course, the name of the church is tucked in there somewhere.

Servant evangelism works to help churches grow. For one, it takes advantage of the "numbers game." In marketing, the law of averages suggests that if you offer almost anything to enough people, someone (or two or three even) will want whatever you're offering. The same holds true for churches. If you personally touch enough people with kindness, there will be some whose interest is piqued and they'll make their way to the church.

However, servant evangelism shouldn't be just a program done by the local church. It needs to be a lifestyle for every Practicing Christian. Practicing servant evangelism on a personal level is a powerful way to let your light shine. It's not about handing out servant evangelism cards in the name of the church, but about doing acts of kindness in the name of Jesus.

Most servant evangelism programs are designed to reach numbers; however, practicing servant evangelism on a personal level is more one-on-one and less programmed. It's developing a habit of doing good works while you're doing something else. For instance, I've developed a habit of returning shopping carts. At most of the local stores near where I live, they have set aside convenient "parking stalls" for their shopping carts. However, there are a lot of people who apparently can't be bothered to return their carts to these stalls, so they leave them hither-and-yon. For the past several years, when I finish my shopping, not only do I return my cart, but I also grab any nearby carts to return along with mine. Recently, one of the store's employee's commented quizzically, "I saw you push return those carts." I smiled, thanked him, and said, "It's just a practical way I do what Jesus teaches."

The key to servant evangelism is giving credit where credit is due. I'm who I am because of who Jesus is through and in me. That relationship makes a real difference in how I behave. When I get "caught" doing a random, senseless act of "good works," I make sure God gets the credit. It may take awhile to get used to saying, "It's just a practical way I do what Jesus teaches," or, as some say, "It's just a practical way to show Jesus' love," but after you've said it a dozen times or so, it comes naturally.

Making a habit of sharing your faith through servant evangelism takes a measure of intentionality. Busy people are geared toward taking care of business, so pausing to think of others amid their daily regimens is not "natural." However, as you practice servant evangelism intentionally, random thoughts of how to be kind will become second nature. Until this *is* second nature, though, you will need to think about and plan acts of kindness that you could do. Use the following thoughts to "prime" your thinking pump.

- Make a list of your coworkers and ponder what simple and unexpected tasks you could do for each one. Sharpen pencils? Bring a snack? Extend a deadline? Empty their trash or shredder? Send an e-card?

- Think about places you frequent and people you regularly see there. What kind act could you do at these places?
- What could you do in your neighborhood? Pick up the litter in front of your neighbor's house? Pluck a few weeds in a neighbor's flower garden? (Make sure you know it's a weed!) For example, we have a very tiny patch of grass in our front yard and I despise yard work. One year my neighbors paid their gardener to cut our grass all summer long. Not only was it a blessing, it was a way for him to show Jesus' love in a practical way.
- What about truly random acts? Feed an expired parking meter as you walk to work. Drop off a box of doughnuts at the courthouse, union hall, unemployment center, or anywhere people stand in line for extended periods of time. When you're in a fast food drive-thru, pay for the order of the car behind you (one of the *few* times having a silver fish on your bumper is a good thing).

With the above in mind, make a list of things you could do. it's simply a matter of taking on one or two acts as habits and practicing them. Then, when someone looks at you funny and asks, "Why'd you do that?" you can smile and say, "It's just something I do because it's something I think Jesus would do."

The Habit of Being Salt

Being a high-lumen light to the world is a grand thing and an effective way to share your faith. But Jesus didn't say we were just the light of the world and leave it at that. He said we're the salt of the earth as well. We're expected to be not *just* a beacon, but to be a seasoning that makes people thirsty for the living water of Jesus–like salted peanuts at the pub.

To practice being salt, you have to give people a taste of what faith is all about. Sharing faith as salt means to open our mouths and share who we are in Jesus. Jesus said that salty salt is good, but salt that's lost its flavor is useless (Mt. 5:13). On the other hand, too much salt can even spoil popcorn, so it's important to strike a balance.

Sharing your faith verbally sounds intimidating, and, the truth is, sometimes it can be. However, most of the time you can be salt without choking either yourself or others. Here are a couple of ways even busy people can be the salt of the earth.

The Salt in Verbal Clues

Remember the earlier nonverbal clues? They were subtle hints dropped here and there to elicit questions. The same is true of verbal clues. They are suggestive phrases woven into the fabric of conversations that may invite further inquiry. They're clues.

Before I go on, let me offer an explanation and an assurance. The point of this section is *not* to introduce you to a Christianized form of subterfuge. I'm not suggesting behavior like those who have represented a particular multilevel marketing soap company made famous by its associates, who would avoid using the name of the company–and sometimes even deny representing that company in order to entice their friends, relatives, acquaintances, neighbors, and coworkers to a presentation. As often as not, those who used these tactics ended up with ex-friends, relatives who wouldn't pick up the phone or answer the door for them, short-lived acquaintances, angry neighbors, and ice-cold coworkers. What I *am* suggesting is about leaving clues about who you are in Jesus–unapologetically and without guile.

So what makes for a good verbal clue? Sharing what's happening or has happened in your faith journey is the most effective hint you can offer. Let me illustrate.

If you bought a brand new convertible sports car, working your exciting new purchase into the conversation wouldn't be a difficult task. Virtually *everyone* would know about it. Well, if you were that excited about something going on at church or in your spiritual life, you wouldn't have any difficulty sharing that either.

So take a few moments and think: What is it about your faith journey that makes your eyes light up?

Hopefully, you immediately thought of something; if not, it may be time for some healthy reflection time. Assuming something came to mind, look for ways to work it into your conversation. For instance, if you're watching the kids play soccer and chatting with the other soccer parents, invariably someone will ask what you're doing for your weekend. If you're excited about something going on at church, you might respond, "Well, on Sunday morning at church we're going to be hearing from a doctor who spent a year in Darfur. They say his stories about what's going on over there are horrifying, but that the work he's doing is making a real difference with local refugees. What about you, what are you doing?" The salt wasn't overwhelming, it didn't offend, and it left a clue to who you are in Jesus. And though your acquaintances might not be interested, on the other hand, they might say, "Tell us more."

But what if you're not in a local church? How can you be salt in a conversation then? Hopefully there's something happening in your faith journey that's exciting. Let's say something you read in the scriptures this morning deeply touched you and someone mentions he or she has to make a tough decision. You might share something like this: "I was reading the Bible this morning and found a couple verses about making tough decisions by taking time for prayer and asking God what to do. But then it said to just hush up and listen. That's always the hard part for me. What do you think you're going to do?"[8]

The key to dropping a verbal clue is to gently let people know you're a Practicing Christian while simultaneously distancing yourself from as many of the negative stereotypes as possible. In other words, present yourself with authenticity and integrity.

Before moving on, here are a couple of other considerations for leaving effective verbal clues.

1. LESS IS MORE. The point is to entice, not to educate. Keep your clue to a sentence or two without adding specifics. Unless someone genuinely asks you to expand on what you've said, let the conversation move along unabated.

2. BE A SPRING, NOT A HOSE. Verbal clues shouldn't be forced. They should bubble up from deep inside and be positive additions to the conversation. If you have to force it, it will be neither natural nor subtle. The point is to make someone thirsty for more, not hose them down.

3. BE REAL. Wanderers are a lot more familiar with believers than they are authentic Practicing Christians. If you're not walking the walk, *please,* start with some other spiritual habit. If you have to fake excitement to work it into a conversation, don't.

4. BE SALT, NOT AN ENTRÉE. A verbal clue is dropped amidst a conversation; it's not the *topic* of a conversation. There are certainly times to share what's exciting at your church or to open up a discussion on how God answers prayer, but unless you've earned the right to have those discussions, leave them to another time. This brings us the last, and perhaps most important, consideration.

5. EARN THE RIGHT. It's a faith-sharing axiom that no one cares how much you know until they know how much you care. Salting a conversation with your coworkers, friends, and even acquaintances is acceptable. But doing the same in a group of strangers only reinforces negative stereotypes of Christians. The rule of thumb is this: If you know the names of the people you're chatting with, salt away (gently). If not, don't add salt. Instead, get to know them first.

Salty Habits

A friend of mine sat across the table from me at a restaurant. There  were three of us at the table, and we'd met for an afternoon business lunch. When the meal was served, but before we started eating, he reached over and took one of the dinner rolls and said, "You know, this bread reminds me of the night my friend Jesus was arrested and killed. At dinner he took bread and gave his friends a piece of it. He said the bread represented his body and that they should eat it to remember him by." Then my friend tore the roll into pieces and gave each of us a bit and he continued. "So when I have lunch with friends, I share some bread with them to remember what Jesus did for his friends." Then we took the bread, ate it, and went on with the meal. There was no juice or wine to "complete" communion, but the impact it made on us at the table was profound.

Now my friend knew that those gathered around the table were all Christians, but later in conversation he explained that he does communion like this whenever there's bread on the table, no matter who he's with. I'll admit, I was taken aback, but the more I thought about it, the more I came to appreciate his candor.

Salt isn't always a subtle seasoning. It's a key ingredient in bacon, ham, and potato chips. Sometimes, what is needed in faith sharing isn't subtlety, but openness of practice. For instance, if you come to our house on a Monday evening, you'll be invited to stay for our home worship time. We have a number of friends who visit with us most Mondays for dinner, singing, praying, scripture study, and communion. If you're in our home on Mondays, you can expect to be a part of it (unless you decide to leave–and so far, no one ever has). It's just what we do. It's not subtle, but it's a key ingredient to who we are.

We have another habit of praying at every meal. We join hands around the table and offer thanks and lift up whatever is pressing on our spirits. But we don't just pray at home. We pray at *every* meal, from ones at McDonalds, to those at the Ritz. If someone joins us for a meal, they're invited to pray with us. No one's ever said no. Some have been uncomfortable with our public praying; however, so far, 100 percent of those who were uncomfortable have been Christians. We don't make a big deal of our prayer time; we simply do it.

There are many different ways to practice faith sharing, but sharing your spiritual habits with others can be a powerful testimony. Steve Necessary shared an experience he had with a business acquaintance:

> I met with an executive recruiter who had his own business in Atlanta. We were business acquaintances, but not anything more than that. We reconnected at a time when he was trying to drum up some business and we went to lunch. He asked, not really knowing me, if he could say a blessing at lunch. I, of course, told him that would be fine, but afterward I asked him about that. He pointed out that this was a way in which he would share his faith very boldly, but not obtrusively, not obnoxiously–my words, not his–in a very routine kind of environment. I was inspired by that level of boldness of somebody who would, mindless of the potential negative consequences from a business standpoint, step out in faith.[9]

In this instance, the recruiter didn't know whether Steve was a believer or not. It was a risk, but it was a risk the recruiter was willing to take for the sake of sharing his faith.

It takes a bit of courage, and perhaps even some bravado, to step up to being this salty. You are, of course, taking a risk when you do so. You risk losing the other person's respect, you could lose the account, and I suppose in some circumstances, you could even lose your job. The question boils down to how seriously you take Jesus' last command about building the infrastructure of the Kingdom of God.

A Special Note about Salt for Pastors

(Before you read any more, get a pen or a pencil.)

On the lines below, list all the Wanderers with whom you are friends. Think "friend" as in having dinner with or going to a movie with, rather than just a passing acquaintance whose name you know; a Wanderer who you've spent time with as a friend sometime during the last four to six weeks.

1. _____

2. _____

3. _____

4. _____

5. _____

6. _____

7. _____

8. _____

If you filled up all the lines, you're a salty pastor. If you filled up half the lines, you've done better than any church pastor I personally know. Even if you filled in just one line, in my experience you're still way, way above average for a North American pastor. And if you had trouble coming up with a single person, you are in the same boat as probably 90 percent of your colleagues.

The fact is, most pastors in North America spend nearly all of their professional time with members of their flock. They're either in their office, at a meeting, or visiting one of the saints. There's so much to do to keep the organization going that most of us don't have time to do anything else.

So we leave faith sharing to our flock. We may preach it and teach it and send people to seminars to learn about it. But, most of the time, it's to no avail, as evidenced by North America's rapidly shrinking churches. Our congregations look to us for leadership and they will charge into battle with us if we lead. But few are actually leading—mostly we're gesturing and pointing.

Jesus had twelve disciples, twelve apprentices. And for three years he showed them how to do what he was doing. He taught some, but mostly he demonstrated. He *did* it. They watched. He watched them do it. Eventually they caught on and began practicing it.

The point is, pastors, we've got to lead in *all* the spiritual habits, and especially in the spiritual habit of faith sharing. And the most effective way to do that is to start spending time with the spiritual Wanderers.

How?

Get out of your office and spend time where the Wanderers are. Personally, I do the majority of my work at my local Starbucks. I wrote most of this book there. I write Bible lessons there. I do my correspondence there. And I schedule as many meetings as I can there. If one of my flock needs to speak to me, I always have my cell phone with me and I'm online at Starbucks, so I can be reached by e-mail or instant message, and, besides, they can always drop by and have a latté with me there—I even buy.

So choose to be salty. Find someplace where your church building and your home office isn't. Instead, go where the Wanderers are. Go ye therefore and be light to the blind and salt for the bland.

SPARKS AND RESISTANCE _____

Questions for Discussion and Reflection

1. Do you agree with the author that Christianity is not just one of many faith opinions? Why or why not?
2. Have you shared your faith in the workplace over the past year? If not, what keeps you from sharing? If so, how did you share?
3. Has anyone ever approached you "out of the blue" and asked you to explain the reason for your hope (or asked what makes you different)? If so, what do you think prompted the question? If not, why do think no one has asked?
4. What nonverbal clues do you think would be effective in your workplace?
5. What could you do as a regular servant evangelism deed? For whom or where would you practice it?
6. When was the last time you offered a verbal clue to your faith? How was it received?
7. Do you have any salty habits you can use to share your faith? What are they and how could you use them? Will you be using them? When?

Practically Practicing the Spiritual Habits

The aim of this appendix is to help you get started practicing some of the spiritual habits. Essentially, what follows is a series of tables you can reference to find a spiritual habit that will fit into your busy schedule and your lifestyle. When you're ready to add a new spiritual habit into your life, check these charts to help you decide which new faith adventure you want to add.

The spiritual habits are broken into these tables:

1. Time of Day
   a. Spiritual Habits for Your Mornings
   b. Spiritual Habits for Your Evenings
   c. Spiritual Habits for Any Time

2. Place
   a. Spiritual Habits for Work (School, etc.)
   b. Spiritual Habits for Home
   c. Spiritual Habits When You're Away

3. Accompaniment
   a. Spiritual Habits Requiring Solitude
   b. Spiritual Habits Requiring Multiple Participants
   c. Spiritual Habits that Work Both in Solitude or in a Crowd

4. Amount of Time
   a. Minimal Time Required
   b. Some Time Required
   c. Significant Time Required
   d. Allow Plenty of Time

5. Suggested Spiritual Aptitude
   a. Basic
   b. Intermediate
   c. Advanced

Bonus material on the spiritual habit of retreating is available online at www.spiritualhabits.com.

Table 1: Time of Day

MORNING	EVENING

A.M. Projection, 19

P.M. Reflection, 23

ANY TIME	ANY TIME (cont.)

10:2b Virus (Accountability Lite), 133
Centering Prayer, 33
Informal Accountability (Accountability Lite), 135
Light of Christian Ethics (Faith Sharing), 151
Light in Nonverbal Clues (Faith Sharing),152
Salt in Verbal Clues (Faith Sharing), 157
Salty Habits, 159
Worship at Work (Incidental Worship), 90
Worship on the Go (Incidental Worship), 92

Micro Retreats, online*

Be Loving Rather than Right (Centricity), 109
Desktop Devotions (Study), 61
Take On Investment, 126
Listen More than Talk (Centricity), 109
R^3 Desktop Devotionals (Study), 64

Servant Evangelism, 155

Discovery Desktop Devotionals (Study), 66
Shared Prayer(Accountability Lite), 132

Journey Group Partnership (Spiritual Accountability), 137
Worship at Mealtimes (Incidental Worship), 87

Church Worship (Intentional Worship), 78
Cursillo Retreats, online*
Good Works Outside of Church (Faith Sharing), 154
Humble Service, 121
Ignatian Exercises Retreat, online*
Mentoring, 124
Passionate Leadership, 120
Small Group Teaching (Leadership), 72

Imaging the Word (Study), 56
Lexio Divina (Study), 53
Other Spiritual Accountability Groups, 144

*See www.spiritualhabits.com.

Table 1: Time of Day (continued)

ANY TIME (cont.)	ANY TIME (cont.)

 (cont.)

Small Group Worship (Intentional Worship), 83
Small Peer Group Study (Participant), 70
Spiritual Director-Directed Retreats, online*

Cheerful Giving, 106
Conversational Prayer, 36
Fasting, 100

Listening Prayer, 34

Quiet Worship Time (Intentional Worship), 85

God-Directed Retreat, online*
Mini Retreats, online*
Praying the Lord's Prayer, 41
Self-Directed Retreat, online*

*See www.spiritualhabits.com.

Table 2: Place

SPIRITUAL HABITS	At Work	At Home	Away
10:2b Virus (Accountability Lite), 133	✔	✔	✔
Centering Prayer, 33	✔	✔	✔
Informal Accountability (Accountability Lite), 135	✔	✔	
Light in Nonverbal Clues (Faith Sharing), 152	✔		✔
Light of Christian Ethics (Faith Sharing), 151	✔	✔	✔
Salt in Verbal Clues (Faith Sharing), 157	✔	✔	✔
Salty Habits, 159	✔	✔	✔
Worship at Work (Incidental Worship), 90	✔		
Worship on the Go (Incidental Worship), 92	✔	✔	✔
Micro Retreats, online*	✔	✔	✔
Be Loving Rather than Right (Centricity), 109	✔	✔	✔
Desktop Devotions (Study), 61	✔	✔	✔
Take On Investment, 126	✔		
R³ Desktop Devotionals (Study), 64	✔	✔	✔
Listen More than Talk (Centricity), 109	✔	✔	✔
Servant Evangelism, 155	✔		✔
Imaging the Word (Study), 56		✔	✔
Lexio Divina (Study), 53		✔	✔
Other Spiritual Accountability Groups, 144	✔		✔
Church Worship (Intentional Worship), 78		✔	✔
Cursillo Retreats, online*			✔
Good Works Outside of Church, 154 (Faith Sharing)			✔
Humble Service, 121			✔
Ignatian Exercises Retreat, online*		✔	✔

*See www.spiritualhabits.com.

Table 2: Place (continued)

SPIRITUAL HABITS	At Work	At Home	Away
(continued)			
Mentoring, 124	✔	✔	✔
Passionate Leadership (Take-On: Serving), 120			✔
Small Group Teaching (Leadership), 72		✔	✔
Small Group Worship (Intentional Worship), 83	✔	✔	✔
Small Peer Group Study (Participant), 70	✔	✔	
Spiritual Director-Directed Retreats, online*			✔
Journey Group Partnership, 137 (Spiritual Accountability)	✔		✔
Worship at Mealtimes (Incidental Worship), 87		✔	✔
Conversational Prayer with a Companion, 38		✔	✔
Discovery Desktop Devotionals (Study), 66		✔	✔
Shared Prayer (Accountability Lite), 132	✔	✔	✔
Cheerful Giving, 106	✔		✔
Conversational Prayer, 36	✔	✔	✔
Fasting, 100	✔	✔	✔
A.M. Projection, 19		✔	
P.M. Reflection, 23		✔	
Listening Prayer, 34	✔	✔	✔
Quiet Worship Time (Intentional Worship), 85	✔	✔	✔
Mini Retreats, online*		✔	✔
Praying the Lord's Prayer, 41		✔	✔
Self-Directed Retreat, online*			✔
God-Directed Retreat, online*			✔

*See www.spiritualhabits.com.

Table 3: Accompaniment

REQUIRES SOLITUDE	REQUIRES MULTIPLE PARTICIPANTS

Centering Prayer, 33
Conversational Prayer, 36

A.M. Projection,19
Listening Prayer, 34
P.M. Reflection, 23

Quiet Worship Time (Intentional Worship), 85

God-Directed Retreat, online*
Mini Retreats, online*
Praying the Lord's Prayer, 41
Self-Directed Retreat, online*

Ignatian Exercises Retreat, online*
Spiritual Director-Directed Retreats, online*

10:2b Virus (Accountability Lite), 133
Informal Accountability (Accountability Lite), 135
Light in Nonverbal Clues (Faith Sharing), 152
Salt in Verbal Clues (Faith Sharing), 157
Salty Habits, 159

Be Loving Rather than Right (Centricity), 109
Take On Investment, 126
Listen More than Talk (Centricity), 109

Conversational Prayer with a Companion, 38
Shared Prayer (Accountability Lite), 132

Journey Group Partnership (Spiritual Accountability), 137

Church Worship (Intentional Worship), 78
Cursillo Retreats, online*
Good Works Outside of Church (Faith Sharing), 154
Humble Service, 121
Mentoring, 124
Passionate Leadership, 120
Small Group Teaching (Leadership), 72
Small Group Worship (Intentional Worship), 83
Small Peer Group Study (Participant), 70

Other Spiritual Accountability Groups, 144

*See www.spiritualhabits.com.

Table 3: Accompaniment (continued)

FOR SOLITUDE OR IN A CROWD	FOR SOLITUDE OR IN A CROWD

Centering Prayer, 33

Light of Christian Ethics (Faith Sharing), 152

Worship at Work (Incidental Worship), 90

Worship on the Go (Incidental Worship), 92

Worship at Mealtimes (Incidental Worship), 87

Micro Retreats, online*

Imaging the Word (Study), 56

Lexio Divina (Study),53

Servant Evangelism, 155

Cheerful Giving, 106

Fasting, 100

Desktop Devotions (Study), 61

R³ Desktop Devotionals (Study), 64

Discovery Desktop Devotionals (Study), 66

*See www.spiritualhabits.com.

Table 4: Amount of Time

MINIMUM TIME	SOME TIME	SIGNIFICANT TIME	PLENTY OF TIME

MINIMUM TIME	SOME TIME	SIGNIFICANT TIME	PLENTY OF TIME
10:2b Virus (Accountability Lite), 133	A.M. Projection, 19	Conversational Prayer with a Companion, 38	God-Directed Retreat, online*
Centering Prayer, 33	Listening Prayer, 34	Discovery Desktop Devotionals (Study), 66	Mini Retreats, online*
Informal Accountability (Accountability Lite), 135	P.M. Reflection, 23	Shared Prayer (Accountability Lite), 132	Praying the Lord's Prayer, 41
Light in Nonverbal Clues (Faith Sharing), 152			Self-Directed Retreat, online*

MINIMUM TIME	SOME TIME	SIGNIFICANT TIME	PLENTY OF TIME
Light of Christian Ethics (Faith Sharing), 151	Quiet Worship Time (Intentional Worship), 85	Journey Group Partnership (Spiritual Accountability), 137	Imaging the Word (Study), 56
Salt in Verbal Clues (Faith Sharing), 157		Worship at Mealtimes (Incidental Worship), 87	Lexio Divina (Study), 53
Salty Habits, 159			Other Spiritual Accountability Groups, 144
Worship at Work (Incidental Worship), 90			
Worship on the Go (Incidental Worship), 92			

MINIMUM TIME	SOME TIME	SIGNIFICANT TIME	PLENTY OF TIME
	Be Loving Rather than Right (Centricity), 109		Church Worship (Intentional Worship), 78
	Desktop Devotions (Study), 61		*Cursillo* Retreats, online*
	Take On Investment, 126		Good Works Outside of Church (Faith Sharing), 154
	R³ Desktop Devotionals (Study), 64		Humble Service, 121
	Listen More than Talk (Centricity), 109		Ignatian Exercises Retreat, online*

MINIMUM TIME	SOME TIME	PLENTY OF TIME
Micro Retreats, online*	Servant Evangelism, 155	Mentoring, 124
Cheerful Giving, 106		Passionate Leadership, 120
Conversational Prayer, 36		Small Group Teaching (Leadership), 72
Fasting, 100		Small Group Worship (Intentional Worship), 83
		Small Peer Group Study (Participant), 70
		Spiritual Director-Directed Retreats, online*

*See www.spiritualhabits.com.

Table 5: Suggested Spiritual Apptitude

BASIC	BASIC (cont.)

  (cont.)

BASIC

10:2b Virus (Accountability Lite), 133
Centering Prayer, 33
Light in Nonverbal Clues (Faith Sharing), 152
Light of Christian Ethics (Faith Sharing), 151
Salty Habits, 159
Worship at Work (Incidental Worship), 90
Worship on the Go (Incidental Worship), 92

Good Works Outside of Church, 154 (Faith Sharing)
Ignatian Exercises Retreat, online*
Small Group Worship (Intentional Worship), 83
Small Peer Group Study (Participant), 70
Spiritual Director-Directed Retreats, online*

A.M. Projection, 19
Cheerful Giving, 106
P.M. Reflection, 23

Micro Retreats, online*

Desktop Devotions (Study), 61
R³ Desktop Devotionals (Study), 64

Quiet Worship Time (Intentional Worship), 85

Journey Group Partnership, 137 (Spiritual Accountability)
Worship at Mealtimes (Incidental Worship), 87

Conversational Prayer with a Companion, 38
Discovery Desktop Devotionals (Study), 66

Other Spiritual Accountability Groups, 144

Church Worship (Intentional Worship), 78
Cursillo Retreats, online*

Praying the Lord's Prayer, 41

---

*See www.spiritualhabits.com.

Table 5: Suggested Spiritual Apptitude (continued)

INTERMEDIATE	ADVANCED

Conversational Prayer, 36
Fasting, 100

Informal Accountability (Accountability Lite), 135

Salt in Verbal Clues (Faith Sharing), 157

Take On Investment, 126

Listening Prayer, 34

Mentoring, 124

Mini Retreats, online*
Self-Directed Retreat, online*

God-Directed Retreat, online*

Imaging the Word (Study), 56
Lexio Divina, 53

Be Loving Rather than Right (Centricity), 109
Listen More than Talk (Centricity), 109

Servant Evangelism, 155

Shared Prayer (Accountability Lite), 132

Humble Service, 121
Passionate Leadership, 120
Small Group Teaching (Leadership), 72

*See www.spiritualhabits.com.

APPENDIX B

R³ Journaling

Date:_____ Passage: _____

Recall
What scripture touched or intrigued you? Write it here.

_____

_____

_____

_____

Reflect
What is it that touched or intrigued you? Reflect on that here.

_____

_____

_____

_____

_____

_____

_____

_____

_____

_____

_____

_____

Respond
Write your prayer response to these insights here.

_____

_____

_____

_____

_____

APPENDIX C

Discovery Devotions

Date:_____ Passage: _____

1. What did you like about what you read?

_____
_____
_____
_____
_____
_____
_____

2. What did you **not** like about what you read?

_____
_____
_____
_____
_____
_____
_____

3. What did you not understand about what you read?

_____
_____
_____
_____
_____
_____
_____

APPENDIX D

The One-Anothers

Mk. 9:50	"Salt is good, but if it loses its saltiness, how can you make it salty again? Have salt in yourselves, and be at peace with each other."
Jn. 13:34–35	"A new command I give you: Love one another. As I have loved you, so you must love one another. By this all men will know that you are my disciples, if you love one another."
Jn. 15:12	"My command is this: Love each other as I have loved you."
Jn. 15:17	"This is my command: Love each other."
Rom. 12:10	Be devoted to one another in brotherly love. Honor one another above yourselves.
Rom. 12:16	Live in harmony with one another. Do not be proud, but be willing to associate with people of low position. Do not be conceited.
Rom. 13:8	Let no debt remain outstanding, except the continuing debt to love one another, for he who loves his fellowman has fulfilled the law.
Rom. 14:13	Therefore let us stop passing judgment on one another. Instead, make up your mind not to put any stumbling block or obstacle in your brother's way.
Rom. 15:7	Accept one another, then, just as Christ accepted you, in order to bring praise to God.
Rom. 15:14	I myself am convinced, my brothers, that you yourselves are full of goodness, complete in knowledge and competent to instruct one another.
Rom. 16:16	Greet one another with a holy kiss. All the churches of Christ send greetings.
1 Cor. 1:10	I appeal to you, brothers, in the name of our Lord Jesus Christ, that all of you agree with one another so that there may be no divisions among you and that you may be perfectly united in mind and thought.
1 Cor. 11:33	So then, my brothers, when you come together to eat, wait for each other.

1 Cor. 12:25	So that there should be no division in the body, but that its parts should have equal concern for each other.
Gal. 5:13	You, my brothers, were called to be free. But do not use your freedom to indulge the sinful nature; rather, serve one another in love.
Eph. 4:2	Be completely humble and gentle; be patient, bearing with one another in love.
Eph. 4:32	Be kind and compassionate to one another, forgiving each other, just as in Christ God forgave you.
Eph. 5:19	Speak to one another with psalms, hymns and spiritual songs. Sing and make music in your heart to the Lord,
Eph. 5:21	Submit to one another out of reverence for Christ.
Col. 3:13	Bear with each other and forgive whatever grievances you may have against one another. Forgive as the Lord forgave you.
Col. 3:16	Let the word of Christ dwell in you richly as you teach and admonish one another with all wisdom, and as you sing psalms, hymns and spiritual songs with gratitude in your hearts to God.
1 Thess. 5:11	Therefore encourage one another and build each other up, just as in fact you are doing.
1 Thess. 5:13	Hold them in the highest regard in love because of their work. Live in peace with each other.
1 Thess. 5:15	Make sure that nobody pays back wrong for wrong, but always try to be kind to each other and to everyone else.
Heb. 3:13	But encourage one another daily, as long as it is called today, so that none of you may be hardened by sin's deceitfulness.
Heb. 10:24–25	And let us consider how we may spur one another on toward love and good deeds. Let us not give up meeting together, as some are in the habit of doing, but let us encourage one another–and all the more as you see the Day approaching.
Heb. 13:1	Keep on loving each other as brothers.
Jas. 4:11	Brothers, do not slander one another. Anyone who speaks against his brother or judges him speaks against the law and judges it. When you judge the law, you are not keeping it, but sitting in judgment on it.
Jas. 5:16	Therefore confess your sins to each other and pray for each other so that you may be healed. The prayer of a righteous man is powerful and effective.

1 Pet. 1:22	Now that you have purified yourselves by obeying the truth so that you have sincere love for your brothers, love one another deeply, from the heart.
1 Pet. 3:8	Finally, all of you, live in harmony with one another; be sympathetic, love as brothers, be compassionate and humble.
1 Pet. 4:8	Above all, love each other deeply, because love covers over a multitude of sins.
1 Pet. 4:9	Offer hospitality to one another without grumbling.
1 Pet. 5:5	Young men, in the same way be submissive to those who are older. All of you, clothe yourselves with humility toward one another, because, "God opposes the proud but gives grace to the humble."
1 Jn. 1:7	But if we walk in the light, as he is in the light, we have fellowship with one another, and the blood of Jesus, his Son, purifies us from all sin.
1 Jn. 3:11	This is the message you heard from the beginning: We should love one another.
1 Jn. 3:23	And this is his command: to believe in the name of his Son, Jesus Christ, and to love one another as he commanded us.
1 Jn. 4:7	Dear friends, let us love one another, for love comes from God. Everyone who loves has been born of God and knows God.
1 Jn. 4:11–12	Dear friends, since God so loved us, we also ought to love one another. No one has ever seen God; but if we love one another, God lives in us and his love is made complete in us.
2 Jn. 1:5	And now, dear lady, I am not writing you a new command but one we have had from the beginning. I ask that we love one another.

APPENDIX E

Journey Group Partnership

Weekly Bible Readings

Each week, read from the suggested book for the amount of time you and your partner have agreed on. If you complete the book, begin reading it again throughout the week. If you don't finish the book, mark your stopping point so you can continue from there in the future. Notice that twelve times per year you and your partner will jointly choose a book to read. You may read any book from the Bible, including ones you've already read. Use the *R³ Journal* to reflect on your reading.

1. Genesis
2. Exodus
3. Luke
4. **Group Choice**
5. Acts
6. Judges
7. 1, 2, 3 John
8. **Group Choice**
9. Philemon, Colossians
10. Psalms 1–61
11. Galatians
12. **Group Choice**
13. James
14. 1 Samuel
15. 2 Samuel
16. **Group Choice**
17. Mark
18. 1 Kings
19. 2 Kings
20. **Group Choice**
21. Psalms 62–72
22. Hebrews
23. 1, 2 Peter
24. **Group Choice**
25. Romans
26. Amos

27. 1, 2 Thessalonians
28. **Group Choice**
29. Psalms 73–89
30. John
31. Micah
32. **Group Choice**
33. Philippians
34. Jeremiah
35. 1 Corinthians
36. Group Choice
37. 1, 2 Timothy
38. Nehemiah
39. Psalms 90–106
40. **Group Choice**
41. Hosea
42. Matthew
43. Habakkuk
44. **Group Choice**
45. Titus, Jude
46. Ephesians
47. Ecclesiastes
48. **Group Choice**
49. 2 Corinthians
50. Isaiah
51. Psalms 107–150
52. **Group Choice**

Additional Readings

Leviticus, Numbers, Deuteronomy, Joshua, Ruth, 1 and 2 Chronicles, Ezra, Esther, Job, Proverbs, Song-of-Songs, Lamentations, Ezekiel, Daniel, Joel, Jonah, Obadiah, Nahum, Haggai, Zephaniah, Zechariah, Malachi, Revelation

Accountability Questions

Instructions:

- Plan on meeting for at least 1/2 hour.
- Same-gender groups only.
- One person reads the questions; both share their answers.
- Question 9 is to help hold you accountable for an issue God is calling you to deal with.
- There is no place here for judgment. Offer each other only support.

Questions:

1. Have you been a verbal witness to someone this week about the good news of Jesus Christ?
2. Have you exposed yourself, either accidentally or intentionally, to sexually alluring material or have you entertained inappropriate sexual thoughts this week?
3. Have you lacked any financial integrity this week?
4. Have you been honoring, understanding, and generous in your important relationships this week?
5. Have you lied or shaded the truth to look better to others this week?
6. Have you given in to an addictive behavior this week? If so, explain.
7. Are you harboring anger, resentment, or bitterness toward someone?
8. Have you secretly wished for someone's misfortune?
9. (Your Personalized Accountability Question)

———————————————————————————————

———————————————————————————————

10. Were you faithful in your reading and praying, and did you hear from God? What will you do about it?
11. During this conversation today, have you lied, left out parts of the truth, or left a mis-impression with me that needs to be cleared up?

My Most Wanted List

"My prayer is not for them alone. I pray also for those who will believe in me through their message, that all of them may be one, Father, just as you are in me and I am in you. May they also be in us so that the world may believe that you have sent me. I have given them the glory that you gave me, that they may be one as we are one."(Jn. 17:20–22)

"The Son of Man has come to seek and save what was lost." (Lk. 19:10)

Each day, pray specifically for these who are Wanderers...

_____

_____

_____

_____

_____

_____

_____

Lord, prepare the heart of _____ to hear the gospel. (Mt. 13:23)

Lord, raise up a worker to bring the gospel to _____. (Lk. 10:2b)

Lord, send me to be a witness to _____. (Isa. 6:8)

Pray daily as Jesus instructed in Luke 10:2b:

"Ask the Lord of the harvest, therefore, to send out workers into his harvest field."

Notes

Introduction

[1]Yotta=1024, as of this writing, Yotta is the largest number with a scientifically accepted name.

Chapter 1: Power Shortage

[1]The Gallup Organization, *Gallup Poll Social Series – Values and Beliefs,* May 2005, http://brain.gallup.com/documents/question.aspx?question=153027&Advanced=0&SearchConType=1&SearchTypeAll=religion.

[2]"Christianity Lite," *The Christian Century* 122, no. 16 (9 July 2005): 6.

[3]Michael Zigarelli, "The Epidemic of Busyness Among Christian Leaders," *Regent Business Review* 16 (March-April 2005), http://www.regent.edu/acad/schbus/maz/busreview/issue16/busyness.html.

Chapter 2: The Spiritual Habit of Projection and Reflecction

[1]"2003 North America Blackout," *Wikipedia,* http://en.wikipedia.org/wiki/2003_North_America_blackout.

[2]William O'Rourke, *Idle Hands* (New York: Delacorte Press, 1981). Cited in online *Simpson's Contemporary Quotations,* http://www.bartleby.com/63/64/5264.html.

[3]From Robert Frost, "Stopping by Woods on a Snowy Evening."

[4]"2003 North America Blackout."

[5]"I Say a Little Prayer," words by Hal David, 1967.

[6]*Closing Time,* Semisonic, Chicago: MCA, 11733, 1998, Audio Compact Disk.

[7]"Ad War Looming in Sleep Aid Market," *CNN.com,* July 26, 2005, http://www.cnn.com/2005/HEALTH/conditions/07/25/sleep.wars.ap/.

[8]"Study Tips: Math Test Anxiety," from Mt. San Antonio College, http://lac.mtsac.edu/mta.html.

[9]Richard Swenson, *The Overload Syndrome* (Colorado Springs: NavPress, 1998), 200.

Chapter 3: The Spiritual Habit of Prayer

[1]"Overview of the Electric Grid," *Gridworks,* US Department of Energy, http://www.energetics.com/gridworks/grid.html.

[2]Yotta=1024, as of this writing. Yotta is the largest number with a scientifically accepted name.

[3]"Annual Study Reveals America is Spiritually Stagnant," *The Barna Update,* March 5, 2001, http://www.barna.org/FlexPage.aspx?Page=BarnaUpdate&BarnaUpdateID=84.

[4]Brother Lawrence of the Resurrection, *The Practice of the Presence of God,* Paraphrased excerpts from the first and second conversations. English translation available at http://www.housechurch.org/spirituality/brother_lawrence.html.

[5]Ibid.

[6]Ibid, paraphrased excerpt from the fourth conversation.

[7]For more on praying the Psalms, see William Paulsell's *Let My Prayer Rise to God: A Spirituality for Praying the Psalms* (St. Louis: Chalice Press, 2002).

[8]The mathematic formula to figure out the available voltage is called Ohm's law: Voltage (V) equals Power (I) multiplied by Resistance (R), thus V=IR.

[9]Bruce H. Wilkinson, *Prayer of Jabez: Breaking Through to the Blessed Life* (Sister, Oreg.: Multnomah Press, 2000).

[10]Steve Necessary, personal communication, August 17, 2005.

[11]Rosalind Rinker, *Prayer: Conversing with God* (Nashville: Zondervan, 1987).

[12] St. Patrick, "St. Patrick's Breast-Plate," *Catholic Encyclopedia,* http://www.newadvent.org/cathen/11554a.htm.

Chapter 4: The Spiritual Habit of Study

[1]"Americans Spend More than 100 Hours Commuting to Work Each Year, Census Bureau Reports," *US Census Bureau News,* March 30, 2005, http://www.census.gov/Press-Release/www/releases/archives/american_community_survey_acs/004489.html.

[2]"Seattle Commute Time Below National Average," *Puget Sound Business Journal,* February 25, 2004, http://www.bizjournals.com/seattle/stories/2004/02/23/daily21.html.

[3]Sam Anthony Morello, OCD, *Lectio Divina and the Practice of Teresian Prayer* (Washington, D.C.: ICS Publications/Institute of Carmelite Studies, 1995),   http://landru.i-link-2.net/shnyves/prayer.html#Lectio_Divina.

[4]Tom Wolf, *Persons of Peace,* http://kncsb.org/ministries/teaching/bibleteachingdownloads/PersonsofPeace.PDF.

[5]Bob Gandrud retired in 2000.

[6]Bob Gandrud, personal interview, August 8, 2005.

[7]Ibid.

[8]Jim Martin retired in 1978 after working thirty-three years for Shell.

[9]Jim Martin, personal interview, August 4, 2005.

Chapter 5: The Spiritual Habit of Worship

[1]"Piezoelectricity," *Wikipedia.com,* http://en.wikipedia.org/wiki/Piezoelectricity.

[2]Blaise Pascal, in Chris Lute, "The Secret that will Change Your Life," *Campus Life,* 56, no.9 (May/June, 1998): 30, http://www.christianitytoday.com/cl/8c6/8c6030.html.

[3]The definition of a local church in our culture, however, is beginning to see significant change from the image of the white-steepled building on the town square. Local churches may be huge megachurches or smaller family-sized churches and everything in between. But they are also house churches, home fellowships, and even smaller, relational churches of three or four Christians who meet for worship and for mutual support. All of these meet the biblical definition of "church" (see Mt. 18:20 and *Under the Radar* by Bill Easum & Bill Tenny-Brittian [Abingdon Press, 2005]).

[4]For more suggestions for tactile worship practices, see William Tenny-Brittian, *Prayer for People Who Can't Sit Still* (St. Louis: Chalice Press, 2005).

[5]For the traditional "Words of Institution" see 1 Corinthians 11:23-26.

[6]See the section on "Small Peer Group Study" in chapter 4 for Bob Gandrud's story.

[7]Author's paraphrase of the traditional words of institution in 1 Cor. 11:24–25.

[8]"Americans Spend More than 100 Hours Commuting to Work Each Year, Census Bureau Reports," *US Census Bureau News,* March 30, 2005, http://www.census.gov/Press-Release/www/releases/archives/american_community_survey_acs/004489.html.

[9]John Wesley, "Directions for Singing," http://www.gbgm-umc.org/BensalemPA/wesley.html,

[10]Cat Stevens, "If You Want to Sing Out, Sing Out," on *Footsteps in the Dark* (A&M, 1984).

Chapter 6: The Spiritual Habit of Giving Up

[1]From "St. Perpetua: Passion of Sts. Perpetua and Felicity, 203. excerpts," *Internet Medieval Sourcebook,* http://www.fordham.edu/halsall/source/perpetua-excerp.html.

[2]Juan Carlos Ortiz, *Disciple: A Handbook for New Believers* (Lake Mary, Fla.: Charisma House, 1995), 35–36.

[3]Carey Benedict, "Hard to Swallow," *Los Angeles Times,* 20 November 2000, S1.

[4]Consult your physician before engaging in a fast for more than three days.

[5]"Facts and Figures About Our TV Habit," *TV-Turnoff Network,* http://www.tvturnoff.org/images/facts&figs/factsheets/FactsFigs.pdf.

[6]Chris Black, personal interview, July 2005.

[7]Ibid.

[8]Gerald Friedman, "The End of Leisure?" *Econ-Atrocity Bulletin,* September 5, 2003, http://www.fguide.org/Bulletin/leisure.htm.

[9]"Table 9: Average hours per day spent in leisure and sports activities," *News,* Bureau of Labor Statistics, Department of Labor, January 12, 2005, http://www.bls.gov/news.release/atus.t09.htm.

[10]Chris Black interview.

Chapter 7: The Spiritual Habit of Taking On

[1]Hans Selye, as quoted in Richard A. Swenson *The Overload Syndrome: Learning to Live within Your Limits* (Colorado Springs: NavPress, 1998), 80.

[2]If you find yourself in the same predicament, the *Personal Ministry Assessment* is available at www.spiritualhabits.com.

[3]Marcia Holland Risch, personal conversation, July 5, 2005.

[4]Chris Black, personal interview, July 2005.

[5]Bob Gandrud interview.

[6]John Dart, "Study: Student Debt Hurts New Pastors," *Christian Century* (August 10, 2004), http://www.findarticles.com/p/articles/mi_m1058/is_16_121/ai_n6159321.

Chapter 8: The Spiritual Habit of Accountability

[1]"Stress Then Burnout," *Smoldering Wick Ministries,* http://www.smolderingwickministries.org/art17.htm.

[2]Jane Lampman, "New thirst for Spirituality Being Felt Worldwide," *The Christian Science Monitor,* (November 25, 1998), http://www. csmonitor.com.

[3]Buck Jacobs, "Confessions of a Christian Businessman," *Regent's Business Review* 7 (September-October 2003), http://www.regent.edu/acad/schbus/maz/busreview/issue7/confessions.html.

[4]A suggestion: Though it may seem that you could ask someone who was *not* sharing a spiritual habit with you, resist the temptation. Partnering with someone who won't practice with you may make it difficult for them to take their role seriously, plus they won't be empathetic to the cause.

[5]Chris Black, personal interview, July 2005.

[6]See chapter 7 and appendix D.

[7]Robert Banks, *Redeeming the Routines: Bringing Theology to Life* (Wheaton, Ill.: Bridgepoint, 1997), 59.

[8]I have spoken with a number of committed Christians who have told me that they feel it is their responsibility to point out the error of other's ways. I've learned not to argue with them, but by the same token, I refuse to put myself into accountability with them. I know when I've sinned–God is really good at convicting my heart. I need my accountability companion to hear my struggles, not to try and fix my problems. If I need advice, I can always ask. Otherwise, it's between me and God.

[9]Journey Group Partnerships were inspired by Neil Cole's Life Transfromation Groups" ©1999. Adapted by William Tenny-Brittian ©2004.

[10]The first dedicated church building was constructed by Constantine in 313 C.E.–nearly three hundred years *after* the birth of Christianity.

[11]Cyprian of Carthage, *The Letters of Saint Cyprian of Carthage,* vol. 1, trans. George W. Clarke (Long Prairie, Minn.: Neuman Press, 1983), 79 (11th epistle).

[12]Justo L. González, *A History of Christian Thought: From the Protestant Reformation to the Twentieth Century,* . rev. ed. (Nashville: Abingdon Press, 1987), 31 and 166.

[13]Neil Cole, *Cultivating a Life for God* (St. Charles, Ill. ChurchSmart Resources, 1999).

[14]Michael D. Henderson, *John Wesley's Class Meeting* (Nappanee, Ind.: Francis Asbury Press, 1997), 118–19.

Chapter 9: The Spiritual Habit of Faith Sharing

[1]Gallup Poll. May 2005, reported on PollingReport.com, http://www.pollingreport.com/religion.htm

[2]Martin Robinson. *The Faith of the Unbeliever* (London: Monarch Books, 1994), 38.

[3]Buck Jacobs, "Confessions of a Christian Businessman," *Regent's Business Review* 7 (September-October 2003), http://www.regent.edu/acad/schbus/maz/busreview/issue7/confessions.html.

[4]Ibid.

[5]Steve Necessary, personal interview, August 17, 2005.

[6]A local Christian pediatrician who specializes in ADHD has placed a copy of *Prayer for People Who Can't Sit Still* in her waiting room. The book has generated a number of conversations that have led people to visit her house church.

[7]Bert Knapp, personal interview, August 2, 2005.

[8]The passage in question is Zephaniah 1:6-7.

[9]Steve Necessary.